History Reborn

VOLUME I

History Reborn

VOLUME I

BY

Vicki Jo Anderson

EDITED BY
  KAREN ARNESEN
  VALERIE HOLLADAY

ILLUSTRATED BY
  LILY RAYBACK
  BOULDER, COLORADO

Zichron Historical Research Institute

1670 Franquero Cottonwood AZ 86326

First Edition. All rights reserved

ISBN 0-9642524-1-4

Copyright © 1994

by Vicki Jo Anderson

Printed in the United States of America

Table of Contents

Table of Contents - *continued*

Table of Contents - *continued*

Preface

Two hundred years ago an historian was treated with the respect and dignity of a sage or prophet. Sacrifice, dedication, love of truth—these were the qualities the historian boasted. Students, thinkers, and philosophers everywhere turned to history as their textbook. Businessmen took risks and statesmen waged war on nothing more than the lessons of the past. History had meaning.

If such faith in history seems unfounded in our day, it is not because history is suspect to modern scholars—but rather because *faith* is. In the 1890s Progressivism (which later become the atheistic/socialistic movement) invaded our colleges and universities. By the 1920s Progressivism was so entrenched that textbooks began telling history differently.

With faith in God no longer *en vogue*, faith in history lost credence. The atheistic historians who considered faith inconsistent with intelligence rewrote history, systematically deleting God from the stories of great men and women for whom God was everything.

While nineteenth century historians sought accuracy in their work, twentieth century historians prostituted their trade as a tool of political correctness. "Never mind the truth," the new historian said, "I will choose the version of history that advances my career."

Thus God was purged from human history. Some of the historians were simply proofreaders: Editing God out of, for example, Napoleon's or Columbus's journals. Others were liars, among the most notable the imaginative biographers of Thomas Jefferson and Benjamin Franklin. Other great heroes of the past, like Louis Agassiz, a contemporary of Charles Darwin, were censored altogether from the pages of history. God, the "historians" assured us, was dead, and no history book would be permitted to challenge that premise.

Enter Vicki Jo Anderson. I first became acquainted with her research when I served on her thesis committee for her master's degree. I became an enthusiastic counselor, then an avid reader, and finally a devoted fan. In a day when historians seem dedicated to "correctness" rather than accuracy, Vicki Jo dares write history from the standpoint of *truth*.

Dedicated to the conviction that "history is God's dealing with humanity," Vicki Jo is the type of historian that Luther or Jefferson would have admired. Not only does her research reflect years of laborious study and meticulous documentation, but the stories she highlights are uplifting and faith-promoting. God inspired the great men and women of history, and they knew it. They wrote it in journals, letters, and even proclaimed it openly in speeches and books. Vicki Jo Anderson has captured the essence of faith in her writing. In a day when atheism, humanism, and secularism are proving false and devoid of hope, this book delivers a much needed antedate of faith, hope, and truth. Finally: an accurate history textbook tells the story of some of the world's greatest heroes—a story where God is the central figure.

Oliver DeMille, Ph.D.
Provost of George Wythe College
Coral Ridge Baptist University

Introduction

Young people of our generation have been deprived of their birthright, which is to be conscious that they are the children of a high destiny in the line of great men who performed great deeds.

FROM THE TIME I WAS YOUNG I HAVE HAD AN INTEREST IN HISTORY, although I didn't like the way it was taught in school. I was a "people person," and so I studied and graduated with a bachelor's degree in sociology, which is the study of people. My background in sociology has greatly influenced the perspective and form I have adopted in writing history. Instead of focusing on dates and places, people are my prime value. I hold the view that history is the biography of men and women; when we read about their lives, we can have an emotionally satisfying experience in recognizing universal truths.

Some of my perceptions about education led me to homeschool all of my children for several years. It was my desire that they study the lives of great men and women so that it might add character to their own lives. Much to my enjoyment I discovered that, as usual, the teacher always learns the most, and as my children moved on to other subjects, I found that I could not settle for a surface knowledge of these historical people. What started out as a curriculum to teach character to my children turned into a ten-year, in-depth, rewarding research project. As I began to dig and to search deeper into their lives, these people actually started to become my friends, and I could see how some of their stories and character had been damaged by modern historians.

In the beginning my motives were purely personal. Then an event occurred in my life that made me realize that I had to share the information I had been collecting. It happened in 1989 when my husband and I had the privilege of visiting Israel. We were midway across the ocean and I looked down at the waves and the vastness of the water. Just then a very strange sensation came over me. I felt as if I was on a wave linking myself with my ancestors, who in 1650 crossed that vast body of water. It was as if I could see their crowded frail vessel being tossed and driven by the wind and the waves. I pondered over their conditions and their privations, which were a stark contrast to my own comfortable air conditioned seat on the airplane. What was the driving force that caused them to strike out into regions unknown and through perils that only the bravest would face? I knew the answer, but I had never before *felt* the answer the way I did that day. My ancestors were fleeing persecution and going to an unknown land in the hopes that one day their children and children's children would be able to live in freedom and be able to worship God as they pleased. Life and privations for them were secondary to this dream and hope.

And so, in an in-depth way I became cognizant that I, their progenitor, was a recipient of all their dreams and sacrifices. This thought touched my innermost soul. It was almost as if they extended to me an invitation to help others to see the past in a way that goes beyond the cold hard facts. I felt a charge to take my research and write up the lives of those I'd researched and to write of the good things they did. I decided that where possible my research would focus on the intent of their hearts and not the headlines of the day. My rule was to avoid tearing down or finding fault.

I discovered that history written before 1920 was often written of great men and women who performed great deeds. After 1920, history seemed to generally highlight the miseries of men. I could see that the youth of our generation have been deprived of a birthright, which is to be conscious that they are the children of a high destiny in the line of great men and who performed great deeds.

As I shared my goal I received a great deal of help. To my amazement doors immediately began to open with new and useful information. Some of the information came in miraculous ways. For example, I was uneasy with using Lord Byron in my list of eminent men. The worldview of him did little to leave one with a good taste.

One day I was in a bookstore in Mesa, Arizona. Although at

first I saw nothing new I did find among the back shelves an old book on the life and poetry of Joachim Miller. One of my cousins liked his poetry—in fact, he was her favorite poet—but because I had already spent so much money on books, I decided not to buy it for her. Instead I called her and told her about the book. The next day she put "go to the bookstore" on the bottom of her list of things to do. However, she felt very strongly impressed to move the bookstore from the bottom of her list to the top, so she switched her priorities and went to the bookstore. When she arrived at the store a moving van was in the front and men were moving all the books out. All the books except those on the far back shelves were already gone. Hurrying to the shelf she found the book by Joachim Miller and was able to purchase it.

That same night, around midnight, I received a phone call from her. "Did you know that Joachim Miller had a life-long admiration of Lord Byron?" she asked in excitement. She continued to tell me that Joachim had traveled to England to visit with friends of Byron and he perused Byron's nearly ten thousand manuscripts. He had also visited Greece where Byron had given up his life and where he was remembered with great admiration. The discovery of the book changed my perspective of Byron.

The incident with Byron was not an isolated one. There were many such interventions. Mary Wagner, a friend of my mother-in-law, hunted me down one day to tell me there was a sale at our small library. I was really not very hopeful but thought I ought to investigate. I found only a few tables of books, but as I thumbed through them I found marvelous book, *Juarez and His Mexico*, which I used extensively in my biography of Juarez.

Mary Jo Salome, a friend who lives almost fifty miles away, found a book in a yard sale and felt it might be of some use. It was a 1901 edition of Goethe's *Conversations with Eckerman*, a priceless book that she purchased for $5. Another book concerning Goethe was found among the antique decor of a restaurant, a 1902 numbered edition of his autobiography, *Truth or Fiction*. Another friend, Stephaney Abney, loves book hunting and from her continual haunts she would send me tidbits of information as she found them. Particularly helpful were her findings on Benito Juarez. Pamela

Morris, of Madera, California, called with information relating to Victor Hugo's adoration of Napoleon. This information led me to confirm other data I had gathered.

While researching Admiral Farragut, I located a book in my public library that gave great insight to the related events of the times, and although I have tried to refer to this book since that time, it is no longer at the library. On another occasion I ordered a book on Sir Joshua Reynolds through an interlibrary loan. Instead of the book I requested, another book came written by a student of Reynolds, printed in 1817. It was a rare and invaluable book. There were other incidences and other people who seemed to have the right information at the right time, as if an "unseen hand" were helping me in my search for truth.

In my study of the lives of these eminent men, I discovered several things they all had in common. First, they all, each in their own way, had an appreciation of God's creations. Second, they were each concerned about the oppressed.

My studies also included the lives of eminent women, and a second volume devoted to them is planned in the near future. I have found that many of these eminent men and women knew each other—even across oceans continents, and countries—almost as if these people were placed where they could come to know of each other and gain from their corresponding strengths. These biographies are but a sample of many great and good people. I believe that the reader can develop the ability to recognize the goodness of other historical figures by comparing them to these lives of greatness.

One cannot appreciate the future unless there is an understanding of the past. It is the intent of this book to illustrate from the lives of these eminent men that one individual can make a difference. It is my hope that this approach will give the reader the courage, determination, and hope needed to fulfill his or her own destiny.

This research has brought me to a new definition of history. History is God's dealings with this earth. God produces that which is good and beautiful, but when humankind is not in tune with God's purposes, it is humankind who produces misery and waste.

With this information in mind, remember that this book is not written to flatter the world of academia. In advance I acknowledge the human frailties contained herein. However, notwithstanding my weaknesses, I have, I hope, in some small way, been true to the spirit of my ancestors and to the spirit of history.

Eminent Men

Louis Agassiz *1807-1873*

SWISS-AMERICAN NATURALIST

> *"It is the job of prophets and scientists alike to proclaim the glories of God."*

THE GREATEST NATURAL SCIENTIST OF THE EIGHTEENTH CENTURY, Louis Agassiz is acknowledged even by current researchers as the greatest natural scientist of his day.[1] He established the Ice Age and thus became known as the "Father of the Ice Age." A noted teacher, Agassiz attracted students from all over the world. His legacy was the comparative method. He established the famous Museum of Comparative Anatomy at Harvard University, and he and his wife established Radcliffe, the great women's institution of higher education.

Although contemporaries of Agassiz and even researchers of today proclaim him as the greatest natural scientists of his day,[2] little is known of this great man today. Charles Darwin, one of Agassiz's later contemporaries, on meeting the poet Henry W. Longfellow, said: "What set of men you have in Cambridge! Why, there is Agassiz—he counts for three."[3] Darwin should know—for it was the great work done by Agassiz in entomology that Darwin used in his formulation of his *Origin of the Species*.

Apparently, Agassiz and his defense of creation were in some way blackballed from the scientific and historical community while Darwin's theories have remained. However, it was not from Agassiz's lack of scholarship or impact upon the world. All evidence points towards Agassiz being ignored because he tenaciously held that nature was a result of divine thought, "the free conception of the Almighty Intellect, matured in his thought, before it was manifested in tangible external forms."[4] For Agassiz, to discover the structure of nature was to engage our brain with thought similar to the Creator's: "In our study of natural objects we are approaching the thoughts of the Creator, reading his conceptions, interpreting a system that is His and not ours."[5]

Darwin, on the other hand, ventured where Agassiz refused to go. Darwin "overstepped the boundaries of actual knowledge and allowed his imagination to supply the links which science does not furnish."[6] This Agassiz steadfastly refused to do. He stated: "A physical fact is as sacred as a moral principle. Our own nature demands from us this double allegiance."[7]

Agassiz saw too well how a scientist who didn't pay especial care to the facts could easily make the jump from the development of embryonic fish to evolutionized man. However, early in his fossil fish research, Agassiz found "the whole history of geological succession shows us that the lowest in structure is by no means necessarily the earliest in time."[8] This is particularly true of the shark family. Anatomically evolution looked sound, but geologically it just couldn't work. The mere existence of the well developed shark (Selachians) family is in direct contradiction to the idea of a gradual (evolutionary) development because the sharks are found abundantly in the earliest of the Palaeozoic fossil beds!

Agassiz believed that "facts are the words of God, and we may heap them together endlessly, but they will teach us little or nothing till we place them in their true relations, and recognize the thought that binds them together."[9] To Agassiz this process of binding facts together was nature's claim to "Divine Conception." Every fact in nature was sacred to him. Even as a child Agassiz felt that God's revelations of Himself were not limited to the writings in the Bible—God also revealed himself through the book of Nature.

Agassiz's ancestors were French Huguenots who had escaped from France during the persecution of Louis XIV. For the previous five generations, his ancestors, including his father, had been clergymen. His mother came from an intellectual and sturdy stock. Born 28 May 1807, in Motier, a Swiss village nestled on the shore of Lake Morat at the foot of the Bernese Alps, Louis John Rudolph Agassiz was blessed with loving parents. They were his only teachers until he was ten years old and they did not try to push him beyond the ordinary achievements for his age. His mother lost her first four children in infancy. Perhaps it was for this reason that she was so close to Louis. She understood his love of nature and all living things. She recognized he had intellectual tendencies and more than a child's normal delight with animals. It appears that early in his life she had been granted an understanding of the great work he was destined to do. This knowledge gave her the position of being his most intimate friend even up to the last hour of her life.[10]

The close relationship Agassiz had with his mother gave him a high opinion of women. He humorously based his Ph.D. thesis "on the argument that woman, being historically the later creation, was an improvement upon man," indicating his humorous approach to life.[11] During his years at Harvard in an age when women were mostly shut out from higher education he supported equal access to education for women. He also employed women as assistants in establishing his several museums.[12]

Agassiz married twice, each time to an unusual and gifted woman. His first wife, Cecile Braun, had a wonderful talent for drawing and sketching. Her talent was very important in Agassiz's work on fossils. After Cecile died, he married Elizabeth Cabot Cary, who was noted for her literacy and executive ability. Elizabeth's organizational ability was a great aid to his career in America. To help support the tremendous cost of Agassiz's extensive research projects, Elizabeth, with the help of Agassiz's two daughters, Ida and Paulene, suggested the idea of beginning a girls boarding school with Agassiz as the main attraction.

He loved the idea of a women's school, and they immediately went to work on it. Agassiz enlisted some of his fellow professors and student assistants at Harvard to come and teach the girls. The school was tremendously successful but had to close during the Civil War. It was reopened years later under the executive ability of Elizabeth and grew into the now famous Radcliffe University.[13]

As a teenager he convinced his sister Cecilia to draw for him any new species of fish he found. She cooperated willingly   by doing his sketch work. At fourteen it was the modest aim of Louis, with the help of his brother, to memorize the Latin names of "every known animal and plant!"[14]

As a child, Louis also loved to collect things. His parents

tolerated much of his valuable "junk," collected and stored in his and his brother Augustus' bedroom. Their yard was alive with animals. They ranged from the family cow and horse to mice, birds, and snakes. Agassiz loved and tenderly cared for each one.

Although Agassiz disliked leaving all his prize possessions, at the age of ten he, along with his brother Augustus, attended a boarding school at the College de Bienne in a town some twenty miles away. After leaving de Bienne he attended the Academy at Lusanne and entered medical school at Zurich. From there he attended Heidelberg and finished at the University of Munich where he received his M.D.

However, Louis studied medicine only to obey his father; his first love was the study of nature, or Zoology as it is commonly called today. With his roommate, Alexander Braun (brother of his wife-to-be Cecile), they formed their own "little academy." With their friends, they sat for hours each evening debating the problems of the universe. Included in this group were many of the later great scientists of Europe. Agassiz would later reflect that "all our members increase[d] their knowledge by sharing."[15]

Under a philosophy professor named Schelling, Louis's faith broadened to a less dogmatic but not a less deep belief in God. Professor Schelling helped instill in Agassiz a growing conviction that the diversity of animal forms could be explained as individual thoughts of the Creator.[16]

As Agassiz approached his graduation as an M.D., he was dismayed by the thought of losing the opportunity for research he had had at the university. He was already well known for his work on the fish of Brazil, a work gathered by botanist Von Martius and J. P. Spix. The latter died before the work could be compiled and published, leaving Agassiz to classify and publish the data. The book was written with beauty and clarity showing that Agassiz would become not only a man of science but also a man of letters. In this one project alone he characterized "nine new genera, embracing forty-two species new to science."[17] By the time of his graduation he had written more than seventy-five theses on anatomy, surgery, obstetrics, and pathology.

Shortly after graduation he went to Paris with a small sum of money loaned to him by a kindly uncle. Here he took residence in a small apartment across from the famous Jardin des Plantes, the center of Natural History for all of Europe. The headmaster, Professor Georges Cuvier, the leading savant in France and master of comparative anatomy, accepted Agassiz with open arms. It was Cuvier who first established the basis of our classification system with its four branches: the Radiatas, Mollusks, Articulata, and Vertebrata. Cuvier classified these groups according to their anatomical structure, not their function.[18] This means of classification Agassiz felt demonstrated that Nature was the work of a "reflective mind," as in the oldest geological formations these four branches of the animal kingdom had always existed simultaneously.

Agassiz prospered intellectually under Cuvier. His one great wish was to help him prepare a book on fossilized fishes. His dream was more than realized: the grateful Cuvier turned the entire collection over to Agassiz and told him to go ahead with the book.

"I work regularly fifteen hours a day," he wrote his parents. He continued this work though he was short on money, often skipping meals to get by. Cuvier, pleaded with him to relax from his research. "Be careful, and remember that work kills," he warned the young man. Cuvier knew whereof he spoke, for shortly after his warning to Agassiz, he was himself stricken with a paralysis and died.[19] His death deeply affected his young apprentice, but instead of sinking in grief Agassiz became the champion of Cuvier's views that nature came about by a "Divine Intelligence." Agassiz never departed from that true principle.

The great patron of all sciences, Alexander von Humboldt, befriended the struggling young scientist and loaned him 1,000 francs. This was but the first time Dr. Humboldt sponsored Agassiz. Von Humboldt also used his influence to obtain a professorship for Agassiz at the University of Neuchatel at the foot of the Aar Mountains in Switzerland. This allowed Agassiz to return to his beloved Switzerland. With the patronage of von Humboldt, and through the magic of his personality and talent, Agassiz transformed Neuchatel into one of the great centers of science in Europe.[20]

He looked upon his students more as co-workers than subordinates. He enjoyed firing their imagination as they hiked through the hills and the fields. He continually talked to them of the marvelous works of God as they walked without a textbook. He taught a living science: "If you study nature in books, when you go out of doors you cannot find her."[21]

A student, Clara Conant Gilson, described him in this way: "His eyes ... would moisten with tears of emotion as thoughts of his Creator came rushing to mind, while he traced his [the creator's] footsteps in the science he studied. His eyes mirrored his soul. I think there was never but one pair of eyes such as Professor Louis Agassiz."[22] He was easily moved to tears or to laughter and made no attempt to hide his feelings.

His summer curriculum, in contrast to his winter curriculum, was always out of doors. He taught his young colleagues the basics of geography by climbing with them and pointing out the vast panorama below. For him, "Geology [was] but an extension of Zoology."[23]

He wanted students to depend on natural objects rather than on statements in books. He drummed his students constantly with "Look, look; to look is to know."[24]   "Go to nature; take the facts into your own hands; look, and see for yourself."[25]

His winter curriculum consisted of placing a specimen, often a smelly pickled fish on a student's desk in a small tin pan. Write down everything they could see, he would tell them before leaving them to "discover." Their only tool was a pencil: "A pencil is one of the best of eyes," he said.[26] The students were instructed to point out similarities and differences. In this way the students gained knowledge that was "theirs"; it could never be taken away. "The mind is made strong not through much learning, but by the thorough possession of something, " Agassiz said.[27]

In order to gain a general view of science, Agassiz recommended   that his students study its history. His advice to his future teachers was to "select subjects that your pupils cannot walk by without seeing them." He said, "Train your pupils to be observers, and have them provided with the specimens about which you speak. If you can find nothing better, take a house-fly or a cricket, and let each hold a specimen and examine it as you talk."[28]

Agassiz's particular strength was his research. It is not surprising that at Neuchatel, nestled in the beautiful Swiss Alps, he turned from fossils to glaciers. He spent his summers studying glaciers; living, working, and sleeping on one. Once he even convinced his co-workers to lower him into a crevasse, to a depth of eighty feet, where he nearly lost his life in an icy underground river.[29] From this research he startled savants of his time with the knowledge that glaciers actually moved.

He went on to advance the theory that Europe at one stage had been completely covered by a solid sheet of ice. He announced this study at the annual meeting of the leading scientists of his day, the Helvetic Society, of which he was president. His presentation was seen as a disaster, and the audience actually booed. Even his mentor, von Humboldt, appeared disappointed. Von Humboldt recommended to young Agassiz that he have all the research and available facts before announcing such a bold new theory. Agassiz was more than happy to accept such good advice. He spent next year in intensive research establishing the proof that there had been an "Ice Age" and eventually became known as the father of the "Ice Age."

Alexander von Humboldt procured the patronage of the King of Prussia for Agassiz in 1846, who sent Agassiz to America to study the zoology of the United States in order to compare it to that of Europe. While in the States he was commissioned to lecture at the Lowell Institute of Boston. His first lecture, to a crowd of 1500, was "God's Planned Creation." Agassiz was deeply touched by the sight of rich and poor seated side by side in a country where individuals had freedom to advance equally in education.

He quickly developed an immense liking for the country and a passionate belief in its future. When his wife Cecile passed away, an event that considerably loosened his ties with his mother land, Agassiz remarried and brought his children to America. Although considerable effort was made to lure him back to Europe—not only by the King of Prussia, but even by the Emperor Napoleon III who offered him a distinguished post at the Jardin des Plantes—nothing could entice him to leave his new-found country. "I've decided,"

Agassiz told his wife, Elizabeth, "that I prefer the gifts of a free people to the patronage of an emperor."[30] So strong was his belief in the future of this country that although this was in the darkest hours of the Civil War, Agassiz chose nevertheless to become a citizen of the United States and a founder of the National Academy of Science.[31] He was also influential in establishing the Natural History Museum in the Smithsonian Institute.

The moment of his arrival in the New World was particularly fortunate and well timed. Before this time, America had been concentrating her efforts and resources primarily in the building of a new nation. America was just beginning to build up her arts and sciences. Agassiz, having read the scientific compilations of America, found them to be generally "not of good execution." His first order of business was to set out for Washington, D. C. (unannounced, in 1846), and help the government set a strict criteria for good scientific work and publications.[32] Many of America's scientific advancements owe their progress to the groundwork Agassiz set and his consistent demand for quality.

Agassiz considered himself to be the "librarian of the works of God."[33] In his records he tells of his unsuccessful efforts to classify a fossil fish partly concealed in a mass of stone. Then for three consecutive nights he had a "dream" in which the characteristics of the fish were shown to him. After the third night Agassiz was able to draw what he had seen in the dream. Using the sketch, the next day he was able to cut away the stone enclosing the fossil, disclosing a fossil hitherto unknown.[34] This occasion led to the modern sciences of icthiology. Geology and paleontology also bear the stamp of his contributions.

Through lecture and essay, Agassiz spent the closing fifteen years of his life defending "creation." The two most direct and complete works Agassiz produced at this time were *Essays on Classification* and *Evolution and Permanence Type*. (Another excellent publication by Agassiz is *Methods of Study in Natural History*).

His defense of Nature's law and Nature's God places him preeminently among the "interpreters of Nature's Divine Conception." Agassiz himself placed the divisions of the animal kingdom as chapter headings in nature's great book that leads man to know God. According to Agassiz the act of translating the "thoughts of God" is the most conclusive proof of our affinity with the Divine Mind. He reasoned: "Is not this intellectual and spiritual connection with the Almighty worth our deepest consideration?"[35] While Agassiz's death brought to an end a tradition of thought scientifically initiated by Aristotle—that of "divine creation," his research has shown that it can endure the test of time. His stand on divine creation is as valid and compelling today as it was in his.

NOTES

[1] See Gould, Stephen Jay. "Agassiz in the Galapagos," *Natural History*, vol. 90, no. 12 (12 Dec. 1981). See also Lane Cooper's *Louis Agassiz as a Teacher: Illustrative Extracts on His Method of Instruction.* Ithaca, New York: Comstock Publishing, 1945, p. 8.

[2] See Marcou, Jules. *Life, Letters, and Works of Louis Agassiz.* New York: Macmillan and Co., 1896, p. 169.

[3] Magill, Frank. *Great Lives from History.* Pasadena, Calif.: Salem Press, 1987, p. 44-45.

[4] Agassiz, Louis. "An Essay on Classification" as compiled in *The Intelligence of Agassiz* by Guy Davenport. Westport, Conn.; Greenwood Press, 1983. Reprint permission by Beacon Press, Boston 1963, p. 38.

[5] Agassiz, Louis. *Methods of Study in Natural History.* Boston: Ticknor and Fields, 1863, p. 14.

[6] Marcou, *Life, Letters, and Works of Louis Agassiz,* p. 209.

[7] Agassiz, Elizabeth. *Louis Agassiz: His Life and Correspondence.* Boston: Houghton, Mifflin, 1885, 3:781.

[8] Agassiz, Louis, *Methods of Study,* p. 202.

[9] Agassiz, Louis, "Evolution and Permanence Type" as compiled in Davenport's *The Intelligence of Agassiz,* p. 231.

[10] See Agassiz, Elizabeth, 1:2-3.

[11] See Cooper, p. 11.

[12] See ibid.

[13] See Agassiz, Elizabeth, 2:526-27.

[14] Thomas, Henry, and Dana Lee Thomas. *Living Biographies: Great Scientists.* New York: Nelson Doubleday, 1941, p. 167.

[15] Thomas, and Thomas, p. 169.

[16] See Cooper, p. 14.

[17] Ibid., p. 16.

[18] See Agassiz, Louis, *Methods of Study,* p. 7-9

[19] Agassiz, Elizabeth, 1:168.

[20] See Thomas and Thomas, p. 173.

[21] Cooper, p. 78.

[22] Ibid., p. 72.

[23] Thomas, and Thomas, p. 175.

[24] Ibid., p 182.

[25] Cooper, p. 78.

[26] Ibid., p. 58.

[27] Ibid., p. 81.

[28] Ibid., p. 82.

[29] See Tiner, John H. *The Ghost Lake: The True Story of Louis Agassiz.* Grand Rapids, Mich.: Baker Book House, 1983, p. 69-70.

[30] Agassiz, Elizabeth, p. 163.

[31] See Cooper, p. 25.

[32] See Marcou, p. 287-88.

[33] Agassiz, Louis, "An Essay on Classification,"p. 3.

[34] See Agassiz, Elizabeth 1:182-83.

[35] Agassiz, Louis, "An Essay on Classification," p. 37

Charles Louis Napoleon Bonaparte, Napoleon III

EMPEROR OF FRANCE

1808-1873

> *"The triumph of Christianity has destroyed slavery; the triumph of the French revolution has put an end to serfdom; the triumph of democratic ideas has caused the extinction of pauperism."*

CHARLES LOUIS NAPOLEON III IS NOT TO BE CONFUSED WITH his famous uncle, Napoleon Bonaparte. For the purpose of this chapter Charles Louis Napoleon will be referred to as Louis Napoleon, as he was commonly called by his family and friends. Louis Napoleon's accomplishments benefited all humankind. Yet, so unobtrusively did he accomplish his mission that his works are scarcely mentioned by historians. Like his famous uncle, he maintained a passionate support of universal suffrage. Louis Napoleon stabilized the nation of France after more than thirty years of despotism and mobocracy. He implemented the Code of Napoleon, written by his uncle, which was based upon republican principles. It was this code that awoke France to the industrial revolution.

His support was sought by the patriots of Italy in their fight for independence. He responded personally by leading a large French army to their aid. With the help of the French, Italy defeated the ruling Austrians, and for the first time in over a thousand years Italy began to be reunited as a country. For his efforts on behalf of Italy he was offered vast parcels of land but he declined the gift.

Louis Napoleon was also one of the first heads of state to respond to the Turks' plea for help in the Crimean War. His premier policy was peace and he proposed a number of treaties in an attempt to establish permanent peace in Europe. Not long after taking the leadership of France he was able to forge a strong alliance with England.

Realizing that laborers had been overworked, contributing to the mobocracy, he issued the following edict relating to the Sabbath:

> The repose of Sunday is one of the essential bases of that morality which constitutes the force and the consolation of a nation.... [It] is necessary for the health and the intellectual development of the working-classes. The man who labors incessantly, and does not set apart any day, ... sooner or later becomes a prey to materialism; and the sentiment of dignity is weakened within him.... Consequently I invite you to give such orders, that for the future, ... public work shall cease on the Sabbath and on holydays.[1]

In a effort to rid the country of old prejudices he ordered a splendid ball given in honor of the market-women of Paris. No effort was spared to make this ball as beautiful and elegant as ever seen in this city of past grandeur. The ball began with a grand march led by the head of police, with the assistance of a graceful and excellent woman who supplied the market with mushrooms. Persons of the most elevated stature danced with those of the most humble and the most humble workers danced with the most elevated officials. The Minister of Interior danced with a seller of vegetables. The Chief of Division danced with a dealer in butter. To those of past hereditary titles this event was an outrage and a debasement of power and authority,[2] and Louis Napoleon was severely criticized for this action.

However, such peace and acceptance were conducive to the prosperity of the French culture and talent. Paris became the cleanest and most beautiful city of all of Europe. People began coming from all over to worship at Lourdes and to admire at the Louve. The sciences in particular received Louis' personal support, the most noted among the French scientists of the time being Louis Pasteur.

As a young man Louis studied and researched extensively. His collected writings fill eleven volumes, the study of which is essential in order to truly understand the intent of the man. His first pamphlet, "Political Reveries," was printed when he was twenty-four. In it he outlines his basic philosophy of government. The fundamental principles of government, he felt, were based in the right of the people to change it when necessary. He called for three powers of State; the people, the legislative corps, and the executive. The people should have elective power and the power of sanction, the legislative corps should have power of proposing and making laws, and the executive should have executive power. Unlike the United States the French people, he felt, still desired some form of a monarchy, based on their tradition, therefore he called for a republican monarchy. There is a supreme judge on this earth, said Louis, for all governments no matter in what form it exists who will sooner or later pass judgment, and that judge is the people.[3]

Louis also wrote "Ideas of Napoleon," a treatise on the principles of the Code of Napoleon I. It went through four editions and was translated into all the languages of Europe. Some of the elements he elaborated on were the protection of religion, the rights of families to insure the freedom of public worship and education, and the protection of property being basic to the stability of a nation.

His public and personal writings reveal that early in his life, he became fixed with a determination to fulfill his uncle's dream. He often reassured his friends that some day he would sit at the head of France and implement The Code of Napoleon I. He never wavered in this belief.

Louis Napoleon's destiny was imbued in him while he was a young child and was often reinforced by his family and friends. His father, Louis Bonaparte, was the younger brother of Napoleon I and his mother, Hortense Beauharnais, was the daughter of Josephine, the wife of Napoleon I. The father of Hortense and first husband of Josephine had been held in prison and murdered by the revolutionary government. Josephine had also been held in prison, but the day before she was to be conducted to the scaffold, there was a new revolution: Robespierre the philosophical leader of the revolution was guillotined, and Josephine, the future empress, was liberated. Josephine remarried Napoleon Bonaparte, the emperor of France, and her daughter Hortense was raised as if she were his own child. Louis Napoleon looked upon his uncle as a beloved grandfather.

The French revolution, ignited by the desire for freedom of the people, dislodged one of the most ancient, and at that time disabled, ruling houses in Europe. Deliberate ignorance of the ancient rule of "law and order" led revolutionary leaders to a complete state of anarchy. Tyranny reigned without check throughout France. The rulers of its surrounding countries—England and Austria, as well as other parts of Europe—fearing the spread of the revolutionary spirit, joined together and marshaled their vast armies to crush the French "king killers."

It is important to understand that faced with tyranny from within and destruction from without, France turned to the man who lead them in their great military victories, Napoleon Bonaparte, who later became known as Napoleon I. In light of the facts, Napoleon I did not, as often stated, usurp the crown of France—the people freely gave it to him. Utmost discipline and order had to be enforced to gain control over the mobs in the street. Therefore, complete authority was given to Napoleon to accomplish this task. In return, the will of the people became his first priority. They clamored for religion, which had been cut off by the revolution; for universal suffrage wherein all had a right to vote; property rights; and economic stability. All these Napoleon attempted to give them.

At a time when the United States granted suffrage to white males only, Napoleon I became the first in modern times to grant universal suffrage. This act enraged the monarchs of Europe, increasing their determination to punish the French people. Napoleon I felt the only way to meet such great odds was to launch an offensive against the allied invaders. This he did to keep them off French soil. Thus ensued the great Napoleonic wars.

In spite of the great drain and demand the war made on Napoleon I, he continued to implement republican principles, and France progressed greatly during his fifteen-year reign. Because of the war, he was unable to install many of the reforms he felt beneficial, however, his goal was to hold off the invaders long enough for the fresh breath of freedom and progress to be felt by the people. His progressive ideas were also felt and experienced by many of the lands he conquered. A feeling of change was beginning to wave over Europe. The kings knew it and did all in their power to suppress it.

The Allies finally succeeded in removing Napoleon I, and the foreign armies once again submitted the people of France to the yoke a king. They restored the "divine right" of kings while suppressing the more divine rights of the people. Exiled from France, the Bonapartes were threatened with death should they return.

During the following years France passed through three tumultuous reigns of three Kings Louis XVIII, Charles X, and Louis Phillip. Each was eventually driven out by the French people themselves. Each reign was accompanied by endless rioting and revolts.

When Napoleon I was re-elected emperor, a grand coronation was held. The emperor ascended the elevated platform, dressed in imperial robes, and by his side was young Louis Napoleon. The soldiers roared their deafening pledges of support, and the crowds filled the air with "*Vive l'empereur.*" Louis Napoleon and his older brother were presented as future heirs to the throne and the crowd enthusiastically cheered. Though he was but seven years old the scene must have produced a profound impression upon young Louis' reflective mind.

Louis Napoleon spent much of his early life in the palace with his famous grandparents where he was affectionately called little "Oui-oui." He charmed all who came and went with his love of people and of life itself. While tending Louis Napoleon, his grandmother Josephine wrote to her daughter, Hortense, that one day they took a walk in the woods. and when they arrived he threw his hat into the air and shouted, "Oh, how I love beautiful Nature!"[4]

Upon the edict of exile by King Louis XVIII, Louis Napoleon's family settled in Switzerland on the southern shores of the lake Constance on the beautiful Arenemberg estate. It was an ideal place for his physical, moral and intellectual training. He studied the ancient classics, modern languages, and the sciences. His mother devoted herself to the education of her son, never allowing him to forget the name he bore or the political principles that his uncle had proclaimed. Included in his studies were the fine arts and the languages, a number of which he spoke with fluency.

As a young boy Louis Napoleon was observed one day coming from the town mill. It was a cold winter day yet he was barefoot and in his shirt-sleeves. Skipping from spot to spot, he was obviously trying to avoid both detection as well as the freezing cold pockets of mud and snow. When he was stopped and asked to give a report of his dress and behavior, he reported that while at the town mill he had seen a family pass by whose poverty and misery so touched him that before he gave it another thought he took off his shoes and gave them to one child and gave his coat to another.[5]

As he grew he was enrolled in the military camps in Switzerland and had advanced schooling in Germany. Reflecting later on these educational experiences Louis Napoleon remarked that having lived on foreign soils had taught him a better understanding of nations and given him an appreciation of their cultures. Having been a boy without a country he felt in some respects a citizen of the world. After finishing his formal schooling, he continued to study and write at Arenemberg. Refusing the comfort of the mansion there, he had built a small, spare room in the garden. Here his studies for a time took a decidedly military turn.

Hearing of the attempted insurrection in Italy in 1830, Louis Napoleon left his comfortable surroundings and traveled to Italy, joined by his brother, and as a simple soldier he began to fight in a war that had little of chance of success. However it provided the great prologue to the later and more successful insurrection that led to Italy's independence

A fever passed through the battle field and Louis Napoleon became terribly ill; his brother died. Upon hearing of her son's condition, his mother traveled immediately to Italy and by disguise took her son back to Switzerland to heal.

As he recuperated, Louis observed the great discontent in France. It was the right time, he felt, for an insurrection. In collaboration with some friends, he led the group to storm the walls of the Fort Strasburg. Their efforts failed and he was captured. A trial was held and he was deported to South America.

After a short time in Brazil and the United States, Louis received word that his mother was dying in Switzerland. In spite of the threat of arrest upon his return, he made it to his mother's bedside in time to receive her dying words. "We shall meet again— shall we not?—in a better world, where you [may] come to join me as late as possible.... I am very calm and resigned.... The will of God be done."[6]

Louis Napoleon moved to England and quietly continued his studies. In 1840, he again felt it was right to return to his land and that the popularity of Napoleonic spirit at that time would carry them to the capital. Like Strasburg this attempt also failed. His small party attempted to return to their ferry but their rowboat capsized and many were shot and killed as they swam. An English gentleman hearing the commotion rushed to the shore. He saw a soldier take aim one of the fugitives who was half drowned in the water, only a few yards from shore. Striking the barrel of the gun and calling the soldier a coward to shoot in such a situation. The Englishman then assisted the drowning fugitive only to discover that he had saved the life of Louis Napoleon.[7]

Louis Napoleon never again attempted to set foot on French soil in such a manner although he never waned in his personal belief that he would one day stand as head of France. Patiently he waited until the people of France drove King Louis Phillip from his throne. Elections were held and Louis Napoleon was elected representative from four separate districts. As he entered France, the Assembly, feeling threatened by his presence, sent word to remind him of the edict of exile. A wiser and more mature man, he withdrew from France and the election. He said: "They will come to me without any effort of my own.... Though fortune has twice betrayed me, yet my destiny will none the less surely be fulfilled. I wait."[8] Soon the demand of the people became so great the exile edict was repealed, and in 1848 he was elected by popular acclaim president of France.

Louis Napoleon's popularity began to grow among the people. The Assembly had not ceased to fear his potential power, and jealous members of the Assembly began to plot his overthrow and even his death. At the same time, the Assembly was guilty of various abuses of the constitution as well, perhaps the greatest of which was arbitrarily removing the right to vote from a large segment of the population.

Feeling that there was no other recourse, Louis Napoleon, with the support of the national guard staged a *coup de etat.* Arresting the plotters, he held new elections, and the people called for an assembly to write a constitution. this assembly wrote a new constitution based on the code of Napoleon. Hastily written, it was nevertheless a beginning. The new constitution called for a vote for the executive office and the people voted for Louis Napoleon. The exiled nephew of Napoleon I was elected president of France by a margin of three million votes. (Later, the people voted him the title of Emperor.) His own identity was so closely allied with the man who he knew as "grandfather," Napoleon I, that his agenda was the same agenda as Napoleon I.

In expressing his feelings he said: "I [was] called to the throne by Providence and the will of the French people, but trained in the school of adversity."9

It was in the area of foreign affairs that he made his biggest mistake. Possessing such a largeness of heart, Louis was very open to helping others. He had seen his efforts in helping the Italians bear fruit, so when he was approached by the intellectual elite of Mexico to come to their aid, he wanted to be of assistance. All knew that Mexico had been engaged in one revolution or another for nearly fifty years. Louis Napoleon was inclined to help but insisted that he would only help if that was the desire of the people of Mexico.

A vote was taken in Mexico of a hastily gathered assembly of friends of the intellectually elite and the vote submitted to Louis Napoleon. However, the vote was deceptive. Louis ordered his troops to Mexico, and the expedition was a complete failure, ending in the death of many, including Maximilian, a good man who was sent to rule Mexico. Nevertheless, the impact of the French upon the Mexicans was such that for the first time since the departure of the Spaniards, enough of them were able to unite to form the first stable Mexican government in modern times.

Because the French army was so weakened by the Mexican experience, upon their return they were easily defeated by the conquering Prussians under Bismark. Louis Napoleon now in his later years, and with a diseased body, rode with his troops. He observed the great losses with a broken heart; gladly would he have taken a fatal bullet alongside his soldiers.

One of the survivors taken captive, Louis was exiled once again to England where he died shortly thereafter. Despite his final defeat, however, due to his influence, France has never since turned her back on republican principles and continues to be a world power.

NOTES

[1] Abbott, John S. C. *The History of Napoleon III.* Boston: B. B. Russell, 1869, p. 73.

[2] See ibid., p. 497.

[3] See ibid., p. 28.

[4] Ibid., p. 136.

[5] See ibid., p. 171.

[6] Ibid., p. 128.

[7] See Encyclopedia Britannica. 11th ed. 1911, 19: 213.

[8] Abbott, p. 280.

[9] Abbot, p. 613.

Lord Henry Brougham

STATESMAN/LORD CHANCELLOR OF ENGLAND   *1778-1868*

> *"God grant that we may not live and die under the present system of things - but I am much afraid."*

THE MOST INDOMITABLE MAN OF HIS TIME, LORD HENRY BROUGHAM was responsible for making slave-trade a felony and he insured Negro emancipation in all his majesty's colonies. His efforts on behalf of reform were indefatigable, and his energy never waned throughout his long life. Upon the success of the Slave Trade Bill, Brougham turned his energies to the education of the poor. He was instrumental in the foundation of the University of London and in establishing the Society of Diffusion of Useful Knowledge.

Some criticized his strong will and drive, but Brougham was also responsible for breaking up the East India British monopoly, which was destroying the economy of India. He was also credited with defeating the continuance of the income tax in England. In 1825, he was elected to the honorary office of Lord Rector of the University of Glasgow over Sir Walter Scott.

Brougham wrote on a variety of subjects, from mathematics, to science to politics. His collected works fill ten volumes. After reading his first paper before the Royal Society at the age of eighteen, Brougham went on to write eighty articles for the *Edinburgh Review*, for which he was a contributing editor. For many years the magazine would affect the public opinion of the British Isles.

Lord Henry Brougham was born in Edinburgh, Scotland, 19 September 1778, where he spent the first twenty-five years of his life. His family was of middle-rank but not wealthy. His great-uncle on his mother's side was the famous Scottish historian, William Robertson, who often guided certain areas of the young man's study. Henry's father taught him to read at a preschool age, and the boy soon began to show signs of precociousness and boundless energy. Indeed, it was a wonderful time in Scotland for a great mind to be educated. Scotland was basking in the sunshine of Scottish Enlightenment. Scotland had already produced such great minds as Adam Smith, David Amy, Sir Walter Scott, Robert Burns, Reverend Thomas Chalmers, and others.

Of her son Brougham's mother wrote "From a very tender age he excelled all his contemporaries. Nothing to him was a labor."[1] He uttered his first intelligible words at eight and a half months old. At the age of thirteen he translated a five-volume work into English for his great-uncle William. His schooling was a wonderful advantage for him, but he seemed to blossom most when he took ill and had to remain home for some time. During this time he read incessantly, assisted by his maternal grandmother, an accomplished woman in her own right besides being sister to William Robertson, the historian. It is to this lady that Brougham gives credit for his success in public life:

> I owe [her] all my success in life. From my earliest infancy till I left college with the exception of the time we passed at Brougham with my tutor, Mr. Mitchell, I was her companion.
>
> Remarkable for beauty, but far more for a masculine intellect and clear understanding she instilled in me from my cradle the strongest desire for information, and the first principle of that persevering energy in the pursuit of every kind of knowledge, which more than any natural talents I may possess, has enabled me to stick to, and to accomplish, how far successfully it is not for me to say, every task I ever undertook.[2]

Brougham's grandmother, like her historian brother, ardently championed the cause of the American colonists.

When Brougham was about twelve, a cousin found him walking with an original volume of mathematics by the French mathematician, La Place, and queried, "What sort of lad [must this] be who not only studied mathematics for pleasure, but through the medium of a foreign tongue."[3] Brougham entered the university at the age of fourteen. His professors were astounded by his extraordinary memory, which could recall details of battles and individuals in history.

At the university a group of Henry's friends organized a debating society called the "Juvenile Literary Society" and debated such topics as the existence of innate ideas in the human mind, the character of Mary Queen of Scots, the act of Brutus in slaying Caesar, and other moral and economic subjects. It was about this time that Henry was invited to present his paper on light and color to the Royal Society. He resented greatly the fact that the secretary made him edit portions of his paper on the grounds that those parts related to art rather than the sciences and he said:

> This was very unfortunate; because I had observed the effect of a small hole in the window-shutter of a darkened room, when a view is formed on a white paper of the external objects. I had suggested that if the view is formed, not on paper, but on ivory rubbed with nitrate of silver, the picture would become permanent... Now this is the origin of photography; and had the note containing the suggestion in 1795 appeared, in all probability it would have set others on the examination of the subject, and given up photography half a century earlier that we have had it."[4]

Brougham finished his courses at the university and entered law school. He practiced for about one year, but by the end of the year he was "disgusted with law."[5]

In 1804, Brougham traveled to the continent under an American passport because of the enmity between England and France. His travel served to further prepare him for his work in Parliament. During this time Brougham was appointed to act as secretary to an army headed to Portugal sent to sustain her against a French invasion. The general took ill and Brougham directed most of the affairs. It was this experience that led to his to later efforts to reform military discipline, particularly the abuse of flogging in the army and navy.

In 1812, Brougham became counselor to the future Queen, Caroline, and she began to consult him on her private affairs. Her husband, the Prince (later George IV) disliked Caroline and separated from her soon after the birth of their daughter. The public thought she had been badly treated by her socializing husband, and the sympathies of the people were strongly in her favor.

In 1814, she left England for extended travel on the continent.

Ultimately, she made Italy her headquarters. On the death of the King George III, the English Ambassadors were given orders to prevent her return and to prevent her recognition in foreign courts as queen. Her name was also omitted in all public ceremonies. These acts stirred up strong public support of the queen, and in spite of all efforts made by the king, Caroline did return to England to claim her rights. The office of the crown tried to buy her silence for £50,000 per year. Failing to accomplish this, a bill was introduced to Parliament to dissolve her marriage with the king on the charge of infidelity to her husband.

These actions drew the attention of the people to the distressed queen and more particularly to the man who came to her aid as her attorney-general. Brougham, as her counsel, came to be regarded as the chivalrous champion of a much-injured lady. By his boldness in denouncing a series of acts of oppression by the highest officers in the land, the queen was fully acquitted. Thus Brougham's reputation rose to the highest esteem in England.

Although Caroline was vindicated and allowed to assume her title, she was refused admittance to Westminster Hall on Coronation Day. She died less than a month later.

Lord Henry Brougham's education and experiences prepared him so well that when he was placed in governmental position, his old friend Sydney Smith, initiator of the *Edinburgh Review,* wrote:

> Look at the gigantic Brougham, sworn in at twelve o'clock, and before six P.M. he has a bill on the table abolishing the abuses of the court.... This is the man who will help to govern you—who [bases] his reputation on doing good to you ... and is a terror to him who doth evil to the people.[6]

NOTES

[1] Duycknick, Evert A. *Portrait Gallery of Eminent Men and Women.* New York: H. J. Johnson, 1873, p. 494.

[2] Ibid., p. 495.

[3] Stewart Robert. *Henry Brougham 1778-1868: His Public Career.* The Bodley Head, London, n.d. p. 6.

[4] Ibid., p. 7-8.

5 Aspinall, Arthur. *Lord Brougham and the Whig Party.* n.p.: Archon Books, 1972, p. 4.

6 Duycknick, p. 505.

Baron Edward George Lytton-Bulwer 1803-1873

ENGLISH NOVELIST, POLITICIAN

> *"Personal liberty is the paramount essential to human dignity and human happiness."*

EDWARD GEORGE LYTTON-BULWER WROTE IN A SHORT autobiography that he was born at the saddest point of his mother's married life.

> Out of jealousy for my mother's love, my father had positively disliked me; for the same cause my grandmother took me into open aversion; and my grandfather, who ought, if conscious of the future, to have welcomed and petted me, as the one of his grandsons destined to live the most amongst books, did not suffer me to be four-and twenty hours in the house before he solemnly assured his daughter "that I should break her heart, and (what was worse) that I should never know my A. B. C." He maintained this ill opinion of my disposition and talents with the obstinacy which he carried into most of his articles of belief; and I cannot call to mind ever having received from him a caress or a kind word.[1]

In spite of such negative beginnings, his early life was not all sorrowful. He spent these years alone with his mother, who lavished on him all the love that she could not share with her husband. Between the two was great affection and sympathy. His mother would recite poetry, particularly that of Goldsmith and Gray, and would read from Homer stories of the siege of Troy. As the little boy listened, he was held captivated and began, even before he could write, to compose verses of his own. He wrote: "Verse fell from my mother's lips as the diamond and rose from the lips of her in the fairy tale. I marveled, and I mimicked. I heard "The tale of Troy divine, the deeds and death of Hector, and my soul was on fire."[2]

It was from this mother's devotion and from her efforts to compensate for a very pained situation that England gained one of her most prolific writers. Lytton is noted for his ability to hold his audience in archeological and historical novels, which were written with astonishing accuracy.

Lytton could converse and make rhyme even in his infant stage. He remembered:

> I used to hear them [the servants] prophesy in low tones of the brilliant futurity of Master Edward. There was one legend concerning me that always came out in these vaticinations, and I repeat it because it had probably its lasting effect on my mind and therefore reacted on my fate. Once, when I was yet in arms, a man with a wild air abruptly stopped my nurse in the streets, and, looking upon me strangely, asked whose son I was. The nurse replied that I was the son of General Bulwer. The stranger then, with much solemnity, took me in his arms, and uttered a prophecy to the purpose that I was to be greater than my father, and something remarkable.[3]

Lytton noted that whether the man was sane or crazy, the maids repeated the incident so often that it influenced his actions and his ideas of the future. He felt that his life had been "entrusted with a mission to the hearts of beings unborn, and that in the long chain of thought connecting age with age my own being would hereafter be recognized as a visible link."[4]

When Lytton was seven years old his grandfather died, leaving a large library, for his grandfather had been a Latin scholar of some note. The books were moved to the Lytton home, where young Lytton spent twelve months of ceaseless undirected reading. Reflecting on this experience Lytton said: "I was Solomon in all his glory, and surrounded by all ... Where I found a book in English it sufficed for me, no matter how dry and how far above my reason; I still looked and lingered read and wondered ... and there, when the flood settled, I rested my infant ark."[5] The extraordinary energy, force, and spirit seemed to drive him all of his life. After a year or more of such exploration he asked his mother: "Pray, are you not sometimes overcome by the sense of your own identity?"[6] This comment prompted her to enroll him in a boys' academy. As the smallest and youngest at school he soon became the favorite target of a gang of bigger boys. His first night at the school, he was gagged and bound and banged against a tree. He was shocked at their low, gross slang and habits. He learned that with the unfeeling, feeling is a crime. His health all but gave way under the circumstances and his mother promptly removed him. Although his time at the school was short, it had an effect on his character. He later stated that it left on his mind a hatred of cruelty and oppression that never faded.

After this experience, he attended several other schools, finally staying at Dr. Hooker's school, where the boys were gentleman, and he began to gain some direction in his studies. But school was not were he wanted to be, and he begged his mother to let him stay home and to give him a tutor. At last she relented.

In this village he loved to wander and one day he crossed two or three fields intent on settling down near a river. There he met a beautiful young girl who, since her mother and sister had died, was much at liberty as was Lytton. They consequently met each day by the banks of the Brent and fell deeply in love; they believed nature intended them for each other. She was well bred and gracious. One day, however, she did not meet Lytton nor the next nor the next. She had suddenly disappeared. Lytton fell into a Byronic state of overwhelming sadness.

Three years later the girl sent him a letter from her deathbed, explaining that her father had forced her into a marriage with a man she never loved. She had tried to make it work and had been a devoted wife as best she knew to be. She hinted that the cause of her approaching death was a broken heart. Lytton visited her grave and after a night of meditating, he felt reborn, gaining a more healthful mind and dedicating his life to literature. This experience, Lytton felt, helped him become more soft and gentle and his boyhood ambitions became subdued.

He attended Trinity College at Cambridge Hall, where he devoted himself to reading history. He began keeping huge notebooks, which afterwards became the basis for his historical novels. After his studies, he left England and traveled throughout Europe studying French, writing Byronic poetry, and working on his first novel, *Falklands*.

In order to write, Lytton required intervals of complete solitude. This need may have influenced his unhappy marriage. Against his mother's wishes, Lytton married a young lady who came from a sadly broken home. As he gained fame for his writing and on his appointment to Parliament, she gained a desire for luxuries. In order to sustain themselves Lytton had to write continuously, which meant he needed more time to himself. Interruptions often caused him to be short-tempered. While his wife was well provided for physically, she had little of his time. She didn't suffer in silence. Two boys were born to their unfortunate marriage, which eventually fell apart.

England at this time was in a state of ease, having won the battles at Trafalgar and Waterloo. Napoleon I was a prisoner at St. Helena, and the Bourbons were temporarily back on the throne in France. King George III, having gone insane, had died, and England was entering a period of peace that was to last one hundred years. In this state of affairs England began to expand her industry and to see extraordinary intellectual achievement. Society too saw great changes.

It was upon these scenes that Lytton's novel entered English society. Lytton's son said that:

> The satire of his earlier novels is a protest against false social respectabilities; the humor of his later ones is a protest against the disrespect of social realities. By the first he sought to promote social sincerity, and the free play of personal character; by the last, to encourage mutual charity and sympathy amongst all classes on whose interrelation depends the character of society itself.[7]

He entered politics and Parliament as a liberal, but as events changed, he became a conservative.

During his first nine years he worked in support of the Reform Bill, which supported local government by election. He also devoted his energies to develop laws to protect copyrights of original works, reducing the cost of postage, and laws affecting dramatic literature. He presented powerful speeches. In 1848, he became Secretary to the Colonies. While holding this office he organized the new colony of British Columbia. About this time he was twice elected Lord Rector of the University of Glasgow.

However, his greatest contribution lay in his novels, plays, and essays. Evidence of his versatile talent and indefatigable industry appear in almost every department of literature. But his novels, his historical romance novels, affected society the most. The expression, *romantic*, in Webster's 1828 dictionary meant "to rise over, to soar, to reach to a distance, to divine, to romance." So it was with Lytton's novels. His *Last Days of Pompeii* was his most popular novel. Of his plays, *The Lady of Lyons* and *Money* held the stage the longest, the latter being performed into the twentieth century. His novel *The Last of the Barons* included so many revolutions, rebellions, and dethronements, one following another so rapidly that, according to one critic, there was enough historical material to make three novels.

In 1843, Lytton's mother died. Her death was a terrible shock to him. Of her he said, "No one else knew my mother as I did, and I never till now knew half her great qualities and noble heart.... After they said she was dead I felt her hand press mine. ... I sought for escape. The physicians said 'travel'.... I had ... to fly into the other world of books, or thought or reverie."[8] He was able to overcome his loss because he could return to his writing.

Lytton wrote over thirty novels and seven plays. Even though some of his earlier novels possessed the morbid sentimentalism that was popular during that age, he exerted a tremendous mental influence on the writers of the time. His later novels would rise above his earlier works to provide worthy models to follow.

Earnest, thoughtful, conscientious, and painstakingly accurate, Edward George Lytton-Bulwer was at the same time the most versatile author of his day.

"Beneath the rule of men entirely great
The pen is mightier than the sword."
Richelieu, Act ii. Sc. 2[41]

NOTES

[1] Commerce, Anne. *Something About the Author*. Detroit, Mich.: Gale Research Company Book Tower, 1981, 23: 126.

[2] Lytton, the Earl of, by His Grandson. *The Life of Edward Bulwer, First Lord of Lytton*. London: Macmillian and Co., 1913, p. 23.

[3] Ibid., p. 26.

[4] Ibid., p. 27.

[5] Lytton, *Bulwer-Lytton,* p. 15.

[6] Ibid., p. 16.

[7] Lytton, Edward Bulwer Lytton, Baron (son of Edward Lytton-Bulwer). *The Works Of Edward Bulwer-Lytton*. New York: P. F. Collier and Son, 1901, p. 21.

[8] Commerce, p. 130

Edmund Burke *1729-1797*

Irish/English Statesman, Political Author

> *"Respecting your forefathers, you would have been taught to respect yourselves."*

THE EIGHTEENTH CENTURY WAS AN ERA OF GREAT POLITICAL polarity. At the apex of each pole stood two men of renown, one who followed ancient political principles, the other who decried the wisdom of the ages. The former was Edmund Burke; the latter, Jean Jacques Rousseau.

Rousseau's philosophies of abstraction, emancipation, and an impotent deity, among others, greatly contributed to the French Revolution. On the other hand, Burke felt that liberty is true liberty only when it has its bearing and its ensigns in the past. Freedom must have a pedigree from time immemorial in order to have a native dignity. Burke's system was one of prescription, experience, duty to old ties, the reign of law, and an omnipotent God. Without such connections, he felt, freedom is not liberty, but anarchy. Although Burke was originally criticized for his beliefs, in time Burke's philosophies and his unwavering stand for the ancient principles of government served to lead the populace of England to a greater conviction of their own principles and a heightened sense of patriotism

Because France's revolution systematically destroyed the past, Burke was concerned about its results. He could see that the leaders of the French Revolution worked for freedom by discrediting any wisdom from the past simply because it was old. He noted that other revolutionists had slain people, but French Revolutionists had slain the mind as well.

Long before Paris was laid to waste, Burke put in writing his concerns about the direction France was heading and his opinions and were strongly attacked. Nevertheless, his prophetic warnings of the potential calamities that would result from France's course came to pass with precisioned accuracy. France's revolution ended in chaos and destruction—not in freedom.

In the American Revolution Burke saw a different course, a cause he ardently supported. The American founders, unlike those of the French, had searched out liberty's ancient pedigree and laid the foundations of the new government accordingly.

Burke lived through one of the most unique times in history. His life spanned not only the American Revolution, the French Revolution, and the corruptness of his own government, but Burke also lived through the destruction of his native land during the Irish Rebellion, events that had enormous historical impact. Burke's writings and observation at this time established him as one of the greatest names in the history of political literature. His writings were a political testament.

Whether or not people are aware of it, Burke was a major contributor to the unchanging fundamentals of sound government. His political preferences were relevant only to his time, but his political principles are timeless. He discerned Divine Guidance in history, and because he was the champion of permanent things, his voice is ageless. Unlike others he is not famous so much for what he did as much as for what he was able to perceive. In an era of revolution Burke was not only a conservator, but a reformer and philosopher as well. These are the elements of Burke's legacy.

Although Burke's public presence and writings are well known, he was very quiet about his private life. There is even some question as to the date of his birth. The most generally accepted date is 12 January 1729, in Dublin, Ireland. As a child he had delicate health and was tenderly cared for by his mother. It was under these conditions that his mother first taught him to read. Burke had a strong affection for his mother, who was a woman of cultivated understanding.[1] She and her family were Catholics and his father's family were Protestant. Despite the religious differences between them, however, he dearly loved them both. During his years as a statesman he was known for his continual efforts in promoting religious tolerance.

As a young boy Burke was sent to the country in the hope that the fresh air would give vigor to his frame. So young Burke went to stay with his maternal grandparents, the Nagles. Part of the Nagle estate consisted of medieval ruins. It was here that he first entered school, and it was here with his Virgil and the estate ruins that his devotion to the classical and the "ancients" began to settle upon his mind in earnest.

Burke had a deep appreciation for those educators and mentors who touched his life. In later years when Burke returned to Ireland for a visit, his old schoolmaster, whose name was O'Halloran, sought out his now famous student and great statesman. When Burke saw his old master he dropped all that he was doing and rushed to take the aged man by both hands, lovingly looking him in the eyes and expressed his gratitude for his old master. [2]

From the Nagle estate, young Burke was sent to a Quaker school at Ballitore since his health still could not take the air of Dublin. This Quaker school was run by a remarkable master, Abraham Shackleton. Burke spent two very productive years with Shackleton and formed a lifelong friendship with Shackleton's son Richard. It is to Abraham Shackleton that Burke always gave credit for anything that he accomplished as a result of education. However, it was not so much the master's skills that impressed him as it was his daily example of integrity and simplicity of heart.[3]

An experience at this time gives a good example of Burke's character:

> A poor man having been compelled to pull down his cabin, because the surveyor of roads declared it stood too near the highway, Burke, who saw the reluctant owner perform his melancholy task, observed with great indignation, that if he were in authority such tyranny should never be exercised with impunity over the defenseless: and he urged his school fellows to join in rebuilding the cottage.[4]

Burke's defense of justice seemed to have come at an early age, and he never departed from the principles he exemplified in this incident.

By the age of fifteen, his health had somewhat stabilized and Burke entered Trinity College. Here he was rather a lackluster student, much to his father's frustration. His father was a lawyer and had high ambitions for his son. He wanted him to practice law. The older Burke may have felt that his young son wasted his life in literature and politics. During this time Burke's attention was drawn to a close examination of literature and the study of theology in a study of the principles of how to govern himself and the commonwealth.

Among his favorite English authors were Shakespeare, Spenser, Milton, Waller, and Young; and among the ancients he favored Virgil, Cicero, Sallust, Homer, Juvenal, Lucian, Xenophon, and Epictetus. Like his contemporary Samuel Johnson, Burke read everything. He later advised more reading of "the writings of those who have gone before us than our Contemporaries ...."[5]

While at Trinity he was accustomed to rise with the dawn and walk out of the city to the fresh countryside until the want of breakfast drove him back. These morning walks provided time for contemplation and evaluation, a time in which his philosophies began to take root in his mind.

In 1750, having finished his degree, Burke was sent to Middle Temple in London to pursue his law studies. He had briefly contemplated remaining at Trinity as a teacher but the character of the professors seemed to have repelled him. He later wrote in the *Annual Register*: "He that lives in college, after his mind is sufficiently stocked with learning, is like a man, who having built and rigged and victualed a ship, should lock her up in a dry dock."[6]

While in England, Burke would sometimes retire to Bath for his health. There he met Dr. Nugent, who was one of the original members of Dr. Johnson's famous literary club. Dr. Nugent took a liking to young Burke and invited him to his home. Burke could not help noticing the doctor's beautiful sixteen-year-old daughter. They courted for some six years before they married. Burke found much solace and strength from this gentle lady and they were deeply devoted to each other. (It is interesting to note that like Burke's mother, Miss Nugent had been raised Catholic. Later, his detractors would use his wife's family's religion against him.)

The study of law was so contrary to his natural desires that he forsook it entirely. This was more than Burke's stern father, with his ambitions for his son, could tolerate. He severed his son's allowance. With this Burke began to earn his way with his writings, which were meager at best. His father's harshness perhaps accounts for the reason Burke remained in England instead of returning to his native Ireland, and for a time Burke even considered emigrating to America.

Little is known about the next nine years of Burke's life. Slowly his writings gained recognition. In 1756 he published *A Vindication of Natural Society,* a satirical attack on a rationalistic approach to religion written by a noted member of Parliament named Bollingbroke. Burke felt it was evident that religion required something more than reason for its foundation. Faith, he wrote, was indispensable to social order—faith in one's fellow citizens, as well as in the system. *A Vindication,* published anonymously, was written so exactly in Bollingbroke's style that many, even the critics, thought that it was Bollingbroke himself who wrote it.

In 1757, Burke became editor of the *Annual Register,* a position he held for the next thirty-two years. The *Register* analyzed the political events of the world at that time and gave Burke a vast store of knowledge of contemporary governments. It was in the pages of the *Register* that readers began to discover men who were to become some of the greatest political writers of the day—Edmund Burke and Adam Smith. Burke and Smith had a great admiration for each other, though it is not known whether they ever met except through their writings.

When George III assumed the crown, Burke entered the House of Commons and began twenty-five years of public service. He stood in opposition to many of the acts of George III. His untiring efforts finally led to the repeal of the Stamp Act, to the resolution against general warrants and seizure of papers, and to the protection of private houses from the intrusion of tax officers by the repeal of the cider tax.[7] He was so committed to following his conscience that at one time he did so at the loss of his own party and Parliamentary friends.

One of his greatest accomplishments came through his role in the Warren Hastings trial. The British governor of India, Hastings, was tried for high crimes and abuses. The atrocities and lawlessness with which Hastings had ruled in India led Burke to, as some have stated, a "divine rage." The trial lasted fourteen years. Hastings, who had many friends and connections in high places, was finally acquitted.

Although Hasting was acquitted, the long trial was not in vain, for England had heard Burke's plea for decency and justice. The influence of Burke's long years of work changed the way in which England began to rule India. By demand of the English public, strong laws of protection were passed. Burke wrote of this event: "If I were to call for a reward, it would be for the services in which for fourteen years without intermission, I showed the most industry and had the least success, I mean in the affairs of India ..."[8]

By his untiring efforts a whole nation was set upon the road to dignity and education. This very act eventually led to the foundations of self-government for India.

Burke was the only statesman member of Johnson's famous literary club. Johnson wrote that although he detested Burke's political party, " I love his knowledge, his genius, his diffusion and affluence of conversation." Johnson went on to say that Burke was "an extraordinary man."[9] Thomas Macaulay wrote that Burke was "the greatest man since Milton."[10]

Burke was gifted to see beyond the temporary governances of the day. He recognized the sacredness of law and defended it with holy fervor. He once noted that "there is a sacred veil to be drawn over the beginning of all governments"[11] and that it was only proper to attempt to thin that veil through the study of history. And that history is a great volume "unrolled for our instruction, drawing the material of future wisdom from the past errors."[12]

NOTES

[1] See Prior, James. *Life of the Right Honourable Edmund Burke.* London: George Bell & Sons, 1889, p. 5.

[2] See ibid., p. 6.

[3] See Morley, John. *Burke.* London: Macmillan and Co., 1904, p. 4.

4 Kirk, Russell. *Edmund Burke A Genius Reconsidered.* New York: Arlington House, 1967, p. 23-24.

5 Ibid., p. 24-25.

6 Ibid., p. 26.

7 See Encyclopedia Britannica. 11th ed. 1910, 4:827.

8 Ibid., p. 830.

9 Ibid., p. 828.

10 Morley, p. 3.

11 Encyclopedia Britannica, 4:832.

12 Harvard Classics. Conn.: Grolier Enterprises, 1980, p. 275.

Robert Burns   1759-1796

SCOTTISH POET

> *"But deep this truth impress'd my mind—*
> *Thro' all His works abroad,*
> *The heart benevolent and kind*
> *The most resembles God."*

NATURE, IN HER HARROWING, OFTTIMES SOWS A CERTAIN SEED full of thundering restraint. That seed is divine, and encased in mortal soil it receives nourishment, deprivation, or both. In 1759, such a seed was born—Robert Burns of Scotland. Burns was born full of celestial messages, yet without the facilitation or means to easily perform his divine mandate. Notwithstanding his station in life, Burns was to become the greatest poet Scotland ever produced and was loved throughout the entire English world.

The life of Robert Burns is a span of paradoxes often contradictory and complex. Although he worked from the first light of day to the last light of sun at night, poverty was ever his lot. Known as an expert plowman, he would follow his plow with a book in hand, and then by candlelight write out his supreme dictates. Nothing escaped the view of this heaven-taught plowman; such works as "The Fall of a Leaf," "To a Mountain Daisy," "To a Mouse," "To a Louse," "Yon Wild Mossy Mountains", all came from his daily communion with his surroundings.

He once described to his friend George Thompson the way his poetry came about:

I walk out, sit down now & then, look out for objects in nature around me that are in unison or harmony with the cogitations of my fancy & workings of my bosom; humming every now & then the air with the verses I have framed: when I feel my Muse [the deity or power of poetry] beginning to jade,

I retire to the solitary fireside of my study, & there commit my effusion to paper.[1]

Burns said, "The poetic genius of my country found me ... at the plough, and threw her inspiring mantle over me. She bade me sing the loves, the joys, the rural scenes and rural pleasures of my native soil, in my native tongue. I tuned my wild artless notes as she inspired."[2] His was tsaid to be the purest and finest of poetry.

One of the greatest lyricists of all time, he was the very soul of Scotland. Because of his love of liberty and justice and brotherhood, he raised all of Scotland to a new state of patriotism. Sir Walter Scott called Burns's work "fine strains of sublime patriotism."[3]

His poem "A Man's a man for A' That" was a clear note for democracy:

"....Then let us pray that come it may,
As come it will
That sense and worth, o'er all the earth,
May bear thee agree
That man to man, the world over
Shall brothers be."

His "Ode for General Washington's Birthday" is a clarion call to his own native land to become sons of liberty:

" ... To thee [Scotland] I turn with swimming eyes;
— Where is the soul of Freedom fled?"

Burns had the ability to turn the Scottish heart to its own land. As Thomas Carlyle noted: "A tide of Scottish [patriotism], had been poured along his veins; and he felt that it would boil there till the flood-gates shut in eternal rest."[4]

Robert Burns was born to William and Agnes Brown Burns on 25 January 1759. A few days later a northwest storm blew a portion of the wall and roof off their little farm home down, driving William to seek shelter for his wife and child with a nearby neighbor. Turbulent was his birth and turbulent was his life.

Burns's father, William, had profound nobility of soul. He was as pure before his maker as ever a man came to be. He was a man of great strength and devotion. He continually supplemented his sons' limited education as they worked on the farm and during evening sessions by the fire. Rooted in the Bible, their lessons included history and grammar. Gilbert, Burns's younger brother, wrote:

> My father was for some time almost the only companion we had. He conversed familiarly on all subjects with us as if we had been men, and was at great pains while we accompanied him in the labors of the farm, to lead the conversation to such subjects as might tend to increase our knowledge, or confirm us in virtuous habits.[5]

No son ever had a more attentive father. Some writers pronounced him stern because of his resolve to do right and be honest. But to classify him in this way is to do him an injustice; his feet were firmly placed upon the path of honesty, integrity, and the hard labor that was the lot of poor Scottish land tenants. To these qualities of his father, Burns was never untrue

It was because of the burdens his good father bore that Burns developed a bitter dislike for the separation of the classes and reflected this in his writings. It was hard for him to accept his father's struggles with poverty and want as the family was continually harassed by the landowner's agent. These reflections of his devout and oppressed father produced in Burns's mind sensations of deepest distress.

Burns's mother, Agnes, was devoted to her husband and children. She worked hard and she sang as she worked. Many of the songs she sang had been passed from generation to generation without ever being written down. Sometimes whole verses had been lost and new verses added, and some lines were altered beyond recognition. The tunes were old and often ancient. Agnes had an excellent voice, sweet and strong. Her memory served her well with an unending repertoire of songs. Her children loved to listen to her, especially Robert who never tired of hearing her sing, and the children often joined her in singing.

But of all the paradoxes in Burns's life, the greatest was that he was tone-deaf. His mother's music could set the melody pulsing in him, but he could not vocally release it. It was not until he discovered poetry that he discovered his own source of release. Had he not been tone-deaf, the world probably would not have received the wondrous gifts from the pen of Robert Burns.

A fortunate accident helped prepare him for his poetic future. An uncle brought what he thought was a letter-writer book to the Burns, but it turned out to be a small collection of the most eminent writers, which exposed Burns to the great masters.

Burns never forgot his mother's songs or the love he had for them. Years later he would search out and collect old Scottish songs and write them down. He also wrote new tunes to old songs. He did this while he remained a poor land tenant, working as an exciseman, being a husband and father and suffering from weakening conditions of health. In doing so he preserved a diminishing heritage.

Arthur Henry King, an English literary scholar has stated: "If a man is a promoter of freedom, he has a generosity of the soul that can lead to a frailty in his actions."[6] So it was with Burns. He had the power of making man's life more honorable and reverenced, but as Carlyle said: "That of wisely guiding his own life was not given."[7] In protesting against hypocrisy he, like Byron, occasionally stepped beyond the limits of prescribed good taste. Nevertheless he was keenly aware of his own mortal failings, and often sought a merciful God repentantly.

Though Burns's sympathies were on the side of right, his personal acts were at times irresponsible and often without excuse, though seldom irreverent. He possessed a strong religious faith in a benevolent Creator. For that reason he was opposed to the Calvinistic doctrine of his day, that of "original sin" with no room for repentance. He felt that the whole business was reversed: "We come in to this world with a heart & disposition to do good for it," but we soon find ourselves "under a kind of cursed necessity of turning selfish" in our own defense. He was "glad to grasp at revealed religion."[8]

Some claim that Burns died of alcoholism; however, stories of his intoxication appear exaggerated. It does not appear documented that he drank more than any other ordinary Scotsman. Mr. Alexander, his superior officer in the Excise office, publicly stated that Burns "was quite capable of discharging the duties of his office, nor was he ever known to drink by himself or seen to indulge in the use of liquor in a forenoon .... and I never beheld anything like the gross enormities with which he is now charged."[9]

The fairer sex was perhaps his greatest intoxication. The very presence of a woman seemed to hold him in a mystical spell. His first poem as a youth was to a young lass with whom he was, in the old Scottish tradition, paired to work in the hay fields at haying time. Burns noted that he had not even had an inclination to be a poet till his heart brimmed with love for "Nell." Once this love awoke his genius, it became the cornerstone of his work: the love of nature, of fellow man, homeland, and especially, of the heart.

As he grew older his father sent him to learn the rudiments of surveying in Edinburgh. Here he became filled with admiration of the lovely daughter of one of the scholars. Upon his return he was asked by a friend, "Well, and did you admire the young lady?"

"I admired God Almighty more than ever!" was the reply: "Miss Burnett is the most heavenly of all his works."[10]

This example expresses Burns's lifelong attitude toward women and their influence in his life and work. He regarded women as "the blood-royal of life."[11]

Auld Nature swears, the lovely dear
Her noblest work she classes
Her prentice han' she tried on man.
An' then she made the lasses.

Burns felt deep loyalty towards his family. When his father died, Burns supported his mother and brother and sisters. In an old Scottish custom, he signed a paper of marriage with Jean Armour. But after she bore twins, her father forbade her to see Burns and tore up the "paper." Devastated Burns decided to leave Scotland for Jamaica. He intended to sell his poems for passage. To his surprise the poems were wonderfully successful, and he decided not to sail.

Jean's father finally relented to a formal marriage after a second set of twins was born. Burns then settled in supervising the construction of a new home for his growing family. He personally supervised the education of his children. When his health began to fail, his chief concern was for his wife and their four living children. In reflecting on home life he wrote the all-time favorite poem "The Cotter's Saturday Night":

The parents pair their secret homage pay.
And proffer up to Heaven the warm request,
That He who stills the raven's clam'rous nest
And decks the lily fair in flow'ry pride,
Would, in the way His wisdom sees the best,
For them and for their little ones provide;
But *chiefly,* in their hearts with grace divine preside.

Burns referred to himself as a Scottish "bard," which, according to Noah Webster's 1828 dictionary, is a poet and singer among the ancient Celts. The occupation of the bard was to compose and sing verses "in honor of the heroic achievements of princes and brave men." Burns fit this definition well for his verses were filled with such declarations.

Statements made by his wife and brother indicate that he had a rheumatic heart condition and often kept a glass of cold water by his bedstand for the time when his heart fluttered. A splash of water seemed to help him catch his breath. This health condition and his early death were in part the result of the privations and strenuous work of his youth.

In 1795, his health gave way. Burns was sent to a distant town for its mineral baths and health. This trip was more detrimental than healthful, and he returned home in an extremely emaciated state. On 26 June 1796, he wrote to Mr. James Clarke:

Still, still the victim of affliction! ... Whether I shall ever get about again is only known to Him, the Great Unknown, whose creature I am.... As to my individual self, I am tranquil, and would despise myself if I were not; but Burns' poor widow and half a dozen of his dear little ones—helpless orphans!— there I am weak as a woman's tear. ...[12]

Burns's short life came to an end on 21 July 1796, at thirty-six years of age. He was buried on 25 July, the same day his widow, Jean, gave birth to a son, Maxwell. Before his death Burns prophesied to his wife: "Don't be afraid. I'll be more respected a hundred years after I'm dead than I am at present."[13]

NOTES

[1] Fitzhugh, Robert T. *Robert Burns: The Man and the Poet: A Round, Unvarnished Account.* Boston: Houghton Mifflin Company, 1970, p. 13.

[2] Duyckinck, Evert A. *Portrait Gallery of Eminent Men and Women.* New York: Henry J. Johnson, 1873, p. 215.

[3] Scott Sir Walter. *The Journal of Sir Walter Scott.* New York: Harper & Brother, 1890, 1:276.

[4] Carlyle, Thomas. *Burns.* Chicago: Scott, Foresman & Co., 1903, p. 89.

[5] Daiches, David. *Robert Burns.* New York: Macmillan,   n.d., p. 46.

[6] Personal correspondence with Arthur Henry King, July 1992.

[7] Carlyle, p. 52.

[8] Fitzhugh, p. 15.

[9] Crichton-Browne, Sir James. *Burns from a New Point of View.* London: Hodder and Stoughton Limited, n.d., , p. 53.

[10] Duyckinck, p. 215.

[11] Fitzhugh, p. 6.

[12] Crichton-Browne, p. 83.

[13] Fitzhugh, p. 12.

Lord George Gordon Byron

ENGLISH POET

1788-1824

> *"The king-times are fast finishing. There will be blood shed like water and tears like mist; but the people will conquer in the end. I shall not live to see it, but I foresee it."*

IN THE GREAT LITERARY WORKS CONFLICT AND TRAGEDY ARE often symbolized by the main characters. Characters may often personify the passing of one era, and the pains of birthing a new one. In Shakespearean tragedies, such as *Hamlet,* the main characters were often troubled by the political and social events of the day. In Goethe's *Faust* the two leading characters represent classical Greece (Helen) and the changing feudal Germany (Faust). *Don Quixote* represents the conflict between the "natural man" and the man given to a "glorious quest."

The life history of Lord George Byron could have fit any number of themes written by Shakespeare, Goethe, or Cervantes. But Lord Byron was not a fictional character. His life was real. Like the fictional Faust, Byron was born into a crumbling culture brimming with hypocrisy and grave injustices. Rumblings of a revolution in France made life among the British Isles uneasy for those of power and position. Lord Byron's restless spirit knew little peace, suffering as a child, a youth, and then a young adult. He thus turned to writing to express and deal with his painful perceptions. As he grew in maturity and talent, Lord Byron became a voice for freedom, using much of his writing to satirize the corruptions of the day. The force of Byron's poetry served to cleanse the culture and influence for the better the morals of the time.

Byron probably had more influence outside of England than any other English poet except Shakespeare; his influence on the continent was far greater than in England. Goethe, in a conversation after the death of Byron, said: "The English may think of Byron as they please; but this is certain, that they can show no poet who is to be compared with him. He is different from all the others and for the most part, greater."[1]

Goethe was fascinated by Byron, who gave his life in Greece defending freedom. Goethe used a Byron-like character to finish his incomplete play *Faust*.

Giuseppe Mazzini, the great Italian patriot of the time, wrote of Byron:

> The day will come when Democracy will remember all that it owes to Byron. England too will, I hope one day remember the European role given by him to English literature. ... Before he came, all that was known of English literature was the French translation of Shakespeare. It is since Byron that we Continentalists have learned to study Shakespeare and other English writers.
>
> From him dates the sympathy of all the true-hearted amongst us for this land of liberty, whose true vocation he so worthily represented among the oppressed. He led the genius of Britain on pilgrimage throughout all Europe.[2]

George Gordon Byron was born in London, 22 January 1788, to Catherine Gordon and John Byron. Not long after this only child's birth, the parents separated. Byron was born with one foot twisted, which caused him to limp. Because of this defect he was taunted and treated unkindly. Tragically, an autopsy performed after his death disclosed that the foot had been merely dislocated, but there had not been enough medical knowledge to set the bones properly.

Living in near poverty, Byron's mother struggled with her mental well-being, often lapsing into fits of violent rage followed by profound indulgence. Because of the mental state of his mother and the absence of a father, Byron did not receive the tenderness and care needed for healthy emotional development. But it created in him a craving for tenderness not only for himself but a tenderness he would give to others, especially those who were oppressed.

Byron was often cared for by a hired nurse, and it was from one of them, who was apparently very religious, that Byron was introduced to some knowledge of the scriptures and stories from the Bible at a very young age.

When not yet five years old Byron was sent to a day school. After day school Byron was placed under the guidance of a clergy-man named Ross. Byron recollects of this time: "Under him I made astonishing progress.... The moment I could read, my grand passion was history."[3] Thereafter he deliberately set out to know something about every country. Byron's subsequent teacher was a kind tutor named Paterson from Scotland.

As a boy, Byron was not always tuned to the dry intellectual work of the private school he attended. He greatly desired to participate in sports, but since he was lame, his participation was limited. He did, however, excel in swimming, which skill would later save his life in a shipwreck in Italy.

At the age of ten, upon the death of a grand-uncle, George Byron became "Lord" Byron because there were no other direct line descendants. This placed him in a position of nobility for which he was neither prepared nor totally accepted because of his former poverty and lack of training. Some have said that if he had been born with wealth and status he might never have become the poet of the Revolution and "the most powerful exponent of the modern spirit."[4]

Byron was always the champion of the oppressed and much of his writings reflect this. One day in school a companion fell under the displeasure of an overbearing bully who beat him unmercifully. Byron happened to be present, but knowing the uselessness of undertaking a fight with the bully, he stepped up to him and asked him how much longer he intended to beat his friend. "What's that to you?" gruffly demanded the bully. "Because," replied young Byron, tears in his eyes, "I will take the rest of the beating if you will let him go."[5]

The title of "Lord" gave Byron ownership of Newstead Abbey, more commonly known to us as Sherwood Forest. The estate was old and in great disrepair, but it was here that Byron found salve for his emptiness. Wandering about in nature, he found companionship among the crickets, birds, and other animals of the field. His retreats to nature continued throughout his life.

When Byron was about nineteen he became infatuated with a girl two years older than he, a Miss Chatworth. Although she looked upon him as a mere schoolboy, she enjoyed his company and his passion led him to believe she returned his feelings. He continued in his delusion until one day he overheard her casual words to her maid: "Do you think I could care anything for that lame boy?"

This comment, as Byron himself describes it, shot through his heart. He darted out of the house and ran until he arrived at Newstead, where he began in earnest to write, trying to rid himself of his pain.

At the age of 17, in 1805, he entered Cambridge. Here again he was drawn to swimming, riding, fencing, and boxing rather than his academic pursuits. It was at this time that he had great difficulty with his mother as her mental condition was becoming more explosive. He found stability in the friendship of the Pigotts, a brother and a sister, who had read some of his writings and encouraged him to write more.

He had written many verses but was too shy to share them until the Pigotts encouraged him. His stimulus for writing seemed to come either from love or defiance. His first publication "Hours of Idleness" received considerable circulation in London. After a stinging criticism appeared in the *Edinburgh Review*, Byron's sensitivities caused him to lash back with a satire entitled "English Bards and Scotch Reviewers." Published only a few days after he took his seat in the House of Lords, Byron's retort became the talk of the town.

Byron is known for a certain boistrousness, as shown when he decided to have a "house warming party" with four of his good friends at Newstead. One member of the group reported that they slept until noon. The afternoon was spent in various diversions such as fencing, riding, playing cricket. They dined about eight. Then in the dark of the night they dared each other to drink wine from a human skull that had been found in an ancient cemetery at

Newstead. The servants, who stayed out of the house until morning, returned to find a week's worth of dishes and a horse in the library.[6]

Soon after this experience Byron left for a tour of the continent. While traveling through the different countries, Byron obtained firsthand knowledge of the changes that were about to take place. Europe was a pot that was about to boil over. He also spent some time in Greece basking in the great history of that conquered land.

Upon his return to England Byron took several manuscripts to his publishers. The publisher was not impressed and asked if he had any more. Byron described a personal paper he was working on, which the publisher asked to see. Excited about this new work, the publisher asked Byron to polish it and get it ready to print. The poem, *The Pilgrimage of Childe Harolde,* accurately reflected the problems of the current century and was an overnight success, not only in England but in Europe as well. His instant fame was like something out of a fairy tale book. Byron himself describes this event: "I awoke one morning and found myself famous."[7] He was now but twenty-four and at the pinnacle of literary fame. Nowhere in history can one find an equal instance of so sudden a rise to such a height.

Now famous, Byron was invited and courted by all the leading members of society. No one was considered a "real" part of society until he had had Byron to one of his parties. The hypocrisy of being courted by people who formerly had snubbed him was offensive to him.

It was during this time that his mother, during one of her violent fits, died. Although their relationship had been a difficult one, her death was hard on him.

In his search for some kind of "normalcy" Byron began looking for a wife, one that was cool-headed and sensible. He set his mind on Miss Anne Milbanke, and in a letter he proposed to her. She replied, also in a letter, that she appreciated his proposal but kindly refused his offer. Byron was not discouraged and wrote again, pleading for the privilege of being her husband. The second time she consented and they were married 2 January 1815. On 10 December of that same year, a daughter, Augusta Ada was born to them.

Byron reported in some of his letters to friends that these two events brought him great happiness. But, bored of the country life, he returned to London. While there Anne wrote to tell him that she and the baby were going to visit her father. This letter was followed by another from her father, telling Byron that she would not be returning and that she wanted a separation.

This separation was the talk of all of England. What caused the separation no one ever knew. To the credit of both Byron and Lady Byron, they both remained silent. In response to one inquiry, Byron merely stated, "The causes were too simple ever to be found out."[8] But the public hungered for reasons and there were a number of people ready to "tell." Although there are to this day many rumors, the facts neither support nor deny them. When Byron, not having seen his wife for many years, was on his death bed in Greece, his final words were: "Go to Lady Byron—you will see her, and say—" Here his voice faltered and gradually faded.[9]

News of the couple's separation unleashed a flurry of scorn. Former admirers threw their star from the sky with an instant death. The press warned the poet through friends not to appear at public events for fear of the mobs. Disgusted with the fickle English, Byron left England, never to return until his death.

Settling in Italy, Byron found a land in the embryo stages of a revolution. At this time Italy was ruled by Austria and, as with the rest of Europe, the desire for independence moved in the heart and soul of the people of Italy.

Byron was befriended by Count Gamba, whose family was deeply involved in the revolutionary movement. Count Gamba had a daughter, the Countess Guiccioli, who was separated from an elderly husband. In time Byron and the Countess became constant companions. He began to write prolifically during this time and found that outside of England, the rest of Europe responded well to him. His sympathy with the oppressed, his sense of the world's past greatness, and his enjoyment of nature appeared in his writings, stripping away the pretenses of greed and tyranny.

Byron felt that a man should do more for society than just write verses. So he directly involved himself in the Italian revolutionary movement, doing things that the Gambas could not do because they were closely watched. During the insurrection of 1820 he said, "Whatever I can do by money, means, or person, I will venture freely for their freedom."[10] The insurrection failed, but the encouragement of the poet helped keep alive a thin hope until the time of Garibaldi, Italy's errant knight, and Count Camillo Bonso di Cavour, who became known as the father of modern Italy.

Byron was then approached to help in the liberation of Greece, he threw himself into the work. Outfitting a boat he sailed with one of the freedom-loving Gamba brothers to Greece, where he found the revolution split into several parties. Byron went to work training men and giving the revolutionists large sums of money. His work helped to bring the rival parties together, and he was appointed governor-general of the enfranchised parts of Greece.

During this time, Byron's health was not good. One day while he was riding it began to rain; by the time he got home he was thoroughly chilled. It was only a couple of days before his friends and a servant knew that he was dying. In his last moments Byron smiled and said: "Oh, what a beautiful scene!" and then he cried "Forward, forward—courage—follow."[11] Finally, when he sought to send a message to his wife, his voice faded out and, he passed away.

It has been said, that in his death England lost her brightest genius and Greece her noblest friend. Byron's heart was buried in Greece and his body sent back to England. The poet Joaquim Miller's admiration of Byron led him to Newstead Abbey where he met with a few of Byron's friends, all of whom spoke of Byron's goodness of heart. And so it is by the intent of his heart that Byron must be judged. Miller found piles of Byron's manuscripts. There were enough manuscripts to cover approximately a ten-acre field and all were written in the same sprawling hand. Miller found that the king of Greece spoke Byron's name with such profound respect, and he mentioned more than once that if Lord Byron had lived he surely would have been chosen by Greece for her first king.[12]

Although Byron's actions were not always as noble as they should have been, in the cause of freedom "he was courageous, he was kind, and he loved truth rather than lies. He was a worker and a fighter. He hated tyranny and was prepared to sacrifice money and ease of life in the cause of popular freedom."[13] Lord Byron was the voice of freedom and the defender of the oppressed.

NOTES

[1] Ward, Thomas. *The English Poets.* New York: Macmillian, 1894, 4: 254.

[2] Ibid., p. 254.

[3] Duyckinck, Evert A. *Portrait Gallery of Eminent Men and Women.* New York: Henry J. Johnson, 1873. p. 509.

[4] *A Dictionary of Arts, Science and General Literatture.* New York: Warner Co., 1900, 5: 605.

[5] Roberts, B. H. *The Gospel.* Salt Lake City: George Q. Cannon & Son Co., 1803, p. 14-15.

[6] See Encyclopedia Britannica, 11th ed. 1910, p. 4:899.

[7] Perry Bliss, ed. *Little Masterpieces.* New York: Doubleday and Mcclure, 1902, p. 95.

[8] Encyclopedia Britannica, 4: 609.

[9] Nichols, John. *Lord Byron.* New Jersey: Harper & Brothers, n.d. p. 174.

[10] Ibid., p. 174.

[11] Ward, p. 527.

[12] Miller, Joaquim. *Joaquim Miller's Poems, Introduction and Autobiography.* San Francisco: Harr Wagner Publishing Co., 1917, p. 216.

[13] Encyclopedia Britannica, 4:904.

John C. Calhoun 1782-1850

AMERICAN STATESMAN

"The union — next to our liberty, the most dear."

JOHN C. CALHOUN IS CONSIDERED TO BE THE THIRD MEMBER OF what has been referred to as the "triumvirate" of his day. In Roman times the triumvirate was a union of three men who obtained power and jointly ruled Rome. The first of these were Caesar, Crassus, and Pompey. The three that ruled Congress in the 1800s were Daniel Webster, Henry Clay, and John C. Calhoun.

Calhoun, like so many of the early leaders of this country, was of Scotch-Irish parentage. His grandfather, James Calhoun, came from Ireland in 1733 as a result of religious and economic friction. The family settled in western Pennsylvania. When the French and Indian War broke out, they moved further south into Virginia and then again into the Carolinas, near the Savannah river, a remote frontier territory. But they seemed only to move from one peril into another. Game became scarce in the Carolinas, and the local Indians joined with defeated Indians from the north to attack the settlement. When James Calhoun died, his son Patrick led some two hundred and fifty settlers away from the area in an attempt to reach the safety of Augusta, Georgia.

They had not been long on the journey when several of the wagons bogged down in the mire. The men set down their weapons to push the wagons and without warning a band of Cherokees swept down upon them, killing fifty and capturing several others. Among those dead were Patrick's aged mother, Catherine Montgomery Calhoun, and two of his nieces. A third niece was captured and lived with the Indians in captivity for fourteen years until she was able to escape. Patrick Calhoun was later made captain over a company of men who were assigned to protect the settlements in the "upper country."

Patrick Calhoun married Jean Craighead, who died in her first pregnancy. In 1770 he remarried, choosing this time Martha Caldwell, the daughter of another Scot-Irish settler. This wonderful woman became the mother of John C. Calhoun.

Patrick found a great disparity in South Carolina between the "aristocracy" of the coastal regions and the lower class of the "upper regions." The upper regions were not represented in the seat of government. They were taxed but otherwise virtually ignored. They had no courts and no protection by the law from criminals who fled to the upper regions to escape justice. Feeling that the situation was intolerable, Patrick led a group of men down from the upper regions, a march several hundred miles. Then with rifles in their hands, they forced their way into the voting poles. Patrick was elected as a representative.

These experiences, told over and over again at the fireside as young John sat at the feet of his father, sank deeply into his heart and soul. This was his heritage of "rough but high-strung men who had challenged oppression" in Scotland, in Ireland, and in this new land. He listened intently as they told of attending their first church in America in a crude log meeting-house, with a guard posted outside, men sat inside with rifles across their laps while the preacher taught with a Bible in his hand and a powder horn across his shoulder.

Calhoun grew up appreciating the suffering his family had gone through to gain and maintain their freedom. One uncle of his uncles was killed at the Battle of Cowpens in the American Revolution: he had thirty saber wounds. Another uncle had been captured by the British and held in the hold of an enemy ship for the duration of the war. Another had been shot down by Tories in his own backyard. General Pickens of Revolutionary fame was his uncle.[1]

Calhoun's father, Patrick Calhoun, was a representative to the state constitutional convention, and he cast his vote against the document saying that it "permitted other people than those of South Carolina to tax the people of South Carolina and thus allowed taxation without representation, which was a violation of the fundamental principle of the Revolutionary struggle."[2] At the age of nine, John remembered his father saying that the best government was that which allowed the individual the most liberty, compatible with order and tranquility, and that the objective of all government should be to throw off needless restraints.[3]

Calhoun was born in 1782, the last year the guns of the revolution were heard in his mountains. His first contribution to his family's existence was to search each evening through cotton and find the seeds. He was required to find an ounce before bedtime.[4]

At the age of seven or eight he trudged through the forest to attend a log school, where he learned to read and write and do a little "figuring." This education lasted but a short time.

A new preacher, named Moses Waddell, began visiting the upper regions, often staying at the Calhoun home. Waddell appreciated the Calhoun hospitality, but more importantly he appreciated the beauty of Calhoun's older sister. One night Waddell dreamed that he would marry Catherine Calhoun, but that death would claim her before their first anniversary. The dream was so real that he was convinced of its truth.

In spite of the dire prophesy the pair were married, and Catherine moved with Waddell to Appling, Georgia, where he ran a school for boys. They invited Calhoun to come and stay with them and attend school. The Waddells had been scarcely married a year when his wife passed away. Waddell was so devastated by her death that he closed the boys school and returned to the preaching circuit, leaving young Calhoun alone in his house. There were no neighbors and often it was days before anyone visited. For six weeks thirteen-year-old John was left alone.

Providentially, Waddell had a circulating library in his home. John became so enthralled with reading the books that he often forgot to eat or sleep. He consumed such volumes as Rollin's *Ancient History*, Robertson's *America, Cooks' Voyages, Browne's Essay*, and a volume and half of John Locke on *Human Understanding*. Although but a lad, he easily digested these works. When Waddell returned home after fourteen weeks of absence, he found John in a poor state of health. The boy had been so engrossed in his reading that "his eyes became seriously affected, his countenance pallid and his frame emaciated."[5] Alarmed, Waddell notified Mrs. Calhoun, who immediately sent for her son.

By the time John returned home on 15 February 1796 he learned that his father had died. Patrick had left the family rather well off with thirty-one slaves and five farms,[6] but John's two older bothers, James and William, were working in Augusta, learning business and trades. This left the day-to-day working of the plantation to John. Since there were no overseers in that day, John worked alongside his slaves, directing the activities, a responsibility which gave him, on a small scale, an understanding of the workings of a community.

As John performed his duties he would place a book on the plow and read as he went. His neighbors watched as he carried on the affairs of the plantation and saw that the son of Patrick Calhoun was no ordinary boy. However, when they suggested to Mrs. Calhoun that he needed to be sent to school, she refused. John, knowing little else, was content to run plantations for the rest of his life.

Although unable to go to school, John loved learning. Once he obtained a copy of the *South Carolina Gazette*, and it became his prized possession. He read and reread it, making notes in the margin. It was his connection with politics.[7]

At the urging of John's two older brothers Mrs. Calhoun at last agreed to send eighteen-year-old John away for an education. But John did not want to go; he wanted to stay home. John finally agreed to go on one condition—that his family support him through the full seven years it would take to obtain a law degree. He was not interested in half an education. James agreed to this arrangement.

Calhoun pursued his studies for two years and then entered Yale College, from which he graduated with honors. After practicing law in his home town of Abbeville, he entered the South Carolina Legislature in 1808. In 1811 he was elected as a member of the National House of Representatives. Relations between the United States and Great Britain were strained, and Calhoun sided with Henry Clay, then speaker of the House, in favor of war. Clay gave Calhoun the second place on the Foreign Affairs committee, and he became the chief spokesman for the war party. He often debated Daniel Webster, who was opposed to the war. Calhoun derided Britain's oppression and coercion and protested that there is nothing about man "that indicates that he must conquer by enduring."[8] The call for war won out, resulting in the war of 1812.

In 1816, Calhoun promoted a protective tariff bill. He felt that new manufacturing could replace the dependence the country had on Great Britaine and that the South would participate in this development, but slavery proved an insurmountable obstacle.

In 1817 he became the Secretary of War, a position he held for seven years. He found West Point to be in dire straits; men were underpaid, food and other supplies were of poor quality or nonexistent. Calhoun felt that a soldier should be well paid. Because of his reform no soldier in the world is better taken care of than the American soldier,[9] and no military academy is more respected than West Point. In 1825, John C. Calhoun was chosen as vice president of the United States under President John Quincy Adams.

When Andrew Jackson became president in 1828, Calhoun remained as his vice president. But their relationship became strained when Jackson found out that Calhoun, as Secretary of War, had requested that Jackson account for his acts in the Seminole War. At this same time Calhoun began to expound states' rights and to warn against power becoming too concentrated in the federal government. He resigned from the vice presidency and returned to the Senate. Here he promoted the right for slavery or "rightfulness."

He based his stand on his interpretation of the old Virginia Resolution of 1789, which stated that the state had a right to take a cause into its own hands, stopping what it considered the general government's violations of the states' proper privileges. Calhoun believed that slavery was a proper institution and that the Constitution was a limited instrument.

He caused so much unrest that President Jackson threatened him with treason. Hoping to preserve the union, Calhoun began to speak for his policy of "nullification." For over twenty-five years he promoted these policies, bringing the country to the brink of the Civil War. "I mean to force the issue on the North," said Calhoun.[10] That in itself may have been his "measure and calling," for the problem of slavery had to be faced. It had to come to an end.

John Calhoun was also helpful in the building of the United States in other ways. In 1844, President John Tyler asked him to be Secretary of State. Acting in this capacity, Calhoun was instrumental in bringing Texas into the Union, settling the dispute over the Oregon territory and the war with Mexico.

When Calhoun died on 31 March 1850, Daniel Webster wrote his obituary. A man of "unspotted integrity and unimpeached honor,"[11] Calhoun was a fierce debater who often sent stunning blows, but never attacked the men themselves. It was for principles he stood and fought for.

NOTES

[1] Coit, Margaret L. *John C. Calhoun.* Boston: Houghton Mifflin, 1950, p. 2-3.

[2] Meigs, William M. *The Life of John Caldwell Calhoun.* New York: Da Capo Press, 1970, p. 56.

[3] See Coit, p. 6.

[4] Ibid., p. 2.

[5] Duyckinck, Evert A. *Portrait Gallery of Eminent Men and Women.* New York: Henry J. Johnson, 1873, p. 204.

[6] Meigs, p. 7.

[7] See ibid., p. 53.

[8] Duyckinck, p. 208.

[9] Morris, Charles. *Heroes of Progress.* Philadelphia: Lippincott Co., 1919, p. 140.

[10] Ibid., p. 142.

[11] Duyckinck, p. 212.

Count Camillo de Cavour

ITALIAN STATESMAN, DIPLOMAT   *1810-1861*

> *"I am the son of liberty; to her I owe all that I am."*

IN 1810, THE FUTURE ARCHITECT AND FATHER OF MODERN ITALY, Count Camillo de Cavour, was born in the northern city of Turin in the region of Piedmont (known also as the kingdom of Sardania). At this time Italy was not the country we know today. It was divided into eight regions much like feudal states. A united Italy had not existed for hundreds of years. At the time of Cavour's birth, Austria ruled most of Italy, except for the Piedmont region, which had been conquered by Napoleon. This new baby, who would become the first Prime Minister of Italy, was born a subject of France, the godson of Napoleon's beautiful sister Pauline Bonaparte, who governed the region with her husband.

Cavour spent many frustrating years working for the unity of Italy. The capstone of all his efforts was his invitation to act as Italy's first Prime Minister in 1852. When Cavour died in 1861, Italy was once again a single kingdom under a constitutional monarchy, save for Venetia and the city of Rome. Eventually these two also joined the new united land.

Cavour's was the brain behind inducing Napoleon III to enter Italy in 1859. This led to the eventual destruction of power in Austria. Cavour's diplomacy kept Italy free from foreign interference while Italy's "errant knight," Giuseppe Garibaldi, won repeated victories against superior numbers of the Austrians and, in one of the most brilliant military campaigns, swept across Italy, overthrowing old feudal kingdoms.

The second son of the Marquis Michael Benso de Cavour, Cavour spent his early life in a large home filled with extended family members. Cavour's views of freedom and liberty were greatly influenced by these relatives, who were French-Hugenots.

As a young boy he was rather impetuous, possessing a strong and even "bossy" character, but he was entertaining and amiable. He often crossed his instructors because his ideas seemed so out of touch with the thinking of that day; actually his ideas ahead of the times. Because he was the second son, tradition slated him for the military, and at the early age of nine he was sent away to military school. Cavour remained in the military school until the age of sixteen.

Cavour was very attached to his close-knit family, and the separation was hard on him. A letter written by Cavour just before his thirteenth birthday speaks of his longing to be at a family reunion:

> Dear Mama: What it has cost me to be the one absent from a complete reunion of the family you can imagine. I am beginning to feel the thorns with which the path of life is sown; ... I shall be able to embrace my aunt next month at Turin; it is true that the shortness of the time I passed with her only made me feel the more the pleasure of her conversation. Goodbye, dearest Mama.[1]

In the summer of 1823, Cavour with some other youths at his school were sent to a hostel high in the mountains. Of this experience Cavour wrote to his mother. In the letter he referred to the strength of her love: "Dearest Mamma: It needed all your maternal love to brave the heat of the sun and climb up here. We shall then be separated for a month." He then writes a line that so amply describes his personality: "You may be sure, dear Mamma, that I am happy, specially when I am not ordered to be so. Please give my love to father, and believe me always. Your affectionate son."[2]

Cavour was especially close to his paternal grandmother. She remained by his side when other family members had difficulties with him. By the time he was twenty-eight years of age, because of his outspoken political opinions, his family—particularly his father—was somewhat estranged from him, and they made some rather harsh remarks about the direction he was heading. He writes to his grandmother, whom he called Marina:

> To you, oh my dear Marina, who bear me such love, I turn and pray you to defend me against the hateful and undeserved

charge brought against me—that I am hard-hearted and that all feelings of tenderness are extinguished within me. I can be accused of much, perhaps even of being inconsiderate and too much of a Liberal, but never of hardness of heart. We understand each other marvelously, you and I, for you were always a little bit of a Jacobian.[3] [The Jacobians were a political club formed after the French Revolution. The original object of this group was to work for the establishment of a constitution that would support the rights of man.]

There were two other members of the family who seemed to wield influence over the political views of young Cavour. One was his uncle, Count de Sellon, who lived in Geneva, and the other a cousin, Auguste de la Rive, a professor whose relatives were Protestants. Sellon was a pacifist. Cavour agreed with many of his uncle's pacifist ideas, particularly those that "the morality of the gospels ought to apply in politics as well as in private behavior."[4] It was his constant exchange with these relatives, some radical, some conservative, which counted for much of his moral and intellectual development. Their patriotic thinking set him on his future path.

In 1831, the Napoleonic government in Piedmont was defeated. The old royalty was restored to the little kingdom, and in the stroke of a pen the king issued an edict that swept away the progress and political structure that had been advanced under the Napoleonic government for twenty years.

This move particularly affected the educational system and the business community. Overnight all progress was gone. Old officials of the royalty were found and returned to their offices. Education for many was eliminated. These events placed Piedmont in the most backward position of all the Italian states. Cavour's observation of these events greatly influenced the young man's opinion of an absolute monarchy.

Cavour, even at a young age, was a voracious reader, and from his reading he began to see the enlightenment that was taking place in other countries, particularly England. He began the task of mastering the English language, and eventually became fluent, speaking with eloquence. This ability allowed him to follow the political events in England. However, he was often punished for possession of "forbidden books," and was placed under house arrest for ten days.

He was fond of mathematics, and he felt that it helped him form a habit of precise thinking. In later life he would often try to reduce political and moral problems to imaginary graphs on which he would try to plot the relevant factors. He felt this exercise helped him draw his conclusions.

As gifted as Cavour was in math, he felt that there was yet a more important area of study to be pursued. One day in his math class the professor complimented Cavour on his great mathematical ability and advised him to become a great mathematician, to which Cavour replied: "This is no longer the time for mathematics; it is necessary to study political economy; the world progresses. I hope to see the day when our country is governed by a constitution, and who knows but I may be a minister in it."[5] As a youth Cavour knew his life's mission and prepared in earnest to fulfill it. He later wrote the following patriotic words: "No, no; it is not by fleeing from one's native land because she is unhappy that one can reach a glorious end... Happy or unhappy, my country shall have all my life."[6]

In his fourth year of military school he was appointed as a page to the royal prince, a much coveted position. But the costume was offensive to Cavour, and he didn't hesitate to say so in public. Because of his outspoken nature, by the end of the year Cavour had lost the patronage of Prince Charles Albert. Speaking of his actions years later Cavour reflected that he had been imprudent and ungrateful.

His parents were keenly disappointed and they had grave concern about the future of their son. When he was sixteen and a sub-lieutenant in the corp of engineers, he was sent to the remote mountain borders to supervise the construction of fortifications. Here he was extremely bored and so read volumes of history and took copious notes.

From Gibbon he copied chapters on religion. He read Hume and Wycliffe and the British Constitution. Cavour was a great admirer of the works of Benjamin Franklin and Adam Smith. One of his favorite writers was Alexis de Tocqueville, author of

Democracy in America. He felt this book was the most remarkable book of modern times and that it showed the direction the world was about to take: "a book full of warning but also hope."[7] He often read and meditated on the Bible during this time as well. His other readings included Shakespeare, Sir Walter Scott, and the novels of Edward Bulwer-Lytton. He thought Byron the supreme poet of the nineteenth century.

He finally convinced his father to let him out of the military, and he returned to oversee one of the family estates at Leri. Here, although he had absolutely no knowledge of agriculture, he threw himself into rising early to work in the fields with the peasants. He studied all there was on agricultural reform. He began working in the surrounding communities to establish a railroad, factories, mills, and even a line of steamers. His energy seemed boundless. At twenty-two he was appointed mayor. Even so, because of his advanced ideas, he was still watched and spied on by the Royalist Government, as one who might be a revolutionary.

For this same reason he was often denied travel permits. However, when he was able to obtain one he would travel to France or England, establishing contact with different statesmen. It was about this time that Cavour and his friends formed the Society of Agriculture and established a newspaper. The society did not deal strictly with agriculture, but discussed and promoted a whole realm of economic and political reform. The newspaper, *Risorgimento*, with Cavour as editor, began to print new and liberal ideas. During this time, news came that England was attempting to pass the famous reform bill. Cavour and his friends anxiously awaited for the final outcome of the English reform bill. Cavour felt that when it passed, it would spawn a wave of freedom for Italy.

In 1848 Cavour and his friends of the agricultural society and leading men of Turin held a meeting to consider the steps that might be taken to petition the king for changes that would permit progress. After a lengthy discussion Cavour stood up and with great vehemence exclaimed: "Why should we ask in a roundabout way for concessions which end in little or nothing? I propose that we should ask for a Constitution."[8] It was agreed, and Cavour himself made the presentation to the King reassuring him that the constitution was to be a constitutional monarchy. Upon receiving petitions from the city of Turin, Charles Albert on 7 February 1848 granted the first constitution in modern Italy. Today this date is celebrated throughout Italy as the date leading to her eventual independence, unity, and freedom.

Cavour was elected to the newly established chamber. His talents and abilities led to his being selected as the leader of this assembly. One of his first priorities was to obtain a treaty between Piedmont and the two countries he felt could help Italy most, France and England. The object of the treaty in Cavour's mind was twofold: one, it would cause Piedmont to be recognized as a European power, an entity in its own right; and two, Austria would be hesitant to come to war against a government that had a treaty with the great nations of France and England.

The constitutional groundwork laid in Piedmont became the foundation for the eventual unification of all Italy. In this work, Cavour met disappointment on all sides. On one hand he had to contend with republicans who wanted no monarchy. But Cavour had a keen sense of the times and knew that Italy was not ready to do away with a royal family. On the other hand, the democrats opposed every action Cavour took, no matter what he tried.

One of Cavour's major moves was to induce Napoleon III to help expel the Austrians from Italian soil. Through Cavour's supreme diplomacy, Napoleon III agreed. Meeting in battle, the French and Piedmont armies began to push the Austrians out of Italy, and for the first time there was a glimmer of hope that Italy would gain her freedom. Then the Emperor of Austria met with Napoleon III, and a treaty was signed without the knowledge of Cavour or his king, then Victor Emmanuel II. This treaty left the Austrians still in control. It was almost more than Cavour could take and in his anger he resigned. For the first time he was tempted to take up arms as a revolutionist, something he had always been against.

His king, however, had heard Cavour's pleadings; he would not sign the treaty, except as it pertained to Piedmont. Even Lord Palmerston, the Prime Minister of England, spoke out in defense of Piedmont and against the Treaty of Villafranca.

Gathering his courage Cavour returned to his public life and in 1851 declared: "Piedmont, gathering to itself all the living forces of Italy, [will] be soon in a position to lead our mother-country to the destinies to which she is called."[9] This was the speech that seemed to turn darkness into light. It gave a new rallying cry to all those parties hoping for independence and unification. Word was sent from Lord Palmerston, encouraging the constitutional experiment in Piedmont, for by so doing, he said, the Italian despots were doomed.

Cavour made secret contact with Garibaldi, who, against insurmountable odds and greatly superior numbers, drove Austria from the Italian borders and freed the last of the Bourbons from control. Cavour, like a master puppeteer, kept the strength of the nation working for the same goal. His diplomacy abroad kept Garibaldi free of international intervention. At last all of Italy, except Rome and one other providence, was united. A plebecite was held and the national assembly met. Cavour was appointed first Prime Minister of the new united Italy. The new government met in Turin.

Due to a number of crises Cavour was invited to become the Prime Minister, a position he held with only two short interruptions until his death. Cavour immediately began to instigate internal reform. One of his first acts was to establish free trade. He made agricultural reform based his education gained during his years at Leri. He also felt it important to build up the military, but calling for the additional taxes as he needed to do so gave fuel to his enemies. When asked to establish a lottery, he replied that lotteries were "a tax on imbeciles."[10]

Cavour knew that in order to completely unite the people, the true capitol of Italy must be Rome. Garibaldi wanted to storm the city, but Cavour set upon another course of action—diplomacy. He proposed that the Pope retain his ruling authority over Vatican City and allow the remainder of Rome to become a part of Italy. He summed up his views in a formula called "a free church in a free state." Cavour did not live to see his goal accomplished. The strain of all he had been doing destroyed his health.

When it was known that the doctors could do no more for him, the family called for the Friar Giacomo to offer the last rites. Even though Cavour had been excommunicated in one of the Pope's mass excommunications, the good Friar came at once. When the throngs outside Cavour's home heard the tinkling of the bell signaling his death, a murmur of uncontrolled grief was heard in the crowd, for their leading patriot was about to leave them. Cavour from his bed addressed Giacomo: "The time for departure is come"; he then kissed the king's hand in a show of deep devotion. His last words were "The thing [the independence of all Italy] is going on; be certain that now the the thing is going on." And as he gradually sank, he was periodically heard to utter, "Italy—Rome—Venice." Then as if he was being greeted on the other side, his last word was spoken in the form of a salutation, he called out the name: "Napoleon!"[11]

Cavour, the boy who became the father of his country, left a legacy that few can follow, but all can be grateful for.

NOTES

[1] Whyte, A. J. *The Early Life and Letters of Cavour.* Conn: Greenwood Press. Reprint 1925. 1976, p. 17.

[2] Ibid., p. 18.

[3] Ibid., p. 4.

[4] Smith, Denise Mack. *Cavour.* New York: Alfred A. Knopf, 1915, p. 5.

[5] Whyte, p. 13.

[6] Orsi Pietro. *Cavour and the Making of Modern Italy.* New York & London: G. P. Putnam's Sons, 914, p. 71.

[7] Smith, p. 9.

[8] Duyckinck, p. 70.

[9] Encylopedia Britannica, 11th ed.. 1910, 5:583.

[10] "Pro & Con: Should We Have State-Run Lotteries?" *Readers Digest,* August 1963, p. 105.

[11] Duyckinck, p. 70.

Thomas Chalmers

SCOTTISH DIVINE, REFORMER   *1780-1847*

"The despisers of godliness are the enemies of the true interest of our nation."

DR. THOMAS CHALMERS IS CONSIDERED BY SOME AS ONE OF four greatest Scotsmen of his time. It was said of him that he was not one man but a thousand. Though a reformer, Chalmers reflected the social traditions of the preindustrial age. As a student in the University of St. Andrew, Chalmers developed the idea that a man's value was based on his contribution to the welfare of society: this in its turn was a function, not of his personal wealth, but of his *principles* and his *integrity*. The well-working society was based on the fundamental social principle of benevolence.

Adam Smith in his Wealth *of Nations* wrote that the pursuit of wealth by the individual stimulated the economy and thereby benefited society. Chalmers felt Smith's theory needed a little revising. He felt that society was really benefited by the works of consciously benevolent men who had liberal dispositions and who with unbounded charity gave to the relief of the poor and distressed.[1]

Amidst the many social reforms in which Chalmers' name stands connected, the most prominent was his effort to return the management of welfare of the poor to the Church. The age of great industrial triumphs had led masses from the countryside to the cities, which created an age of appalling social deprivations of before unknown proportions. Chalmers felt that if the essence of the gospel of Jesus Christ could reach these people their lives could improve. This great churchman believed that the salvation of his nation, Scotland, lay not merely in preserving traditional rural values but somehow in reintroducing them into the cities. Character, he said, is the parent of comfort, not vice-versa; the strong economic condition of the masses is dependent on their right moral condition.

In 1820, the chance came for Chalmers to implement his belief. He was transferred to the largest and poorest parish in Scotland, where he convinced the town council to give him the right to administer welfare funds raised by the church rather than funds from forced taxation. He divided the parish into districts and subdistricts, much as was done in the Law of the Covenant under Moses. He chose laymen of Christian character, officer-bearers of his own church, to establish Sunday and day schools where needed.

Two schools and fifty new sabbath schools were established. There were twenty-five districts, each with 50 to 100 families, over which an elder and a deacon were placed. The elder worked with the families' spiritual needs, and the deacon addressed their physical needs. Chalmers personally supervised the whole program, making an effort to visit every family in the entire parish. His efforts were highly successful.

Chalmers believed that "compulsory assessment," or taxation for welfare as we know it today, only resulted in the swelling of the welfare rolls and that relief should be *raised* and *administered* by voluntary means. Taxation for welfare did more to create the very monster of welfare than it did to eliminate it. He was highly criticized at the initiation of the program, but he persevered, knowing that it was founded on ancient and sound principles.

The deacon interviewed each family in his district who were making application for help. Every effort was made to enable the poor to help themselves. "When once the system was in operation, it was found that a deacon, by spending an hour a week among the families committed to his charge, could keep himself acquainted with their character and condition."[2] Chalmers taught them to analyze their resources and share with others within their district.

Within four years, Chalmer's method showed its advantages. In the beginning, the poor of the parish were costing the city £1400 per annum. Through the adoption of Chalmers method, the welfare cost to the city was reduced to £280 per annum. The results were accompanied not only by an economic success, but also by an increase of morality as well. Drunkenness decreased, and parents took an increased interest in the welfare of their children. Chalmers pleaded with the city to allow him to continue, but a new council had taken over and a law was passed taking control out of the church's hand and placing it back into the hands of the government.

Thomas Chalmers began his life 17 March 1780, in Anstruther, Scotland. He was the sixth of fourteen children. His father was a shipowner, general merchant, and provost of the town. His mother was an energetic woman, visiting the homes of the poor on a regular basis with parcels of food and clothing.

When Chalmers was but two years old, the family hired a nurse, whose cruelty and deceitfulness haunted his memory throughout his life. When he could bear no more of her cruelty, he would run to tell his mother. The nurse would stop him and hug him and shower him with pleading tenderness, all the while extorting from him a promise not to tell. Once he made such a promise, she would turn around and treat him more harshly than ever.[3]

At the age of three he began to attend school, not because he wanted to but because of the fear he felt towards his nurse. But even here the schoolmaster had a "thirst for flogging." At this little parish school Chalmers was known as "one of the idlest, strongest, merriest, and most generous-hearted boys."[4] Reading came easily to him and to his lifelong advantage he absorbed many of the books in his father's large library. His favorite was *Pilgrim's Progress.*

Even before he could read, stories and sayings from the Bible became a part of his knowledge. One evening when he was about three years old the family could not find him. It was late and dark. He was discovered in the nursery, "pacing up and down, excited and absorbed, repeating to himself as he walked to and fro the words of David: 'O my son Absalom! O Absalom, my son, my son!'"[5] Thus the gifts and talents which were to make him so famous in his life were observed in childhood.

During these early years Chalmers declared his heart's desire to become a minister. Not only did he set his heart on becoming a minister, but he decided what was to be his first sermon: "Let brotherly love continue."[6] A neighbor girl recalled that as a child she burst into the room where her brother and Thomas were playing. She found the future great religious orator standing upon a chair and preaching most vigorously to his captive audience, her brother.

In his eleventh year, Chalmers was enrolled as a student in the University of St. Andrews. This early age of entrance was not uncommon for that time. Chalmers had a tremendous struggle during the first two sessions because of his faulty early education. He was also still given to old habits of idle and boyish ways. It was not until the third session when he enrolled in a math class that he discovered one of the great passions of his life and began to grow serious about his studies. Mathematics and science held such a fascination for his mind that for some time he did not pursue his goal to be a minister.

In 1798, young Chalmers was sent to be a tutor of a family. The experience proved a great trial for the young college student. He worked from seven in the morning until six at night. The children had no discipline; and the parents treated Chalmers as nothing more than a mere domestic. He wrote his father often pleading for the opportunity to quit. One of the servants accused him of having far too much pride. Chalmers replied with the air of youth: "There are two kinds of pride, sir. There is that pride which lords it over inferiors; and there is that pride which rejoices in repressing the insolence of superiors. The first I have none of—the second I glory in."[7]

After the summer he returned to school, and at the age of fifteen he entered divinity school. Some aspects of his education there disturbed him. He was disconcerted with lecturers who lacked sincerity and doubted the value of listening to mere intellectual power that had no basis in the heart. He also objected to Christianity being promoted as a system of authority, rather than as a faith which is nurtured through personal experiences.

Chalmers completed his studies by the time he was nineteen; however, the minimum age for licensing was twenty-one. His father, anxious for his son to be on his way, petitioned some of his influential friends to waive the age requirement. Thus, at the age of nineteen, Thomas Chalmers received his doctor of divinity.

In 1803, he became a minister of Kilmeny. Along with his pastoral duties he continued to give lectures in chemistry and math. This was very disconcerting to the presbyter. Chalmers merely responded that they had no jurisdiction over his weekday activities.

It was about this time that Chalmers went through a very profound spiritual experience. Because there is no record given of the event, we know of it only because Chalmers occasionally referred to the incident.

As his health began to fail, Chalmers started to brood about the purpose of life, and these two forces created great unrest in his mind. As his health continued to deteriorate, he engaged upon the task of researching and reading the scriptures to prepare an article for the *Edinburgh Encyclopedia* entitled "Christianity." Chalmers found peace for his troubled mind finding as he reflected that salvation was in Jesus Christ alone. This changed the course of his life, marking the beginning of his taking the principles of morality and self-sufficiency to the poor.

Chalmers maintained that it was essential for a Christian church to possess the right of self-government, undisturbed by the intrusion of secular government. This belief led to the great disruption in 1843, with Chalmers and others separating from the Church of Scotland and forming the Free Church of Scotland. Following Chalmers, four hundred and seventy ministers resigned their livings and joined the Free Church.

Chalmers' teachings were unique for his day. He felt that social evils are cured by character rather than legislation; that though "Christianity may only work the salvation of a few.... It raises the standard of morality among many."[8] If parents do not teach their children to "seek the kingdom of God and his righteousness," then when that child enters the world in the work force, "the parent is guilty of offering up their children at the shrine of the idol of the world, because inevitably they will perish."[9] The salvation of their children should be a parent's challenge in life, their best and their dearest interest. Chalmers urged everyone to question himself to see if he cooperates in an orderly society out of good manners or out of goodness of his heart. Manners will not sustain society when control is lost! Finally, he felt "that unless a sabbath-school apparatus be animated by the *spirit* of God, it will not bear with effect on the morals of the rising generation."[10]

Chalmers was highly respected by Sir Walter Scott, the most noted man of Scotland. Scott detested being flattered by anyone about his works. One evening at a dinner party, a man said to Scott: "Well, Sir Walter, I was dining yesterday, where your works became the subject of very copious conversation."

Scott merely replied, "Well, I think, I must say your party might have been better employed" Chalmers was identified as the speaker, and Scott said, "Dr. Chalmers? That throws new light on the subject. To have produced any effect upon the mind of such a man as Dr. Chalmers is indeed something to be proud of. Dr. Chalmers is a man of the truest genius."[11]

Chalmers spent Sunday, 30 May 1847, with his beloved family and several guests. He bade all a good night and laid down to a slumber from which he never woke.

While Dr. Thomas Chalmers was a man of his time, he was perhaps ahead of his time. His socioeconomic experiment should not be dismissed, for Chalmers, endowed with divine connections, showed "the truest genius."

NOTES

[1] Brown Stewart J. *Thomas Chalmers and the Godly Commonwealth in Scotland* London: Oxford University Press, 1982, p. 6.

[2] Encyclopedia Britannica. 11th ed. 1911, 5:810.

[3] See Hanna, William Rev. L.L.D. *Memoirs of the Life and Writings of Thomas Chalmers, D.D, .L.L.D.* By His Son-In-Law. Published for Thomas Constable. Edinburgh: Sutherland and Knox, 1849, 1:5.

[4] Ibid., 1:7.

[5] Hanna, p. 8.

[6] Ibid, p. 9.

[7] Ibid., p. 32.

[8] Chalmers, Thomas D.D. *A Sermon Preached in St. John's Church, Glasgow, on Sabbath the 30th of April.* Glasgow: William Whyte & Co., 1820, p. 38.

[9] Hanna, p. 191-92.

[10] Chalmers, p. 41.

[11] Scott, Sir Walter. *The Journal of Sir Walter Scott.* New York: Harper & Brothers, 1890, 1:175.

Henry Clay   *1777-1852*

U.S. STATESMAN, "THE GREAT COMPROMISER"

> *"If any one desires to know the leading and paramount object of my public life, the preservation of this union will furnish him the key."*

BORN IN 1777, AT THE BEGINNING OF THIS COUNTRY'S STRUGGLE for freedom, Henry Clay became deeply affected by the circumstances of the time. When Clay was just four years old, his father died and his mother was driven from her home by British troops under the command of Tarleton. Even as an adult Clay remembered being visited by the troops of Tarleton, who ran their swords into the new-made grave of his father and grandfather, thinking they contained hidden treasures.[1] Tarleton's cavalrymen ransacked the house, tearing open chests, breaking dishes, and filling the air with mattress feathers.

The memory of this catastrophe so marked Clay's thinking that much of his adult life was spent in devising compromises among the members of Congress in an effort to avoid another bloody war among the people of this land.

Henry's father, John Clay, was a Baptist preacher whose undying efforts in the cause of religious freedom were reflected in the American Revolution. Reverend Clay was an agitator for "soul liberty."[2] He preached against "diabolical, hell-conceived' religious tyranny, defying a tax-supported state church.

Henry Clay was born on 29 June 1777 in Hanover County, Virginia. The region of Virginia where the Clay family lived was a swampy area called "slashes." Clay was the fifth of seven children. After John Clay's death, Mrs. Clay remarried Captain Henry Watkins, a kindly gentleman.

As a child Clay saw the foundations of the new country laid. He heard the impassioned speeches of Patrick Henry. At the age of twelve he saw Madison, Wythe and others debate the Constitution in his home state of Virginia. Washington, Adams, and Jefferson were his presidents. Henry Clay was, as he said, "rocked in the cradle of the revolution."[3]

As an adult, he sat in the governing councils in Washington for many years. He authored the great compromises that held this nation through Southern threats of separation over the slavery issue. These compromises bought valuable time so that Webster and others could establish the constitution as a viable working document. No one knew that in a few years the constitution would have to pass the supreme test of a terrible civil war.

As a child, Clay attended the "Field School" for three years. This was a dirt floor log cabin. The teacher was rarely sober, but he was able to give young Clay a basic education.

Perhaps his greatest education came through listening to the great orators of the day, particularly Patrick Henry. The power of speech captivated him. To master such power became a passion with him. He began reading political and historical works and then practiced reciting them before the cows and horses in the barn. He gained a fluency of speech and had an unusual dose of self-confidence.

As a young boy he discovered a runaway slave hiding in the forest and struck up a friendship with him. He gave him food and other assistance. When the runaway was eventually killed while resisting arrest, young Clay wept disconsolately.[4]

With the Revolutionary war over and the Constitution established, the young nation began looking west. In 1791, Clay's parents pulled up stakes in Virginia and pioneered the frontiers of Kentucky. But Clay stayed behind, working at his first job as a "counter-boy" in a small retail store. Then through the influence of his stepfather, Captain Watkins, Clay was able to obtain a position as a clerk in the office of Peter Tinsley, clerk of the High Court of Chancery. This position became a major turning point in his life. He copied legal documents, did general writing, and learned order. At first he received a few chuckles from other clerks for his homespun appearance; he was now fifteen and "very tall and very awkward." But his co-workers soon learned to respect and like him well. Even though Captain Watkins had had to "lean" on his friend to make an opening for young Clay, in short time he proved to be the brightest and most studious of the office boys. Night after night he would burn the candle down while reading a book. He sought learning in any form, and particularly enjoyed the recorded wisdom and events of the past

Because of his diligence and quickness in learning, Clay began to attract the attention of none other than George Wythe, who was then the most eminent jurist in America. Wythe was one of the most cultivated and refined minds in Virginia. It was he, who years before had taken another young law student, Thomas Jefferson, under his wings. Wythe's influence can be seen in the writings of the Declaration of Independence, which he signed. As a jurist Wythe routinely traced law to its most remote source, both to Roman and Latin times, and his decisions were among the most noted ever given. Wythe's decisions were among the most noted ever given. Clay became Wythe's personal clerk, and for four years he regularly copied Wythe's decisions. A deep and abiding friendship grew between the two.

In this setting Clay also learned etiquette. A debating society was formed in Richmond, which gave Clay the opportunity to practice publicly the many things he had gathered and stored in his mind. All of this proved to be "better than an education."[5] In November of 1797 when he was approaching his twenty-first year he became licensed to practice law.

He immediately went to Kentucky to be near his family and to try his luck in the fast-growing new state. He settled in Lexington a small village of about fifty houses. It was not long before he became very successful. People from all around loved to hear him talk. In his farewell address to the Senate in 1842, Clay referred to these early days in Kentucky: "Scarce had I set my foot on her [Kentucky's] generous soil when I was seized and embraced with parental fondness, caressed as though a favorite child, and patronized with liberal and unbounded munificence."[6]

In 1799 he married Miss Lucretia Hart, the daughter of

Colonel Thomas Hart, a respected citizen of Kentucky. A woman of great dignity, she inspired respect. The union, which lasted 53 years was a happy one. Although they had eleven children, five sons and six daughters, only two daughters lived to womanhood. One of these, Anna, passed away while he was serving in Washington, D. C. Her death affected him so deeply that he fainted and was on his bed for several days. It was only by exerting himself that he was able return to work. He was said to have remarked: "My country and my state need my services, so why should I bow down to my private grief."[7]

In 1806 Clay purchased the beautiful farm of Ashland. He wrote of Ashland: "I am in one respect better off than Moses. He died in sight of and without reaching the Promised Land. I occupy as good a farm as any he would have found had he reached it, and 'Ashland' has been acquired, not by hereditary descent but by my own labor."[8] The Clays resided at Ashland for nearly fifty years. It became a labor of love by both the husband and his wife. (However many of the day-to-day duties and the actual overseeing of Ashland was left to Mrs. Clay because her husband was away so often in Washington.)

Clay soon became active in local politics, advocating the policies of President Jefferson, for whom he had great admiration. In 1798, Clay made earnest efforts for the eventual phasing out of slavery in Kentucky. Even though he was not successful in his efforts, Clay felt that his proudest memory was the effort he had made at the very outset of his career to free Kentucky from slavery.

His political career began in 1803 when he was elected to the legislature in Kentucky. During this time he defended Aaron Burr, who was charged with treason. He accepted no fee, thinking it was an occasion for generosity toward an eminent man in misfortune. Although he had first obtained a pledge in writing from Burr concerning the facts, he later learned that Burr had deceived him.

Clay had a tremendously successful law career. It was so successful that he won even most of the criminal cases. Near the end of his life, however, he regretted being so successful in obtaining freedom for criminals who truly deserved punishment.

Service in the Kentucky Legislature lasted until 1806, when he was appointed to fill a vacancy in the United States Senate. (History now shows that he was under the age limit to serve in congress, being only twenty-nine at the time.) He plunged into legislative activity as if he had been there all his life, pushing for the protection of American interests which were being threatened by England. When his term expired in 1807, he returned home and re-entered the Kentucky Legislature. It was at this time that he became embroiled in a political dispute with a Mr. Marshall and according to the foolish custom of the time the two men fought a duel in which both were wounded.

Clay returned to Washington in 1811, this time to the House of Representatives. He began his career in the House as the Speaker of the House, the only man in history to do so. It was his political leadership that left its mark upon the destiny of the United States. Unlike Webster and Calhoun, Clay loved a crowd. He would walk across a street to converse with a group there. He absorbed the public pulse and responded to it.

The first thing Clay tackled was the growing troubles between England and the United States. England had been forcing American seamen on the high seas to serve on British ships. Britain lamely excused its action by saying it did not have a mark by which it could recognize its own defected sailors. Clay spoke positively for war as did John C. Calhoun. Nevertheless, although Clay pushed for war, he was ready for peace at the first moment. He was appointed as one of the commissioners to the signing of the peace treaty at Ghent. His negotiations brought about peace between the two countries.

Next Clay turned his energies to other pressing problems. He pushed relentlessly for the cause of the South American revolutionists, who, he believed, were entitled to recognition as independent republics. In a speech before Congress he said of their cause: "Spanish America for centuries has been doomed to the practical effects of an odious tyranny. If we were justified, they were more than justified."[9] He then teamed up with Daniel Webster to push for the recognition of Greece.

Clay also played a prominent part in the famous controversy

between the North and the South which arose with the debate over the admission of Missouri as a slave state. It was by almost superhuman effort and through his gifted leadership that he was able to bring about "The Missouri Compromise." This compromise kept slavery out of the area acquired by the purchase of the Louisiana Territory north of Missouri and "pacified" for a time both the North and the South.

In 1824, Andrew Jackson, John Quincy Adams, William H. Crawford, and Henry Clay were candidates for the U.S. Presidency. Because of a lack of a majority it became necessary for the House to vote on the top three candidates. Clay used his influence for the votes to go to Adams. Adams was elected president and subsequently appointed Clay to be Secretary of State. Immediately Jackson's supporters said that Clay had been "bought" for his influence. History has shown that the charge was malicious and false. But it hurt Clay for the rest of his political career.

Clay's integrity, however, remained intact. He was so given to a principle that he sometimes voted against old political friends. This habit had an adverse affect on his opportunity for the Presidency and when warned about it he replied: "I would rather be right than be President."[10]

Upon his retirement from government he said: "I have honestly and faithfully served my country; that I have never wronged it; and that, however unprepared I lament that I am to appear in the Divine presence on other accounts, I invoke the stern justice of his judgment on my public conduct, without the smallest apprehension of his displeasure."[11]

NOTES

[1] Duyckinck, Evert A. *Portrait Gallery of Eminent Men and Women.* New York: Henry J. Johnson, 1873, p. 228.

[2] Mayo Bernard. *Henry Clay Spokesman of the West.* Boston: Houghton Mifflin, 1937 p.1.

[3] Ibid., p. 1.

[4] See ibid., p. 15.

[5] Clay Thomas Hart (grandson). *Henry Clay.* Philadelphia: George Jacob Co. , p. 20.

6 Ibid. p. 23.

7 Caldwell, Howard. *Henry Clay: the Great Compromiser.* Chicago: Union School Furnishing Co., 1912, p. 1.

8 Clay, p. 29.

9 Ibid., p. 40.

10 Ibid., p. 174.

11 Ibid.

Richard Cobden

ENGLISH LEADER OF THE FREE TRADE   *1804-1865*

> *"Peace will come to earth when the people have more to do with each other and governments less."*

RICHARD COBDEN EARNED HIS PLACE IN HISTORY AS AN ambassador of good will, advocate for free trade, and enemy to injustice. He is perhaps best known for his work on the repeal of the Corn Law, which opened the way for free trade. Established in 1436, the Corn Law had worked moderately well under the stewardship of Sir Issac Newton. However, by 1815 it had become extremely prohibitive, restricting the importation of grain and keeping domestic prices low. This one law had literally strangled the farmers in England as well as the people of Ireland. After seven long years of dedicated work, through his efforts, the Corn Law was repealed.

Richard Cobden was born on a farm near Midhurst, Sussex, England, on 3 June 1804, the fourth of eleven children of a poor farmer. The farm did not do well and Cobden's father died while Cobden was a child and he was raised by his relatives who helped him get the beginnings of his education. Outside of this education, Cobden was virtually self-taught.

At the age of fifteen, Cobden went to work in his uncle's warehouse in London. In spite of his uncle's warnings that it would interfere with his success in business, Cobden spent every spare hour studying. At twenty he began to travel as a salesman and became known for his great energy and lively discussions on political economy. He also became know for his genteel speech. He never indulged in the crude talk of the men on the road, always seeking a higher tone in his discussion.[1]

In 1830, he joined with two friends to buy out the cotton print business of some retiring gentlemen. The three young men having little capital were able to convince the retiring gentlemen to remain in the business as silent partners until enough cash was generated to buy them out. Once this was agreed upon, Cobden immediately introduced into the business a new system of management. This led to the opening of several new stores. The business became so successful under his direction that it became known as "Cobden Prints."

Cobden's excellent business sense brought success to all his efforts, and he was soon on his way to becoming extremely wealthy. In spite of this success he had a great desire to give his heart and soul to the betterment of his fellowmen, to lift the status of every citizen.

In 1840, he married Miss Catherine Anne Williams, by whom he had five daughters and one son. Devoted to his family and his religion, he thoroughly valued the religious character in others and he deeply loved his country. His work, he felt, supported the best purposes of Providence.

Cobden wrote several clear and concise articles on commerce and economics which he submitted to the *Manchester Times* under the pen name "Libra." His understanding of countries and governments grew as he traveled on business, going as far as Russia, Greece, Egypt, Turkey and America.

Upon his return to England he published a pamphlet entitled "England, Ireland, and America, by a Manchester Manufacturer." This pamphlet created quite a stir, for in these articles Cobden outlined certain issues that became the hallmark of his life work. The most prominent themes were peace, non-intervention, and free trade. He also warned England that her developing fear of Russia would allow her to be drawn into an unnecessary war. His fears proved correct when England involved herself in the Crimean War.

It was the establishment of the railroad by Stephenson that enabled the lecturers of the League to talk with people in all parts of the country. The whole country was informed because of this new mode of transportation.

In 1838 the Anti Corn-Law league was established in

Manchester. Though not one of the original members, Cobden put a large amount of energy and money into this group and was assisted by a good friend John Bright. (These two men had already worked to promote public education.)

In 1841, Cobden was elected to Parliament. Because of his opposition to the Corn Law, he was treated with great contempt by the other members. He was not intimidated by this attitude, however, and he began almost immediately presenting his argument to repeal the Corn Law. His speeches were interrupted with jeers. But he compelled attention and respect by his thorough knowledge of the subject. Because of his knowledge of economics and commerce and the difficulty of the times, Cobden soon became a major force in Parliament.

The power source of the movement to repeal the Corn Law, Cobden used up his wealth in the pursuit of the repeal of the Corn Law. To show their gratitude, his friend, admirers, and supporters collected funds for him in recognition of his services. All together some £80,000 were raised.

In 1846 after the great Potato Famine in Ireland, the Corn Law was repealed. Simultaneously, in order to avoid total devastation in Ireland, Sir Robert Peel, the Prime Minister, established the policy of Free Trade. Cobden's plan had worked—an injustice had been stopped and free trade begun.

When Lord John Russell offered Cobden a seat in the cabinet, Cobden declined preferring to be free of government obligations in order to serve his fellowmen as he saw fit. Since Cobden felt that he would best serve by teaching the principles of free trade, he went to the continent to promote free trade, traveling as far as Russia. As he traveled he visited with rulers and statesmen. To a friend he wrote:

> Well, I will, with God's assistance during the next twelve months, visit all the large states of Europe, see their potentates or statesmen, and endeavor to enforce those truths which have been irresistible at home. Why should I rust in inactivity? If the public spirit of my countrymen affords me the means of traveling as their missionary I will be the first ambassador from the people of this country to the nations of the continent. I

am impelled to this by an instinct emotion such as has never deceived me. I feel that I could succeed in making out a stronger case for the prohibitive nations of Europe to compel them to adopt a freer system than I had here to overturn our protection policy.[2]

Upon his return Cobden was again entered Parliament. Free trade having been established, Cobden now turned to the promotion of peace. In 1849 he presented a plan for the establishment of international arbitration and the reduction of arms. He participated in the Peace Congresses held in Brussels, Paris, London, and other cities.

When Louis Napoleon took over France in 1851, the English people feared an invasion. Cobden openly protested against such alarms, giving speeches and writing a pamphlet "1793 and 1853." Once the popular spokesman for free trade, Cobden quickly became one of the most abused men in England because of his stand for Louis Napoleon. However, Cobden's reservations proved wise, for it was not long until the Emperor became the ally of Great Britain. The British, left without an enemy, turned their fears and energies against Russia and her dispute with Turkey.

This was another action against which Cobden had warned. He had been in Turkey and had an understanding of its difficulties. He also knew that the dynasty which ruled Turkey had become decadent. He conceded that it was right and proper to recognize Turkey as a country, but repeatedly counseled Parliament not to support such a vicious and cruel government. He pleaded with them not to be hasty in their decision to join with Turkey in a war against Russia. England refused to see the logic of his arguments and was drawn into the Crimean War.[3]

It was in this parliamentary seat that Cobden remained for over ten years, advocating among other things parliamentary reform, free hold land societies, suffrage and, as always, peace with other nations. In 1857, news reached England of a conflict in China where a British Admiral destroyed the river forts and 23 ships of the Chinese navy. Upon thorough investigation, Cobden became convinced that the British had not acted in a defensive manner but were actually the aggressor. He submitted a motion in Parliament to this effect. A long debate followed, in which he was supported by several notables of Parliament including Disraeli and Gladstone. It all ended in the defeat of Lord Palmerston then Prime Minister. Cobden also, however, lost his seat.[4]

Cobden took advantage of his time away from Parliament to once again visit the United States. When he returned he was sought out and invited to sit in government. He again refused the honor, preferring on his own initiative to negotiate a freer trade agreement between England and France. The English press greatly maligned his efforts, but undaunted, Cobden preserved and completed the treaty. He was offered the honors of royalty for his accomplishment but that had not been his purpose and these too went unaccepted. He felt the highest moral purpose on earth was not monetary gain but "peace on earth and goodwill among men."[5]

Concerned about the hatred and the fear that the press was promoting, Cobden wrote a pamphlet entitled "The Three Great Panics." In an effort to expose the absurdity of some of the power plays of the press, these pamphlets traced patterns of the press through history.

When the Civil War broke out in the United States Cobden was deeply distressed. His sympathies were wholly with the North for he detested slavery. His concerns grew as he realized that his own country of England was detaining American ships. He vigorously opposed all schemes that were continually made in an effort to aid the South. His life had been of such integrity to correct principles that he fought to keep his country from any unworthy course.

Cobden had for some years been suffering from bronchial irritation and, during this stressful time, he became seriously ill. In spite of his illness Cobden returned to Parliament to oppose a bill designed to build large defensive forts along the Canadian border. Had they been built, the North would have had to defend itself on two fronts, thereby dividing its strength.[6] He was able to stop the bill, but the demands of doing so left him physically vulnerable. When he caught a chill, its effect coupled with his bronchial weakness caused his strength to give away entirely He died on 2 April 1865. His last act was to seek for peace in a country that was not his own.

Richard Cobden's name now rarely appears in the annals of noted men. But the imprint of his character has been felt by all the world. Without him, Ireland might have been completely annihilated. He led the crusade for free trade, for international arbitration, for disarmament of nations, and for universal peace. He was always a just and good man. Peace and understanding were always his national and international aims, the hallmark of his life.

NOTES

[1] See Encyclopedia Brittanica. 11th ed., 1910, 6: 608.

[2] Ibid., p. 609.

[3] See Lambertson, J. P., ed. *Characters and Famous Events of All Nations and All Ages.* Boston: B. Millet, 1902, p. 205.

[4] See Encyclopedia Brittanica, 6:610.

[5] Ibid.

[6] See ibid., 6:611.

Christopher Columbus

> *"God made me the messenger of the new heaven and new earth of which he spoke in the Apocalypse of St. John after having spoken of it through the mouth of Isaiah; and he showed me the spot where to find it."*

COLUMBUS DID NOT SEE HIMSELF AS SOLELY RESPONSIBLE FOR THE discovery of what he felt were the Indies. He acknowledged the hand of God in his work. "When I was very young," wrote Columbus "I went to sea to sail and I continue to do it today.... I have found Our Lord very well disposed towards my desire, and I have from him the spirit of intelligence for carrying it out. He has bestowed the marine arts upon me in abundance and that which is necessary to me from astrology, geometry, and drawing spheres and situating upon them the towns, the rivers, mountains, islands and ports, each in its proper place."[1] To King Ferdinand and Queen Isabel, Columbus wrote:

> I spent six years here at your royal court, disputing the case with so many people of great authority, learned in all the arts. Finally they concluded that it all was in vain, and they lost interest. In spite of that [the voyage to the Indies] later came to pass as Jesus Christ our Savior had predicted and as he had previously announced through the mouths of His holy prophets.[Here Columbus's Book of Prophecies contains some scriptural references Psalm 2:6-8, Psalm 18: 43-44, Psalm 22:27-28, Isaiah 14:1-2, John 10:16, etc.]

> If what I myself say does not seem to be sufficient evidence of this, I offer that of the Holy Gospel, which says that everything shall pass save for His marvelous Word. And in saying that, it says that everything must come to pass as it has been written by Him and by the prophets.... *I have already said*

*that reason, mathematics, and mappaemundi were of no use to me
in the execution of the enterprise of the Indies. What Isaiah said
was completely fulfilled.*[2]

Columbus's efforts to convince his king and queen to let him do
what God had for him to do are reminiscent of Moses' efforts to
fulfill his divine role. Like Moses, he sought permission from his
sovereign with relentless persistence, then led the people out of a
captivity of ignorance. Columbus even "parted" the waters so the
children of Israel could cross to the promised land. And like
Moses, Columbus sought to lift the veil of paganism to give the
people a knowledge of the Christ.

Little is known of Columbus's family, but there has been much
speculation about it. Columbus was the eldest son of Domenico
Colombo, a weaver, and Suzanna Fontanarossa. He was born in or
near Genoa. From his home Columbus gained a depth of feeling for
spiritual things. His brother Bartholomew, a noted navigator of the
time, was devoted to Columbus and to Columbus's work.

Columbus wrote to a member of the royal court: "I am not the
first Admiral of my family. Let them call me, then, by what name
they will, for after all, David, that wisest of kings, tended sheep and
was later made king of Jerusalem, and I am the servant of Him Who
raised David to that high estate."[3]

Columbus had a somewhat ruddy complexion and is reported
to have had blue eyes and a freckled fair complexion which stood
out in contrast to some of his darker companions. He left to sail the
seas at the age of fourteen. His son Ferdinand described an incident
that occurred to his father during this time. Columbus was on a ship,
returning from Flanders when it engaged in battle with a foreign
ship. The two ships grappled and men crossed from boat to boat;
the slaughter on both sides was without mercy. The fight lasted
most of the day until the ships began to burn. To keep from being
burned alive the survivors had to jump overboard, even though, for
many this meant certain death. An excellent swimmer Columbus
was able to swim to shore, although land was more than two leagues
away (the equivalent of six miles). He found an oar, which, his son
writes, fate provided to preserve his father for greater things.

Since his ships usually sailed from Portugal, Columbus made his home there and worked as a map maker. While on shore, Columbus frequented the Convent of the Saints, where he attended mass. There he met a religious lady of minor nobility, Dona Felipa Moniz Perestrello, whom he later married. It was only fitting that he should find her in his chosen place of worship.

Columbus's deceased father-in-law had been the governor of an island belonging to Portugal, an island situated near the edge of the known parts of the western ocean. He had also been a sea captain and had a good collection of maps. The young couple moved in with Felipa's widowed mother, who saw the interest Columbus had in the maps and she gave him her husband's collection. These maps excited him and strengthened his conviction of a western route to the Indies. Marriage seemed to mature Columbus's convictions, and he began in earnest to bring about the work to which he had been called.

Columbus and his wife soon moved to the island of Santo Porto. Here he learned that strange items had been washed upon the shores of the local beaches including carved pieces of wood unlike any in Europe. There were huge hollowed out carved pine-tree trunks, which he would later discover were made by Indians and called "canoes." Most significant, two bodies of dead men washed up on shore. Their features differed from those of the known races, the known world of Columbus's day extending on the north to Iceland and Scandinavia, south to a cape 100 miles south of the Equator, to the east as far as China and Japan, and to the west as far as the Azores.

After Marco Polo's travels were highly publicized, Columbus felt it was an opportune moment to approach the king of Portugal. But the King of Portugal merely sent him to a board of "learned men," who scoffed at his ideas and turned down his request for a western voyage. Soon after, Columbus's wife died, and Columbus returned to Spain with his young son.

In Spain Columbus became again the subject of criticism. Many churchmen assailed him because he maintained the existence of inhabited lands on the other side of the earth. His presumption implied to them the presence of nations not descended from Adam, because it was impossible for those inhabitants to have crossed the ocean. According to the ecclesiastical leaders, Columbus's belief was an attempt to discredit the Bible.[4]

In spite of such criticism, Columbus worked steadily to obtain his goal. He sent his brother to England, in the hope obtaining support for his ideas. He also knew that if he were to convince Queen Isabel and King Ferdinand, he would need the backing of learned men of the day. With that in mind, he wrote to Paolo Toscanelli, the leading savant of Italy and probably the most knowledgeable cosmographer of his day. Toscanelli responded with a copy of a letter that he had previously written to a friend in Portugal. He stated that from all his research and knowledge, there definitely had to be land to the west.

Armed with this information, Columbus approached the sovereigns of Spain. But Spain was in the mist of one of the last great battles against the Moors, and so they, too, referred Columbus to a board of learned men. Again, Columbus's visionary plan was rejected. Queen Isabel, feeling impressed that Columbus's work was of great importance, told him not to give up and to try again, and for six long years, Columbus appealed to the court. However, the court would not listen while Spain was at war. Some believed that God gave victory to Isabel and Ferdinand in the Battle of Granada so that they would be able to support Columbus's plan.

Hopeful that the king and queen would personally listen to his proposal, Columbus returned to court and was again referred to the group of learned men. In despair Columbus decided to visit the King of France, having already sent his bother to seek support from the courts of England.

In his Book of Prophecies, Columbus quotes an ancient writer who prophesied that the person who would open the way for the return to Mount Zion would come out of Spain. Columbus felt that his voyage to the west would help open the way for the reinstatement of Jerusalem and the fulfillment of the prophecy.[5] Nevertheless, the mission itself mattered more than from where the support came, and so he set off for France.

Stopping at the mission of La Rabida to pick up his son, Columbus gained the sympathetic ear of the friars, particularly the good Prior Perez (who had been the queen's confessor). The prior believed Columbus and sent for his very educated friend, Dr. Garcia Hernandez. Dr. Hernandez agreed with the prior, and at last Columbus received support from some ecclesiastical and secular leaders.

Prior Perez left immediately for the royal court, and his endorsement convinced Isabel to grant permission for Columbus's voyage. After meeting with Perez, she sent a messenger to bring Columbus back. Columbus told the queen what he needed for the trip and also asked for certain rewards. Some people point to these rewards as evidence that Columbus sought only glory and wealth. However, Columbus was to be granted the rewards only if he discovered something of value that was approved by the king and queen. Columbus wrote, "I want it understood that I will not put prices high or low to valuables or land that I discover. I have the authority from your Royal Highness to decide or not to decide but only under your authorization."[6]

Many people in court did not believe Columbus's theory, but they still felt Columbus was greedily asking for titles and tenths (the rewards that Columbus had requested). Ironically, those in court who felt he was greedy in asking for titles and tenths were the same people who believed there was nothing on the other side to be found.

Upon obtaining approval from the royal court, Columbus went to Palo, Spain, to purchase ships and obtain supplies. With the help of the Pinzon brothers, who became captains, they were able to take on fairly good crews. The three ships, *Nina*, *Pinta*, and *Santa Maria*, set sail on 2 August 1492.

The crew left Spain filled with great apprehension about the trip. The voyage lasted much longer than Columbus expected, rations ran low, the men became mutinous and wanted to turn back. During this time Columbus wrote that he stood in need of God's help as much as Moses had when he was leading the children of Israel out of Egypt. The Israelites dared not lay violent hands upon Moses on account of the miracles God had wrought in his behalf, and the crew dared not resort to violence towards Columbus for much the same reasons. Soon the grumbling returned, and the other two captains met with Columbus in his cabin. They informed him that they could no longer restrain the men. Columbus asked for three more days, and the two captains agreed.

Columbus did not record what happened after he shut the door behind the two captains. Surely he must have poured his heart out to God as he had never done before. They were so close to victory, and he knew it. He seems to have received some sort of assurance. That night Columbus entered into his journal that his name was now to be *Christo-feren,* meaning Christ bearer.[7]

The next day, the crew pursued what they thought was land. All day long they followed the sighting only to discover that it was a cloud. However, this pursuit was not in vain as the ship covered more than double the leagues ever traveled in one day. Birds began appearing in abundance, and the crew found a branch with berries on it, floating in the water. They knew that land was not far away.

The Pinzon brothers felt that they should turn northward. But Columbus's sense of "dead reckoning" had them stay on course. On 11 October, at about 10 o'clock P.M., Columbus was walking on the deck, when he suddenly saw a light straight ahead that seemed to rise and fall as if someone were walking with a candle or lantern. Columbus called to those near him, and they agreed the light was definite enough that it must have come from land. About two hours after midnight, they spotted land.

At daybreak they saw an island. On shore there were people running to see their ships approach. After the anchors were dropped, Columbus and his men went ashore in their finest silks and velvets. With royal banners of their sovereigns in hand, Columbus knelt on the sand and kissed it. Tears of joy streaming from Columbus's eyes, as he rendered thanks to Almighty God and christened the island San Salvador, in honor of his Savior.[8]

Columbus explored several islands, and established a fort at La Navidad, then set sail for Spain. The return trip was not without danger. As his ships came near the Azores, there arose the worst storm ever recorded in history. The storm raged for fifteen days. Finally, they were able to put in at the Azores, but when they left these islands, they were met by another raging storm that caused critical damage to the vessels. It required all Columbus's skills and experience to guide his broken ship into the Lisbon port. The people there were ecstatic to greet Columbus and his crew. The king of Portugal treated him kindly. What a glorious day for that great kingdom and for the Christian queen who had always believed in Columbus!

Columbus made three more trips to the new world, and then his health gave out. Disheartened with the greed and lust that were wreaking havoc in the newly discovered land, in 1496 he wrote to the king and queen, begging that the same laws existing in Spain be applied to the islands, and that all people—including the Indians—have the same justice.

He wrote: "Procure for the Indians, that are coming under our rule, the same rules and protections as those we have been speaking of [here in Spain]. These rules are to apply to those in power and those not in power equally. I want them to have the same protection like I have as if they were my own flesh."[9] In 1497, he pleaded again: "

> I worry immensely about the future. I do not know what will happen in years to come. But we will discover new lands and we will negotiate in some of them according to the law of Castile and if this is not ruled by a strong hand then we will lose and rip apart our future and we will lose everything. I am afraid we will be misunderstood. I tell you to do it this way because gold is not everything.[10]

To his good friend, Amerigo Vespucci, Columbus said: "I feel persuaded, by the many and wonderful manifestations of Divine Providence in my especial favor, that I am the chosen instrument of God in bringing to pass a great event-no less than the conversion of millions who are now existing in the darkness of Paganism"[11]

Columbus died on 20 May 1506 in the city of Valladolid, Spain. His dying words were "In manus tuas, Domine, commendo spiritum meum,"[12] which translated means "Into thy hands, God, I commend my spirit."

NOTES

1 Watts, Pauline Moffitt. "Prophecy and Discovery: On Spiritual Origins Christopher Columbus's Interprise of the Indies." *American Historical Review* (Feb. 1985), p. 95.

2 Ibid, p. 96.

3 Columbus Ferdinand. *The Life of Admiral Christopher Columbus by His Son Ferdinand Columbus.* New Brunswick, N.J.: Rutgers University Press, 1959, p. 8.

4 See Lester, Edwards. *The Life and Voyages of Vespucci.* New York: New Amsterdam Books, 1903, p. 75.

5 Watts, p. 95.

6 Columbus, Christopher. *Letters to King Ferdinand & Queen Isabel 1496 Raccolta Collection.* Racolta Di Documenti E Studi Publicicate Dalla R. Commissione Colomiana Pel Quarto Centenario Dalla Scoperta Dell America, Appendix Roma 1894, p. 270.

7 Marshal, Peter. *The Light and the Glory* New Jersey: Fleming H. Revell Co., 1940, p. 39.

8 See Columbus, Ferdinand, p. 59.

9 Columbus, Christopher, p. 270.

10 Ibid, *Letters,* Dec. 1497, p. 270.

11 Lester, p. 79.

12 Columbus, Ferdinand, p. 284.

John Filpot Curran

Irish Statesman

1750-1817

> *"Depend upon it, my dear friend, it is a serious misfortune in life to have a mind more sensitive or more cultivated than common—it naturally elevates its possessor into a region which he must be doomed to find nearly uninhabited"*

NOW AND THEN PROVIDENCE SEEMS TO SMILE UPON THE EARTH BY providing her with an individual possessed of truly great wit and humor. John Filpot Curran was the wittiest and most eloquent constitutional lawyer of his time. He came into public service in the Irish Parliament at a time when the government was most reprehensible. As part of the opposition party courageously he used his wit and humor to bring new hope. For the people of Ireland, the days seemed a little brighter, the oppressed had a champion.

Curran was born in Newmarket, in the county of Cork, Ireland, on 24 July 1750. His beginnings were humble. His patriarchal line is said to have come from an English soldier in Cromwell's army, the same army that subdued Ireland. In Curran's account of the family, he paid his highest tribute to his bright and intellectual mother. (Her maiden name of Filpot became his middle name.) "If the world has ever attributed to me something more valuable ... than earthly wealth," Curran stated, "it was that ... a dearer parent gave her child a portion from the treasure of her own mind."[1]

From Curran's account she must have been an extraordinary woman. Because of her station in life she was uneducated, but she did not allow this to be a disadvantage. She was filled with enthusiasm for life and readily used her numerous gifts and talent to help others. Witty and eloquent, she was the delight of all those who came within the circle of her influence. Many would sit with her in the evening just to hear her tell the legends of "olden times," spiced with her wit. But none were more entertained than her son "little Jacky," as she affectionately called her son. In childhood play he would often imitate her.

One day the traveling puppeteer in his area lost his voice and could not continue the performance. Young Curran, having memorized the entire play, asked if he could not be the voice of Mr. Punch. The puppeteer agreed. Curran greatly amused the crowd— until he began changing some of the lines, adding satire on the local politics. Becoming braver with each performance young Curran's dialogue eventually went too far, touching too many sensitive nerves. Mr. Punch had to move on.

With such a sense of humor, Curran was naturally given to some mischief. He was often involved in the neighborhood escapades. "Heaven only know where it would have ended," Curran wrote. "But, as my poor mother said, I was born to be a great man."[2] Eventually the pride of the Senate and the courtroom, Curran responded to all compliments that any merits he possessed he owed to the affections of his gifted mother.

While playing marbles with the neighborhood boys, Curran was seen by the rector of Newmarket, who was a kindly gentleman. For some unknown reason unknown, the kindly rector took an interest in him. The rector, "Boyse," as Curran called him, invited the young lad to his home to visit and the two became fast friends. In this favored environment Curran learned his alphabet and grammar and was introduced to the classics. The rector taught Curran all he could and then made it possible for the young lad to attend school at Middleton. Of "Boyse," Curran said, "He made a man of me."[3]

Years later after he had gained eminence, Curran related that he came home from Parliament one day to find an old gentleman sitting in his drawing-room. "He turned around," recorded Curran. "It was my friend of the ball alley, Boyse! I rushed instinctively into his arms. I could not help bursting into tears. Words cannot describe the scene which followed. 'You are right, Sir; you are right; the chimney-piece is yours—the pictures are yours—the house is yours: you gave me all I have-my friend—my father!'"[4] When they had finished dinner that evening, Curran observed a tear glistening in the eye of the old gentleman. He was grateful to see his bounty and kindness resulted in goodness in his young recipient.

As in the lives of eminent men, Curran's life was touched by other great men. When he left the influence of Boyse, he came under the influence of a gentleman named Mr. Carey. Not only did Mr. Carey befriend young Curran, but he also had a profound knowledge of the best of the ancient literature. He shared with young Curran his great store of classical learning.

Upon finishing his courses at Middleton, Curran entered Trinity College, a theological college. It had been his mother's wish that he become a preacher. However, an event at Trinity changed his career. Guilty of a schoolboy prank, Curran was brought before a Dr. Duigenan, who was the enforcer of the law. Curran's punishment was to pay a fine of five shillings, or translate an article into Latin. He chose the latter assignment. But upon the appointed day he had not done the assignment. As a result the consequence was increased, he was to stand before the professor and give a recitation in Latin from the pulpit in the college chapel.

Curran prepared his Latin sermon and gave it. He was not far into his speech before Dr. Duigenan realized that it was a satire on himself! As soon as Curran finished, he was sent to the provost to be reprimanded. The provost listened in amusement to the Latin presentation and dismissed him with only a slight reproof. Curran's comrades all declared him born to the profession of a lawyer and not a preacher. He accepted their pronouncement, changed his courses and pursued a law degree.

In 1773, with a Master's degree in hand, Curran went to London to enter law school. Letters written during this time give a taste of his life then. "I still read," he wrote to his friend, "ten hours every day, seven at law and three at history, or the general principles of politics; and that I may have time enough, I rise at half after four." In order to keep such a rigorous schedule, Curran contrived an "alarm" to wake himself up at four every morning.

Exactly over my head I have suspended two vessels of tin, one above the other; when I go to bed, which is always at ten, I pour a bottle of water into the upper vessel, in the bottom of which is a hoe of such a size as to let the water pass through so as to make the inferior reservoir overflow in six hours and a half. I had no small trouble in proportioning those vessels; and I was still more puzzled for a while how to confine my head so as to receive the drop, but at length I succeeded.[5]

Those familiar with the cold, damp winters of Ireland will find this method to be a rather "chilly" way to wake up.

Curran obtained his law degree and married in 1774. In 1775 he was called to the Irish bar, where he soon obtained a fair practice. However, for all his wit and talent, he had a weakness. In presenting his first cases he would become extremely nervous and he would stammer and stutter. One day the judge asked him to read more clearly. This flustered him to the point of being unable to proceed. At last he paused for a moment, then revived his courage and proceeded without any noticeable nervousness.[6] Curran then joined a debating society and practiced until he had mastered the elements of good speaking.

During these early years, Curran struggled with poverty. A judge once chided him on his poverty. Speaking of this time Curran said, "my wife and children were the furniture of my apartments; and as to my rent, it stood pretty much the same chance of its liquidation with the national debt."[7] Due to the sympathetic assistance of a fellow attorney, Bob Lyons, he was able meet his rent. Soon Curran's practice began to grow and he became known for his eloquence.

A less reported but just as formidable talent was Curran's ability to do cross examinations. In this he could not even be imitated. Those who committed perjury were usually exposed by the time Curran finished questioning them. Just as stratagem is important in war, it was important to Curran in his pursuit of justice. During one trial a witness suffering under Curran's verbal drilling, pleaded with the judge to have counsel stop putting him in such a "doldrum." The judge asked Curran what the witness meant by a "doldrum," to which he replied that it was merely "a confusion of the head arising from a corruption of the heart."[8]

As Curran's fame as an orator at the bar grew so did his association with other notables of his time. Those with time on their hands would come to court when Curran was presenting or defending a case just to be entertained. One of his contemporaries, Reverand George Croly said of his oratory skills:

Of all orators, Curran was the most difficult to follow by

transcription. The elocution—rapid, exuberant, and figurative in a singular degree—was often compressed into a pregnant pungency which gave a sentence in a word. But his manner could not be transferred, and it was created for his style;—his eye, hand and figure were in perpetual speech.[9]

Curran soon became the most popular counselor in all of Ireland. Serving poor and rich alike. One time he defended an aged Roman Catholic clergyman, who acting in his position had given a religious reprimand to the brother of the mistress of an Irish nobleman. The nobleman assaulted the aged priest. No one would take the case because of the powerful political position of the nobleman. Curran offered his services and was able to obtain a verdict in favor of the reverend. The poor priest's health soon gave way, and he asked that Curran come to his bedside.

> The poor priest had neither gold nor silver to bestow [recorded Curran's son] but what he had, and what with him was above all price, he gave the blessing of a dying Christian upon him who had employed his talents, and risked, his life, in redressing the wrongs of the minister... He caused himself to be raised for the last time from his pillow, and, placing his hands on the head of his young advocate, pronounced over him the formal benediction of the Roman Catholic Church...[10]

Part of the blessing was prophetic. Although he participated in the shooting duels of the days, Currant was promised that he would not be harmed and he never was.

The bar had always been the training ground for Parliament so it was natural for Curran with his popularity to enter politics. At this time Ireland had its own Parliament, and it was here, upon this battle field of liberty, that Curran displayed his noblest defense of constitutional principles and the oppressed. At the very outset of his parliamentary career his standards became fixed. Parliament seats being owned by the leading families, Curran was given a place in Parliament by one of these borough owners. It was not long before Curran found himself differing radically in principle from the gentleman who bought his seat for him. With great difficulty, Curran gathered a large sum of money to buy another seat.

Curran vigorously defended such issues as liberty of the press and national representation. In speaking of the liberty of the press he said, "The liberty of the press, and the liberty of the people, sink and rise together; that the liberty of speaking, and the liberty of acting, have shared exactly the same fate..."[11]

Although he was a Protestant, he fought for Catholic Emancipation as no Catholic could vote or be elected to Parliament. (At this time Ireland was eighty percent Catholic.) Curran also maintained the most rigid principles when it came to money matters therefore he could not be bribed.

Curran served in Parliament with another "eminent" Irishman, Henry Grattan, to better Ireland's conditions under King George III of England, who had severely limited Irish industry. Private ownership of property was prohibited. The Protestants were permitted ninety-nine year leases and Catholics only thirty-one. The one staple food was the potato, because England had limited other agriculture. This led to a great famine during the potato blight.

In an effort to change many of these injustices, Curran supported many of the proposals by Grattan, and worked for the repeal of these deadly restrictions. The repression by England finally pushed Ireland to the brink of a revolution. But England could ill afford another revolution on the heels of the American Revolution, so she conceded a number of rights to the Irish people.

Grattan and Curran were not only political allies but also intimate friends to their death. Some twenty years after Grattan and Curran had worked together, Curran wrote to Grattan about their years in Parliament he wrote: "I made no compromise with power..."[12]

Curran's biographer, a personal acquaintance, Charles Phillips, stated of Curran: "Whatever might have been the fate of his eloquence, it was impossible for his votes to be misrepresented; and the friend of liberty will never look for him in vain wherever freedom or religious toleration was endangered."[13]

Once in a courtroom he approached the jury with an admonition that would do us well to follow. "I have a right to call upon you in the name of your country, in the name of the living God of whose eternal justice you are now administering in that portion which dwells with us on this side of the grave, to discharge your breasts, as far as you are able, of every bias of prejudice or passion."[14]

In 1798, military oppression broke out supported by the leading party. Much to Curran's dismay Ireland began to resemble the bloodthirsty days following the French Revolution. No person or property was safe. Despite the danger, Curran did not cease to speak out against the government's diabolic actions, often acting as counsel in the cases of those accused of high treason. Yet, Providence preserved him. Reportedly because of his "unstained" reputation, he was never a victim of the bayonet or dungeon.

His speeches were full of illustrations from the scriptures. No irreverent word against religion was ever heard from Curran.

He was a devoted father. At home, "He was a little convivial deity," reported a visitor.

> He soared in every region, and was at home in all; he touched everything, and seemed as if he had created it; he mastered the human heart with the same ease that he did his violin. You wept and you laughed, and you wondered; and the wonderful creature who made you all at will, never let it appear that he was more than your equal.[15]

Curran was by nature extremely sensitive. Like many who live upon this earth, Curran was not free from tragedies that beset mankind. His family suffered much sorrow.

Curran knew no fear in defense of those he felt were wronged, and the heavens protected him from retribution. John Filpot Curran: orator, humorist, constitutionalist, and, most important, champion of the rights of individuals.

NOTES

[1] Duyckinck, Evert A. *Portrait Gallery of Eminent Men and Women.* New York: Henry J. Johnson, 1873, p. 504.

2 Phillips, Charles. *Recollections of Curran & Some of His Contempories.* New York: C. Wiley & Co., 1818, p. 9.

3 Phillips, p. 10.

4 Phillips, p. 10.

5 Duyckinck, p. 399.

6 Encyclopedia Britannica. 11th ed. 1910. 7:647.

7 Phillips, p. 31.

8 Phillips, p. 41.

9 Duyckinck, p. 407.

10 Duyckinck, p. 403.

11 Phillips, p. 175.

12 Ibid., p. 130.

13 Ibid., p. 136.

14 Ibid., p. 155.

15 Duyckinck, p. 408.

Michael Faraday *1791-1867*

ENGLISH SCIENTIST—FATHER OF ELECTRONICS

> *"Let others attend to the harnessing of the forces of nature. I am content merely with the study of the correlation of these forces."*

KNOWN AS THE FATHER OF ELECTROMAGNETISM, MICHAEL Faraday established the law of electromagnetism, laying the foundation of the science of magneto-electricity. "Faraday stands at the head of scientific observers of the nineteenth century, and his discoveries have left their indelible mark on the progress of mankind. To him must be given the credit for the solid foundation of electrical science as it is known today."[1] One of the most distinguished pioneers in the field of chemistry as well, Faraday was outstanding in the nineteenth century for his genius as an experimenter.

Michael Faraday was born in Newington Butts, Surrey county, England, 22 September 1791. His father, James, was a blacksmith. His mother, Margaret Hastwell, had grown up on a nearby farm. They belonged to a small religious sect called the Sandemanians and were very devout and humble. Faraday records of his father's smith shop that "nail making ... is a very neat and pretty operation to observe. I love a smith's shop and anything relating to smithery. My father was a smith."[2] Faraday loved his mother and father very much, but times were hard; he was often hungry. During one particularly difficult year, young Faraday was allowed but one loaf of bread each week to eat. Consequently, his frail frame was too puny to follow his father's trade.

Faraday writes of his meager education that it was one of the "most ordinary description consisting of little more than the rudiments of reading, writing, and arithmetic at a common day school. My hours out of school were passed at home and in the streets."[3] At the time he was securing his education, Faraday's family moved to a rather poor section of London and lived over a coach house. When not in school Faraday spent much of his time taking care of his younger sister Margaret and playing marbles.

Because of a defect in his speech, Faradays's formal schooling came to an abrupt end. Unable to correctly pronounce his "R"s, Faraday was corrected again and again by an old maid school teacher who loved precision and hated children. When correction failed, she resorted to ridicule. Finally, when the these two methods failed she ordered Faraday's older brother Robert to go and buy a cane for her with which she promised "to give Michael a public flogging."[4] Robert pitched the half penny over a wall and ran home to report the teacher's cruelly. Mrs. Faraday refused to let her boys remain in such a situation and promptly removed them from school.

Faraday's youthful adventures were severely curtailed due to the poor circumstances in which the family found themselves. He went to work full time as an errand boy for the neighboring bookseller, a kindly Frenchman named Mr. Riebau.

His first assignment was to deliver newspapers early in the morning and pick them up again when the people had finished reading them. Then he would deliver them to other customers. On Sundays he hurried extra fast so that he might get cleaned up in time to attend church with his family. Because of his experience delivering papers, in later years he rarely saw a paper boy that he did not go out of his way to acknowledge in a kindly way.

After observing the diligence with which young Faraday worked, Mr. Riebau decided that he was an exceptional young man who would make a good apprentice. This opportunity would give young Faraday a trade that would fit his physical ability. Riebau's offer, contrary to the custom of the day, did not require a premium or form of tuition, which made it possible for Faraday to accept and provided him with an opportunity to read and handle many books. Faraday reports his own feelings: "Whilst an apprentice, I loved to read the scientific books which were under my hands, and amongst them, delighted in Marcet's *Conversations in Chemistry*."[5] One of his favorite set of books was the Encyclopedia Britannica because of the vast amount of knowledge contained therein. He told a friend that Watt's *On the Mind* taught him to think.

On occasion Mr. Ribeau allowed young Faraday to attend Mr. Tatum's lectures on Physics. The required shilling for each lecture was provided by Faraday's older brother Robert. Faraday kept copious notes of each lecture. He even studied "perspective" (sketching) in order to illustrate parts of the lecture notes with his drawings. Along with this notebook he kept a scrap book which he called the "Philosophical Miscellany." In it he collected articles from newspapers and magazines, as well as notices of events relating to the arts and sciences. Also found in the scrap book was Sturm's *Reflections on the Works of God.* (Faraday's *Diary* totals seven volumes and is one of Britain's most prized scientific treasures).

His first exposure to the Royal Institute of England, a scientific organization, of which he later became its most distinguished member, came one day when a regular customer of Mr. Ribeau's, Mr. Dance, engaged young Faraday in a conversation. Learning of Faraday's fascination with science, Mr. Dance gave him tickets to four lectures by the noted Sir Humphrey Davy. Again, Faraday made copious notes of the lectures and illustrated them. Upon seeing the notes Mr. Dance was impressed and recommended that Faraday forward them to Sir Joseph Banks, the President of the Royal Society. This Faraday did, and as he expected, there was no response.

In 1809 Faraday's father died. He had been weakened by years of strenuous work, and his health had finally given way. Deeply concerned for their mother and sister, Faraday and his brother supported them on their own meager incomes.

During the little time he had after long hours of his apprenticeship, Faraday attempted several experiments in chemistry and physics. This included construction of an electrical machine, using glass cylinders and other electrical "apparatus," many years prior to Edison's experiments.

Towards the end of his apprenticeship, Faraday began a regular correspondence with a friend named Benjamin Abbot. Abbot came from a higher class and had the advantage of a good education. Faraday enjoyed "trying out" some of his unusual ideas and experiments on his friend. Abbot had the good sense to preserve letters from Faraday, thereby adding great depth of understanding into Faraday's life. These letters reflect a simple charm and earnestness as well as give a view of his straightforward search for truth as do the records of his lectures. In speaking to future scientists, Faraday said: "Truth should be [your] primary object. If to these qualities be added industry, he may, indeed, hope to walk within the veil of the temple of nature."[6]

Having finished his apprenticeship with Mr. Ribeau, Faraday sadly parted from this kind man and his wife. He became a journeyman book-binder to a Mr. de La Roche, a violent-tempered French refugee. The situation soon proved unbearable for Faraday's gentle spirit. He stayed with de La Roache until he could stand the cruelty no longer. Then he left, seeking to establish a career for himself. This was a difficult time, for his mother was in dire circumstances, living in poverty.

In a desperate attempt at any position, Faraday, being modest but not timid, again sent a copy of his notes, this time to Sir Humphrey Davy. His perseverance paid off, for Davy hired the young man to work in the Royal Institute. It was later said Sir Davy's greatest discovery was the discovery of Faraday.

It did not take long for Sir Davy to observe the young man's quick mind. He soon allowed his young assistant to participate in his experiments, some of which backfired, with both sustaining minor injuries. So pleased was Davy with his new assistant that he invited Faraday to accompany him on a lecture-tour of the European Continent.

This was the opportunity of a lifetime for this young man, who had only seen the edges of London. Having made his way into the scientific world with his notes, he again began to make minute notations of everything he saw and heard. The habit of making written observations became a habit he continued to the end of his life.

Faraday was only fifteen years old when he returned from the Continental tour. He was to become an integral part of the Royal Institute, which was known as the home of the highest kind of scientific research. The Institute was also known for its specialized lectures. He now earned twenty-five shillings a week, and as an assistant, was given a room in the attic in which to live. It was in this room that a half-dozen of his friends gathered to read, criticize, correct, and help improve each other's pronunciation and construction of the language. These sessions continued for several years, greatly enhancing the education of all of the participants.

Among his good friends were the older brothers of a lovely young lady known as Sarah Barnard. The Barnard family were members of the Sandemanian faith to which Faraday belonged. Faraday was quite taken by Sarah but was unsure of the direction he should head. One evening while visiting Faraday, Edward Barnard, Sarah's brother, picked up Faraday's notebook and read notes of the young bachelor's on the subject of love. "What is love?" wrote Faraday. "[It is] a nuisance to everybody but the parties. A private affair which everyone but those concerned wishes to make public."[7] Edward saw the humor and repeated the lines to his then twenty-one year old sister.

Faraday, who was intent on asking Sarah's hand in marriage on their next meeting, found that upon asking her a strange look came in her eye and she changed the subject. What could be wrong? he wondered He knew she cared for him. However, the next few months were hectic ones and they had little opportunity to see each other. Faraday persisted after Sarah's hand almost to the point of becoming a nuisance. When he wrote her a letter with a formal purpose of marriage it was returned with a note written in the margin: "Love makes philosophers into fools."[8] However, Sarah finally consented to his proposal and the union proved to add strength to the marvelous works of the scientist Michael Faraday.

Faraday's research can be divided into three periods. During the first period his discoveries and experiments were in the field of chemistry with occasional jaunts into magnetism. His conviction of the harmony in the unity of nature led him to the second period, which dwelt exclusively with magnetism and electricity. It was during this period that he succeeded in converting magnetism into electricity. His third period was concerned experiments into the relationship between electricity and light.

However, Faraday paid a dear price for the discoveries he made during this period. He had worked so long and hard at his experiments that he had taken little time out, even for his meals. His mind and body completely exhausted, he was incapable of any work, and forced to leave his beloved laboratory for an extended trip to the continent. The doctors ordered him not to read or to write anything, but to completely relax. So severe was this physical collapse that it took five long years before he could go back to experimenting. When he finally did come back, he began working only two hours a day. He gradually built his strength, until he could work longer hours.

This began his third period of discovery. The most important work of this time was the discovery of the relationship between electricity and light. During his long period of rest, his mind still sought to record the laws of nature.

He went back to work with an inner conviction that these two forms, of energy—light and magnetism, were related in some way. His idea at this time was regarded as almost heretical, and he was mocked for his persistence Today his discoveries for the relationship between light and magnetism are recognized as perhaps his greatest. It was from the inspired mind of Faraday that Edison first received the idea of the electric spark that now illuminates our homes.

In 1824, Faraday was elected a Fellow of the Royal Society. In the next year, 1825, he was appointed Director of the Laboratory of the Royal Institution. Then in 1840, he was elected an Elder of the Sandemanian Church and preached for four years every other Sunday. Both positions were an honor for him. In his Sabbath preaching, he used the words of the scriptures as much as possible using as little of his own words as he could.

Though a commoner, in 1858 Queen Victoria gave Faraday the use of one of Her Majesty's houses at Hampton Court in honor of the great contribution he had made to his native land.

Most of his time was now spent in lectures. He did not talk about his religion unless the subject was brought up. But once in a lecture on mental education Faraday expressed the relationship between science and his religious beliefs. He said:

I must make one distinction which, however it may appear to others, is to me of the utmost importance. High as man is placed above the creatures around him, there is a higher and far more exalted position within his view; and the ways are infinite in which he occupies his thoughts about the fears, or hopes, or expectation of a future life, I believe that the truth of that future cannot be brought to his knowledge by any exertion of his mental powers, however exalted they may be; that it is made known to him by other teaching than his own, and is received through a simple belief.[9]

Dr. Bence Jones, Faraday's biographer, made this observation on the effect of Faraday's religious conviction on his scientific discoveries: "His standard of duty ... was formed entirely on what he held to be the revelation of the will of God."[10]

Michael Faraday died on 25 August 1867, at the age of seventy-six. He had not sought for glories or honors. His scientific purpose had been, as he said, to "let others attend to the harnessing of the forces of nature. I am content merely with the study of the correlation of these forces."[11] Failure, to Faraday, merely proved that he had not yet asked Nature the proper question. Rarely did he talk to assistants or others; his primary dialogue was with nature herself. His science was to search for manifestations of the unity found in nature. That he, a poor, uneducated son of a journeyman blacksmith was permitted to glance into the beauty of the eternal laws of nature was a never-ending source of recognition for him. Faraday's true humility lay in the profound consciousness of his indebtedness to his Creator.

NOTES

[1] Faraday, Michael. *The Chemical History of a Candle—The Popular Educator*, No. 18. National Education Alliance Inc., Washington D.C., 1939, p. 1572.

[2] Stephenson, Leslie, & Brown-Chalner, Sidney Lee, eds. *Dictionary of National Biography.* MacMillan, New York, 1908, p. 1055.

[3] Jerrold Walter. *Michael Faraday, Man of Science.* Fleming H. Revell, New York, n.d., p. 14.

[4] Thomas, Henry and Dana Lee Thomas. *Living Biographies of Great Scientists.* New York: Nelson Doubleday, Inc. n.d., p. 118.

[5]Duyckinck Evert A. *Portrait Gallery of Eminent Men and Women.* H. J. Johnson, New York, 1873, p. 174.

[6] Ibid., p. 184.

[7] Randell Wilfrid L. *Michael Faraday.* Small, Maynard & Co., Boston, n.d., p. 87. YEAR

[8] Thomas, p. 124.

[9] Encyclopedia Britannica. 11th ed. 1910, p. 174.

[10] Ibid., p. 174.

[11] Thomas, p. 12. See also *Faraday as a Discover* by John Tyndall (London: Longsman, Green, 1870) and *The Life and Letters of Faraday* by Dr. Bence Jones, Secretary of The Royal Institution. (London: Longman, Green, 1870).

Admiral David Glasgow Farragut

AMERICAN NAVAL OFFICER   *1801-1870*

> *"God forbid, that I should have to raise my hand against the South."*

"IN THE CIVIL WAR, CONTROL OF THE SEA WAS A PRICELESS ASSET to the Union. The navy maintained communications with the outside world, severed those of the South, captured important points on the coast, and on the Western rivers cooperated with the army like the other blade to a pair of shears."[1] Filling such a role in American naval history was Admiral David Glasgow Farragut.

In March 1776, George Farragut, David Farragut's father, immigrated from his native island of Minorca, in the Mediterranean Sea, to America. Of Spanish descent, George Farragut arrived to find America deep in the Revolutionary War. Farragut's father immediately devoted himself to the cause of the colonists and served gallantly in the war. He served first as a cavalry officer and later in the navy. When the war ended he took his family to settle in the wilderness of Tennessee. It was here that David Glasgow Farragut was born. Life on the frontier was not only rugged but also extremely dangerous. David recalls a time when his mother sent him aloft to watch an approaching Indian party while she stood ready at the barricaded door with an axe.

After the United States completed the Louisiana Purchase, the family moved again to help settle New Orleans. One day his father returned home struggling with an elderly man he had rescued near the lake who was suffering from "heat prostration." This singular incident led directly, both physically and mentally, to Farragut's entrance into the navy. The sufferer, David Porter, had been a seaman and as young Farragut helped nurse him, he listened to Porter's stories of the sea. Farragut began to dream of going to sea.

Mr. Porter did not recover but died while in the care of the Farraguts. Mrs. Farragut had contracted yellow fever while Porter was there and she died also. The funerals of the two were held the same day. Although life was harsh for settlers on the frontier, its very harshness gave strength and hardiness to a youth of spirit.

Commander Porter, son of Mr. Porter, soon visited the family and offered to adopt young Farragut. Dazzled by the Commander's uniform and filled with a sense of destiny, young David agreed to go with Commander Porter and his family. Shortly thereafter nine-year-old David was sent to school in Washington, D.C., for there were few educational opportunities in Louisiana where the Porter family lived. He never saw his father again. He passed away before David could return home.

In 1811, David was commissioned a midshipman and was ordered to serve on the frigate *Essex* which was under his mentor, Commodore Porter.[2] Great Britain was harassing American commerce on the seas, so the *Essex* was sent to Valparaiso, Chile, to protect the American whaling ships from the British.

They captured several British ships, and because of a shortage of officers young Farragut was made prizemaster, or temporary captain, of one of those ships, the British whaler, the *Barclay*. His orders were to return from the coast of Peru to Chile. The captured English captain was greatly disturbed that a lad of thirteen was given command of the ship and he to overawe the boy into surrendering his authority.

> When the day arrived for our separation from the squadron [Farragut wrote] the captain was furious, and very plainly intimated that I would find myself off New Zealand in the morning, to which I most decidedly demurred..... I considered that my day of trial had arrived (for I was a little afraid of the old fellow, as everyone else was). But the time had come for me at least to play the man; so I mustered up courage and informed the captain that I desired the main top sail filled away, in order that we might close up with the *Essex Junior*. He replied that he would shoot any man who dared to touch a rope without his orders ... then he went below for his pistols. I called my

right hand man of the crew and told him my situation. I also informed him that I wanted the main top sail filled. He answered with a clear "Ay, ay, sir!" in a manner which was not to be misunderstood, and my confidence was perfectly restored.[3]

As Farragut returned to the *Essex* in the harbor at Valparaiso, he participated in one of the bloodiest battles in naval history. The British ships the *Phoebe* and the *Cherub* completely destroyed the *Essex*. Farragut was slightly wounded. Young as he was, Farragut seems to have distinguished himself in this engagement. His name is mentioned with honor as one of the officials who "exerted themselves in the performance of their respective duties, and gave an earnest of their value to the service."[4]

In his fourteenth year, his orders separated him from his guardian. He was left to his own strength of character to guide his steps. In reflection, he gratefully recalled the influence of, first, a young first lieutenant named Cocke and, later, a messmate named William Taylor. Farragut noted of Taylor: "He .... counseled me kindly, and inspired me with sentiments of true manliness, which were the reverse of what I might have learned from the examples I saw in the steerage."[5]

In 1815, Farragut's orders sent him with a fleet to the Mediterranean. The following spring he was transferred to the *Washington*. The United States Minister to the Court, Mr. William Pinkney, was on board. This experience allowed him to round out his limited education. The travels of the squadron and his habit of observation did much to fill his mind with information that he had been unable to get earlier in his brief schooling. The chaplain in those days was often the only schoolmaster the young midshipmen had; and the degree of commitment to that schooling depended on the attitude of the Captain. In spite of these drawbacks, Farragut exhibited a natural desire to learn.

It was this characteristic as well as his ability to resist temptation that attracted him to a Mr. Folsom, who, appointed to the consul of Tunis, obtained permission to take Farragut with him to Tunis for the winter. Here Farragut remained under Mr. Folsom's tutelage for nine months, pursuing his studies on the site of the ancient maritime empire of Carthage. The subjects that were of particular interest to him were mathematics, English literature, French, and Italian. Mr. Folsom, who lived to the end of the Civil War, was able to follow the successful and great career of the young orphan boy he once befriended.

Farragut was not yet eighteen when he was appointed acting lieutenant on board the brig *Shark*. Reflecting on this event he recorded, "I consider it a great advantage to obtain command young, having observed, as a general rule, that persons who come into authority late in life shrink from responsibility, and often break down under its weight."[6]

After four and a half years at sea, Farragut returned to the United States. He settled in Norfolk, Virginia, and married Susan C. Marchant, with whom he was very happy until she died after suffering a terrible illness. His devotion and his tenderness in assuring to his wife's every comfort, through the sixteen years of her illness, was reported as a striking illustration of his gentleness of character. When not at sea, he was constantly by her side and proved himself a faithful and skillful nurse.

His kind and compassionate nature extended to all he knew, inspiring admiration in all who interacted with him. A lady of Norfolk was reported to have said: "When Captain Farragut dies, he should have a monument reaching to the skies, made by every wife in the city contributing a stone."[7] After Susan's death, Farragut married again, this time to a lovely southern belle, Virginia Loyall, by whom he had a son, Loyall.

After a thirteen-year absence, his orders allowed him to pay a visit to New Orleans to see his brother and sister. Ironically, the ship he was on carried the first load of bricks to build Fort Jackson, at New Orleans. Years later Farragut would attack this same fort, achieving the surrender of New Orleans during the Civil War.

Farragut spent the following years suppressing piracy in the West Indies. In August 1825, while commanding the famous *Brandywine*, he returned the great General Lafayette to France after his memorable visit to the United States. The time spent with this devoted patriot of freedom was of no minor consequence.

Farragut was always careful to see that his ship's boys received their educational studies and were treated with respect. Many men, unaccustomed to such kindness, gave loyal support in return.

The United States sent Farragut's fleet to Mexico with the American Ambassador on board to help negotiate and observe the battle between France and Mexico. Here he was able to observe firsthand the taking of the fort of San Juan de Ulloa in Vera Cruz. The observations and analysis he made of the battle were helpful to him years later in taking the forts in New Orleans and Mobil Bay.

Notwithstanding all that Farragut had been through, the Civil War proved to be perhaps the greatest test of principles he would ever pass through. Virginia was still wavering in her decision to secede, but while Farragut was home in Norfolk awaiting orders the South took Fort Sumter. When President Lincoln ordered U.S. troops to retake it, the pro-secession party garnered enough votes to cause Virginia to leave the Union.

As a Virginian, Farragut felt great pride in and loyalty toward his state. He was a native of another southern state, Tennessee, and had spent part of his childhood in the extreme southwest. When not at sea, he had spent his adult life, in Norfolk, Virginia. Since Virginia likewise claimed many illustrious men, including George Washington, these sentiments overpowered reason and principle.

Farragut, despite the strong pull of his state, had no trouble deciding his course. He had seen what revolution had done to the countries in South America and dreaded the possibility of that type of destruction in his own land. He was not swayed by sentiment and reason but by the Constitution, the Union, and the destiny of the Republic. The day Virginia seceded, he was informed that because of his allegiance his life was no longer protected. "He at once went to his house and told his wife the time had come for her to decide whether she would remain with her own kinsfolk or follow him North. Her choice was as instant as his own and that evening they, with their son, left Norfolk, never to return to it as their home."[8]

The Navy Yard was in flames as they fled, narrowly escaping imprisonment. Part of the railroad tracks out of Baltimore were destroyed. This slowed the family's departures. Then, when they finally arrived in New York they were met with suspicion. The people there needed time to learn to trust these Southerners. In spite of these difficulties, Farragut was soon working for the Navy department on a "retirement board" for older officers.

When the navy was reinforced by the building of additional ships, Farragut, then a captain, was ordered to the Gulf of Mexico to command a blockading squadron which would go up the Mississippi River to take New Orleans, his childhood home. New Orleans was guarded by two forts, Fort Jackson, and on the opposite bank, Fort St. Phillip. Farragut and his fleet of seventeen vessels made a daring run past the two forts, subduing thirteen gunboats and two ironclads of the Confederate flotilla. Leaving Colonel Porter, grandson of David Porter, to accept the surrender of the two forts, Farragut proceeded with a portion of his fleet to New Orleans. New Orleans surrendered without a fight.

Farragut was then sixty years old, and he spent the next five years in constant blockade of the whole coast, except for Mobile, Alabama. Under his command was a fleet of eighty ships. Managing the commands of all these ships was a Herculean task. Farragut wrote wearily: "They must think I am made of iron, ... [but] as I am always hopeful; put my shoulder to the wheel with my best judgment, and trust to God for the rest."[9]

Orders came for him to take the forts at Mobil Bay. The mouth of the bay was protected by two formidable forts, Fort Morgan and Fort Gaines. The narrow channel leading into the bay was obstructed by piling and lines of floating torpedoes. Farragut's fleet amounted to thirty ships. Against his better judgment Farragut allowed his officers to convince him to place his flagship third.

He gave the first ship orders to proceed around the torpedoes in a narrow opening made for blockade runners. The captain disobeyed the orders and changed his course in pursuit of the southern ironclad, the *Tennessee*. A torpedo hit the ship, which sank quickly, taking with it the entire crew. The next ship, in fear and confusion, began backing up, and in turning almost collided with Farragut's flagship.

The great British naval officer, Lord Horatio Nelson, said: "Five minutes may make the difference between victory and defeat." "Lost moments," wrote Napoleon, "are the determining elements of naval campaigns."[10] The course of this battle depended upon the prompt decision of the admiral. Standing on the top deck Farragut appealed to Heaven for guidance. He recorded: "O God, who created man and gave him reason, direct me what to do. Shall I go on?" And it seemed as if in answer, he said, a voice commanded, "Go on!" God had spoken to him and personal danger could not deter him.

Edging his ship around the others and taking the lead, he shouted his now famous lines: "Damn the torpedoes! Full speed!"[11] As they passed between the buoys, many on board heard the casings of the torpedoes knocking against the copper of the ship's bottom. Many of the primers snapped audibly, but no torpedo exploded.

During the battle for the forts, in order to get above the smoke of the battle to better direct the maneuvers of the fleet, Farragut took a position in the main rigging. He had the quartermaster lash him there so that if he were wounded or lost his footing, he would not fall to the deck.

In this engagement the Confederate fleet was destroyed, all ports to the South were closed, and twenty-six hundred prisoners were taken. This victory also helped re-elect President Abraham Lincoln. Lincoln's presidential opponent, General George B. McClellan, a man whom Lincoln had dismissed as leader of the northern armies, had campaigned that Lincoln was a country bumpkin who did not know how to end a war he had started. The battle of Mobile Bay proved otherwise.

This battle was one of the greatest feats in naval history. Farragut differs from leaders of other great battles in one significant way. Civil War leaders Generals Grant and Sherman were not yet forty-five years old.

Nelson and Napoleon were but forty-six at Trafalgar and Waterloo. Farragut was sixty-one when New Orleans surrendered and sixty-five in the Battle for Mobil Bay. But age did not deter him, so exceptional was his strength and stamina. As a reward for his brilliant achievement congress created the rank of "vice" admiral and conferred it upon Farragut.

When the war ended Farragut was put in charge of the European fleet. This command allowed his wife to accompany him. Before he left on his European tour, Congress created the office of Admiral, the first ever in the United States. A grand reception was held for him on board his flagship. The President and many of his cabinet attended the party.

Europe received Farragut with the honor befitting a hero. Everywhere he was received with honors, particularly from fellow naval officers. In England he was presented to Queen Victoria. But nowhere was he received with more acclamation than on the island of Minorca, the land of his ancestors. Going there filled his great desire to return to the land of his father. His personal secretary recorded that people thronged the street, each trying to get a better look at the admiral. The air filled with cheers and acclamations. The walls, housetops, and balconies were crowded with anxious onlookers. The force of the crowd became so great that Farragut's party had to proceed on foot under armed guard. Arriving at the home they were to stay, Farragut went out on the second balcony and spoke to the crowd in their native tongue. The crowd was deeply touched. "One old man with tears streaming down his weatherbeaten face, stamped sincerity itself upon the nature of the welcome by shouting aloud: 'He is ours! He is ours! But I shall never see him more.'"[12]

Farragut brought had honor not only to himself, his country, and his profession, but also to the land of his forefathers.

It has been said that Farragut had the energy and spirit of the ancient Vikings. Yet, after a battle when those who had been killed were laid out on the quarter deck for him to review, he wept like a little child. His biographer, Captain Mahan, wrote this tribute of him:

> [Farragut] has left on record that, in the moment of greatest danger to his career [Mobil Bay], his spirit turned instinctively to God before gathering up its energies into that sublime impulse whose luster, as the years go by, will more and more outshine his other deeds as the crowning glory of them all.[13]

Farragut's dignity of character and simplicity of heart combined with his profound submission to the Almighty makes his life worthy of emulation.

NOTES

[1] Morison, Samuel Eliot. *The Oxford History of the American People.* New York: Oxford University Press, 1965, p. 642.

[2] Se Mahan, Capt. A. T. *Admiral Farragut.* New York: D. Appleton and Com., 1911 p. 11.

[3] Ibid., p. 25- 26.

[4] Duyckinck, Evert A. and Henry J. Johnson. *Portrait Gallery of Eminent Men and Women.* New York: Henry J. Johnson, 1873, p. 504.

[5] Mahan, p. 53.

[6] Ibid., p. 61.

[7] Ibid., p. 88.

[8] Ibid., p. 112.

[9] Ibid, p. 250.

[10] Ibid., p. 316.

[11] Ibid., p. 277-78.

[12] Ibid, p. 302.

[13] Ibid., p. 325- 26.

Frederick the Great

KING OF PRUSSIA   *1712-1786*

> *"A man that seeks truth, and loves it, must be reckoned precious in any human society."*

A STUDENT OF HISTORY, FREDERICK II OF PRUSSIA, OFTEN CALLED Frederick the Great, concluded that history was an excellent teacher but drew few pupils. He wrote: "It is in the nature of man that no one learns from experience. The follies of the father are lost on their children; each generation has to commit its own."[1] Frederick's own knowledge of history led him to establish a new era. In his memoirs of the House of Brandenburg, written in 1758, he wrote a startling new philosophy of state that the ruler was in reality the servant of his state. The concept of royalty serving the people was unknown to the people of that age. Frederick helped inaugurate the age of enlightenment. The rulers of state could not easily turn their backs on this leadership style for Frederick proved it so highly successful.

The grand enterprise of Frederick, one of his biographers, Thomas Carlyle, tells us, was making the populace happy. He proclaimed to the public of Berlin: "Our grand care will be to further the Country's well-being, and to make every one of our subjects contented and happy. Our will is, not that you strive to enrich us by vexation of our subjects; but rather you aim steadily as well towards the advantage of the country..." He further wrote: "My will henceforth is if it ever chance that my particular interest and the general good of my countries should seem to go against each other, —in that case, my will is, that the latter be preferred." [2]Unlike many rulers, Frederick meant what he said. The day after his ascension to the throne, he began his startling reforms.

That first year Prussia experienced an extremely cold summer. Many of the crops froze, and famine threatened parts of the land. Frederick opened the public granaries and ordered grain to be sold at reasonable rates to the suffering poor.

Having traveled rather extensively throughout the land as crown-prince, he was a keen observer of the conditions of the people. After opening the granaries he appointed an "Inspector of the Poor" who was charged to do something immediately; particularly to assist the poor, homeless women. "The destitute of Berlin" were "set to spin" at Frederick's expense, and "vacant houses, hired for them in certain streets and suburbs, [were] new-planked, partitioned, warmed; and spinning [was] there for any diligent female soul..."[3] Justice, the opening of the granaries, and the care of the destitute were the first acts of Frederick's reign.

Frederick gave economic reform and reconstruction priority in time and money. Cities that had been devastated by war were relieved of paying taxes anywhere from six months to two years. When the Seven Year War was over, a goodly portion of the military horses were sent to the farmers for plowing. Immigrants were paid to come to the land of Prussia and her new possessions for the purpose of settling new lands.

He pronounced that the common soldier would no longer be treated with harshness when not deserved and abolished the use of torture in criminal trials. He freed the peasants from servitude. His courts became known as the most incorruptible in Europe. He set upon a revision of the criminal code which was very advanced in its approach. Included in this code was religious freedom. Frederick wrote concerning this matter: "All religions must be tolerated and the fiscal must have an eye that none of them make unjust encroachment on the other; for in this country every man must get to heaven in his own way."[4]

The struggling Protestants throughout Europe greeted this proclamation with shouts of "bravisimo." Soon after this the Pope obtained permission to build a large cathedral in Berlin. Frederick supported freedom of religion although he felt much of religion was cloaked in superstition from which it needed to be freed.

Frederick's tolerance extended to the press and he made one of the first attempts to give freedom to the press. This freedom, however, was not the freedom of the press we experience today; nevertheless, in practice it always had some form of a real existence throughout his reign.

Education was especially important to him, and in this cause he was very active. Every child in Prussia, from five to fourteen was to attend school. It is said that he founded as many as sixty schools in one year. Because of his military leanings, old soldiers were appointed as schoolmasters and Latin was dropped from the curriculum. Much of the learning was in military drill style. Frederick wrote: "It is a good thing that the schoolmasters in the country teach the youngsters religion and morals...."[5]

Frederick's love for education was formed in his youth by his mother and his tutors. He long had the idea of building up or re-establishing the Academy of Sciences. When he became king he sought for the finest minds in Europe to come and teach and direct the Academy. Among those who came were Voltaire, the French philosopher, Maupertius, the brilliant scientist who became president of the Academy, and Herr Wolf, who had been exiled by Frederick's father.

As a youth Frederick had been rather free and easy-going, but upon assuming the crown many of his old friends were astonished to find him every inch a king. Many came to approach him in a casual way as they had done before and were instantly reproached for their lack of respect toward the position of the throne. It was not for himself that he made these demands, but out of repsect for the throne he required it. Carlyle relates that one of Frederick's old friends encouraged him to vices with women in return for favors. But Frederick was born to be a king and a king he was. The old companion stood much reproved; it is reported that in despair he hung himself.

Because of his restraint for the sake of the ruling position of the country, Frederick is often seen as heartless and without personal attachment. But there were two people we know for whom he held great tenderness and affection this was his sister and his mother. When his mother approached him after he had been made king, she addressed him as "Your Majesty." He responded to her, "Call me son; that is the title of all others most agreeable to me!"[6] He also refused to have her called "Queen Dowager" as was tradition for widowed queens. Her title was to be "Her Majesty the Queen Mother." He never approached her except with his hat in his hand,

and when in Berlin regardless of how busy he was, he seldom failed to visit her daily.

Frederick's mother was the Princess Sophia-Dorothea, daughter of King George I of England, who was actually a German from the Hanoverian line. Frederick was born on 12 January 1712. His father, Frederick William, was terribly disappointed in his son's below average size. The father was further annoyed when his son spent his days in a dressing gown, reading French history, philosophy, and literature, and playing his flute. Frederick's father was a man who loved military exactness and ran his family and country accordingly. He was especially fond of his palace guards, a crack regiment consisting of what was considered at that time as "giants." All of the guards were over six feet tall. Frederick William had recruiters go through Europe continually seeking tall recruits for this regiment. He also built a fine army.

Though young Frederick wasn't the least bit interested in military drill he was forced to memorize the entire military history of the royal family in detail. Because his father considered many of Frederick's actions effeminate, he abused his son. He forbade Frederick, eventually, to read or study in French. And when he did not measure up, his father shouted at him in public and often as not, a handy item was thrown at him.

Much to his military father's dismay Frederick learned to excel in playing the flute. His love of music extended into his reign. He composed over 120 songs in his free time. He constructed an opera house and brought in Italian operas. He was unceasing in his efforts to lift his people. He loved to play flute sonatas with Johann Sebastian Bach at the harpsichord.

By the time Frederick was eighteen, he had determined to flee to his relatives in England. With the help of a loyal friend, Lieutenant Latte, Frederick reached the borders of Prussia, but the pair were discovered by the King and both were locked up and placed under guard. Latte was marched in front of young Frederick's door and executed by order of the Kings. A tribunal was held on young Frederick, and he was sentenced to die. Through the pleading of the kings of Sweden, Austria, and others, the crown-prince was saved.

However, he was released only to be a prisoner in a small town from which he was not free to leave. He was dismissed from his military rank. The king ordered soldiers to refrain from saluting him. He had to take his meals alone. It was his duty to learn the management of the government of that small town, even to the balancing of its books. Though this was a devastating and traumatic experience it was providential, for through it Frederick learned the very innermost workings of government. However, Frederick was never the same after this ordeal. His boyhood had swiftly been broken with intense pain. His grief was so great at the loss of his loyal friend that he wrote: "In this world of ours, one must love nothing too much."[7]

His father died in 1740, and as the new king Frederick began his sweeping reform by dismantling his father's "giant" regiment. The ruling powers in Europe saw this action and hoped that in King Frederick II they had a weak ruler who might be overpowered. But in this hope they were sadly mistaken. Frederick knew their intent and established an elaborate network of spies. He did not disband the army as many had hoped, but doubled its size and readiness.

Before his death, Frederick's father had signed the Pragmatic Sanction with Austria, granting the right to make the daughter of King Charles queen, because there was no male heir. This Sanction was signed by Prussia on the condition that Austria would help Prussia obtain Berg and Julich, but Austria had not fulfilled her part of the bargain and gave the territory away. Because of this action Frederick did not feel he was bound by the sanction.

In 1741, he entered with his army into the province of Silesia, which is now part of Czechoslovakia, and took possession of the whole of it. Silesia at this time was a part of Austria. This invasion has often been called the most unwarranted act in history. However, it was not without its precedent in Europe. At one time Silesia had its own ruling family. Austria was devoutly Catholic and most of Silesia was Protestant. In 1707 the Silesians had pled with the Swedish King Karl, who was marching through with his army, to pressure the Kaiser of Austria to allow them to be free from persecution. When Frederick and his army approached the little country, the Silesians offered little resistance, for they looked upon the Prussians as Protestant liberators. Some even exclaimed: "Bless God for raising such a defender."[8]

But Austria returned the fire, and in the heat of the first battle Frederick was seen leaving the battle, fleeing into the night. He remained in a small village nearby not seeing anyone. When Frederick appeared again, he was not the same man. Something had gone through the very soul of Frederick in that short time.

He knew what he had to do. He said; "The ox must plow the furrow, the nightingale must sing, the dolphin must swim and I must fight."[9] And then prophetically he announced: "This small event changes the entire system of Europe. It is the little stone which Nebuchadnezzar saw, in his dream, loosening itself, and rolling down on the image made of four metals, which it shivers to ruin."[10]

So began the Seven Years Wars, the war that changed the face of Europe, breaking down the old and setting up the new. Though Frederick's army was set against the major armies of Europe, he prevailed, outnumbered by more than two to one. A brilliant strategist, he was not afraid of his purpose and personally led his army. In one skirmish he had two horses shot out from under him. His clothes were riddled by a hail of shrapnel. And once, as he took out his silver snuff-box, it was crushed by a bullet.

Though the boundary lines of Europe changed but little, the changes that resulted from this war were great. France lost India, and the English drove the French out of North America. France was bankrupt. Spain had lost Havana and Manila. England was glad for peace. She needed to turn her attention to her colonies, for she was now the ruler of the seas and in an ascendancy which was to last for many years. Perhaps the greatest gain was for German patriotism and nationalism, which was essential for progress. It was soon after the reign of Frederick that the great names of Germany began to appear: Goethe, Shiller and others.

Upon his return to Berlin, a battle weary Frederick was deeply moved by the sight of his people, whom he had not seen for six years. "Long live my dear people!" he cried. "Long live my children."[11] Truly they were his children, for he had none of his own. Frederick died in 1786.

Napoleon, after defeating the Prussians at Jena sought out the tomb of Frederick. And in a fitting tribute, Napoleon turned to his generals and declared, "If he were alive we should not be here."[12]

NOTES

[1] Durant, Will, and Ariel Durrant. *The Story of Civilization*. New York: Simon & Schuster, 1967, 10:529.

[2] Carlyle, Thomas. *History of Friedrich II of Prussia, Called Frederick the Great*. Boston: Dana Estesa & Co., n.d., p. 151-52.

[3] Ibid., p. 153.

[4] Ibid., p. 158.

[5] Durant and Durant, p. 500.

[6] Carlyle. p. 168.

[7] Thomas, Henry and Dana Henry. *Living Biographies of Famous Rulers*. New York: Nelson Double Day, Inc., 1941 p. 207.

[8] Carlyle, p. 319.

[9] Durant, p. 60.

[10] Carlyle, p. 286.

[11] Durant, p. 63.

[12] Ibid., p. 530.

David Garrick *1717-1779*

ENGLISH ACTOR AND DIRECTOR

> *"Let others hail the rising sun, I bow to that whose race is run."*

DAVID GARRICK HAS GONE DOWN IN HISTORY AS PERHAPS THE greatest English actor of his age. An excellent playwright his acting talents lay equally in tragedy and comedy. His performances of Shakespeare helped to revive the influence of this great master. In 1769, Garrick organized the first Shakespearean festival at Stratford-on-Avon. Born in a time in which acting and actors were at the lowest point of social acceptability since the 1400s, Garrick lifted the profession to a new respectability.

David Garrick was born in the rural town of Lichfield, England, the birthplace of Samuel Johnson, who was at one time his schoolmaster. Although these men were both born in poverty and obscurity, they were to become the most commanding personalities of the eighteenth century in the world of literature and drama.

Garrick's reputation was not limited to England. Garrick toured France just before his retirement, where he created an admiration for Shakespeare's works that burst into the greatest awakening of the French to an appreciation for Shakespeare. Garrick's fame still echoes in the literature of France. It was perhaps in the creation of this bond between England and France that Garrick performed the work for which he was born. He is considered as one of those who did the most to dispel the clouds of prejudice which kept France and England separated.

Considering Garrick's role in bringing France and England together, it will perhaps seem no coincidence that the nationality of Garrick's grandparents was French and the nationality of his birth was English. Garrick's paternal grandparents were French Huguenots, who were driven to seek shelter in England after the repeal of the Edict of Nantes. The Edict of Nantes had granted religious freedom to Protestants in France in 1598, but it was revoked in 1685. Thousands fled France.

The Garrick family (whose name at this time was De La Garrique) escaped to England from Bordeaux separately and with great difficulty. Eventually the family, including a brother and a sister, was reunited. A fragment of a journal kept by the grandfather, also named David Garrick, lists the births and deaths of the family, recognizing the hand of the Lord in all things.

To this first David Garrick was born Peter Garrick. In 1707, Peter married Arabella Clough who was of Irish descent. This couple had ten children, seven of whom lived. David Garrick was their third child. Peter Garrick became a captain in the king's army. His wife was greatly devoted to her husband.

Clever and bright, with an engaging personality, David was an observer of people. He often entertained his friends with his imitations. He did not find school much to his liking for he had a restless spirit. When Garrick was about ten years old, he watched a company of strolling players and decided to put on a play. The play he chose was *The Recruiting Officer*. The cast consisted of his friends and a little sister.

It was not long after this that he received an invitation from his Uncle David, his namesake, to come and live with him in Portugal. Uncle David was a prosperous wine merchant and was willing to train young Garrick in the business. Garrick's stay in Portugal seems to have been more a success in the social aspect of his life than in the commercial aspect. He entertained the English community at their evening events with his imitations and his ability to give from memory long speeches and other acting tidbits. Samuel Johnson was to say to Fanny Burney that "off as well as on the Stage, [Garrick] is always an Actor."[1] This "education" of life abroad gave him an early glimpse of the world, and his interaction with people there was of invaluable training. However, his work with the ledgers did not prosper. Garrick was sent back home.

Garrick's father was unable to support his large family on his captain's "half-pay," so he volunteered for overseas duty. He was gone for five years. Because the eldest brother had also left for the service, the responsibility of helping the family fell upon young David Garrick. He was fifteen years old.

His mother's health was poor and Garrick did all in his power to relieve the trials of his mother. When Garrick's father returned home, his health, too, was so broken that he lived only a short time. When Garrick's uncle David died, leaving him £1,000, a family council was held and Garrick and his elder brother Peter decided to use Garrick's inheritance to go into the wine business, of which Garrick had some knowledge. Garrick was to warehouse the products in London and Peter would retail them in Litchfield.

When Garrick left for London he carried with him a letter of introduction from Gilbert Walmesley, the Registrar of Diocese, who had a keen interest in the bright young lad. He wrote of Garrick: "as ingenious and promising a young man as ever I knew in my life," who "has been much with me, ever since he was a child, almost every day; and I have taken great pleasure often in instructing him, and have a great affection and esteem for him."[2] (However, because of the death of his father, Garrick's educational experience had lasted less than a year.)

Garrick's place of business was close to Convent Gardens theater. He attended all the plays that he could and became a friend with actors, stagehands, and directors. One of the leading actors who became a friend of Garrick's said: "The stage possessed him wholly; he could talk or think of nothing but the theater."[3] Garrick submitted to the theater at Drury Lane a farce he had written and it was accepted.

One night at Goodman's Field the leading man suddenly took ill, and Garrick offered to fill in for him. He did so well that the audience did not notice the substitution. However, Garrick found the acting of the time very stifled, rigid. It seemed more a place for speech giving and straightforward declarations than a place of acting. This troubled Garrick, for he felt that the stage should hold a mirror up to nature, showing its complexities. He felt it was his calling to effect a revolution.

Garrick continued to act with some of the players from Goodman's Field, and his confidence grew. He began to immerse himself in his parts, acting with emotion and feeling. His voice was strong and melodious, his body light and agile, and he had a commanding set of eyes. He soon became known as the new wonder. When Garrick acted the theater was always full; when he did not, it was half empty. Through jealousies of the rival theaters Goodman's Field was closed down by government decree and the only two remaining registered theaters were Convent Garden and Drury Lane. Garrick signed a contract with Drury Lane, which gave him a salary that far exceeded any previously granted to an actor.

Nobles and titled people flocked to the theater to see this new wonder. Alexander Pope observed Garrick's fresh and forceful style and commented, "That young man never had his equal as an actor, and he will never have a rival." Mrs. Porter, a great actress of the time, prophetically stated after watching Garrick, "All hail, hereafter. He is born an actor, and does more at his first appearance than ever anybody did with twenty years' practice.... What will he be in time!"[4]

Garrick eventually became the manager and owner of Drury Lane. He was an excellent money manager and began to be one of England's wealthiest men. Known for his generosity, he gave away more money than any man in England. He established charities for which he would often give benefit performances, and cared for his brothers and sisters.

Garrick married Eva Marie Viegel, one of the finest and most advanced dancers in the world. Their marriage was an everlasting courtship. She soon retired from the stage to support her husband in his management of Drury Lane. Garrick did not make decisions without consulting Mrs. Garrick.

During Garrick's twenty-nine years as manager, he produced seventy-five plays and revised twenty-four of Shakespeare's dramas. At last he announced his retirement and for three months gave farewell performances to packed houses. Then he and his wife left for his famous tour of France. Their tour coincided with the important translation of Shakespeare by Letourneur. The combination of these two events cemented Shakespeare's reputation in that country. Because of the great admiration France developed for Garrick, new conciliation grew between England and France.

Upon his death, all of England mourned. Johnson wrote: "I am disappointed by that stroke of death which has eclipsed the gaiety of nations and impoverished the public."[5] Garrick's social gifts, his quiet integrity, and his private virtues combined with his great talents to give the dramatic arts the dignity it had previously lacked. His body was taken to Westminster Abbey by members of the highest nobility and placed in the Poets' Corner at the very foot of Shakespeare's monument. Samuel Johnson was observed "standing by his grave, at the foot of Shakespeare's monument, and bathed in tears."[6] Goldsmith eulogized him by writing: "Here lies David Garrick, describe me, who can, an abridgment of all that was pleasant in man."[7]

NOTES

[1] Parsons, Clement. *Garrick and His Circle.* New York: G. P. Putnam's Sons, 1906, p. 5.

[2] Ibid., p. 32.

[3] Duyckinck, Evert A. *Portrait Galley of Eminent Men and Women.* New York: Henry J. Johnson, 1873, p. 109.

[4] Ibid., p. 112.

[5] Parsons, p. 15.

[6] Duyckinck, p. 122.

[7] *The Oxford Dictionary of Quotations.* 3rd Ed. New York: Oxford Press, 1979, p. 231.

Sir Edward Gibbon

"The history of empires is that of the misery of man. The history of knowledge is that of his greatness and happiness."

THE *HISTORY OF THE DECLINE AND FALL OF THE ROMAN EMPIRE* by Sir Edward Gibbon has been said by many to be the greatest history ever written. But such an accomplishment was never dreamed of, "So feeble was my constitution," says Gibbon, that his father named each succeeding son Edward in hopes of an heir. Gibbon's early years were plagued by frail health. His propensity towards illness prohibited many of the regular activities common to most youth. He was the first of seven children, all his siblings died during infancy. His mother died in 1747 due to complications of her seventh pregnancy. Gibbon was then nine years old. From the time of his birth until her death his mother regained her health only during occasional brief periods.

Gibbon was born in Putney, England, on 27 April 1737. The chief source of information about his life comes from his autobiography. Gibbon actually wrote or began six autobiographies, which have been compiled by different individuals. The most popular is a compilation made by his good friend Lord Sheffield. The result was *Memoirs* (1796), sometimes known simply as his *Autobiography*.

Upon the death of his mother, Gibbon's father moved, leaving the boy to the care of a maternal aunt, Catherine Porten, whom he calls the "true mother of my mind," as well as of his health.[1] He never forgot this dear aunt's instruction, devotion and care. Gibbon gratefully stated, "Many anxious and solitary days did she consume with patient trial of every mode of relief and amusement. Many wakeful nights did she sit by my bedside in trembling expectation that each hour would be my last."[2] "To her kind lessons I ascribe my early and invincible love of reading, which I would not exchange for the treasures of India."[3]

Much to his father's dismay, Gibbon was never strong enough to encounter the rigors of a regular classroom. The home in which he stayed was his grandfather's and here the future scholar made much use of the well-stored library. His indiscriminate appetite for reading fixed itself more and more decidedly upon the area of history. "I was led from one book to another, till I had ranged round the circle of Oriental history. Before I was sixteen I had exhausted all that could be learned in English of the Arabs and Persians, the Tartars and Turks."[4] However, "my childish propensity for numbers and calculations was totally extinct!"[5]

In 1749, his Aunt Catherine's father's bankruptcy left him destitute. Unwilling to live a life of dependence, Catherine opened a boardinghouse for students at Westminster School in hopes of obtaining some educational benefits for young Gibbon. But again, his health was too frail to attend, and so his aunt continued educating him privately.

Somewhere towards his sixteenth year nature displayed in his favor "her mysterious energies" and his infirmities seemed suddenly to vanish. His unexpected recovery revived his father's hopes for his son's "education," hitherto neglected if judged by traditional standards.[6]

He entered Magdalen College, Oxford, England, where he did little but read theology. He always had a deep interest in religion. The desire to learn about theology resulted in his becoming a Roman Catholic at the age of sixteen.[7] The Bible and history, he felt, justified the existence of the Catholic Church. His union with the "Universal Church" precluded him from attending Oxford, for this was a time when it was almost treasonous for a Protestant to convert to Roman Catholicism. This brush with the "Church from Rome" appears to be the beginning of Gibbon's search for the original church as established by Christ.

His father lost little time in devising some method which, if possible, might effect the cure of his son's "spiritual malady." He was sent to Switzerland to board in the home of a Calvinist minister named Pavilliard, where it was hoped that the atmosphere and teaching would bring young Gibbon back to the protestant faith. The minister went about this task of reconversion with the greatest tact and caution. He knew little English and young Gibbon knew practically no French, but under Pavilliard's tutelage Gibbon not only returned to the religious views of his father but he also became competent in French, Greek, and Latin.[8] These latter two languages allowed him to read the original works that were so essential to his monumental work, *The Decline and Fall of the Roman Empire.* Gibbon continued to live in the home of his clerical advisor for five years, devoting himself to study. The amount of historical and other data which he stored in his prodigious memory during that period was miraculous. "This independent and unguided way of learning made him the greatest scholar of his day."[9]

Returning to England, he spent a large part of his income on books and "gradually formed a numerous and select library, the foundation of my works, and the best comfort of my life."[10] Gibbon read the classical historians especially Herodotus, Xenophon, Tacitus, and Procopius. During his mandatory "aristocratical" and idyllic military service he perfected his Greek and read Homer and Longinus.

On a trip to the European continent in 1764, he spent three months in Italy and more particularly in Rome. "It was at Rome, on the fifteenth of October, 1764, as I sat musing amidst the ruins of the Capitol, while the barefooted friars were singing vespers in the Temple of Jupiter, that the idea of writing the decline and fall of the city first started to my mind."[11]

In England he did further research before composing the first volume of his monumental work. In 1776 after five years of reading and three years of writing the *History of the Decline and Fall of the Roman Empire* was published. Although his work absorbed most of his time, he did take an occasional break to attend "Johnson's Club" where great minds of the day met for intellectual stimulation. This "club" was frequented by such great contemporaries as Oliver Goldsmith, Samuel Johnson, Sir Joshua Reynolds, and David Garrick, among others.

Gibbon's main concern was his history, and he found it difficult to think seriously about anything else. He rewrote the first chapter three times. Upon his completion of the first sixteen chapters the publisher refused to publish the work because the cost was prohibitive. Two other booksellers pooled their finances in order to print the first volume. The literary world, usually split by its factional jealousies, united in praising this ponderous work.

The timing of its publication was providential, for the writers of the Constitution of the United States scoured history books in order to glean the best and avoid the worst principles of governments as experienced by past civilizations.

The final volume, not as thorough as early volumes, was completed twelve years later in 1787. Gibbon's footnotes and documentation are impeccably accurate and much can be gained in a study of the notations alone. Dissatisfied with secondhand accounts when primary sources were accessible, Gibbon said, "I have always endeavored," he said, "to draw from the fountainhead; my curiosity, as well as a sense of duty, has always urged me to study the originals; and if they have sometimes eluded my search, I have carefully marked the secondary evidence on whose faith a passage or a fact were reduced to depend."[12]

The first part of the *Decline and Fall* (a majority of the whole work), supplies a very full history of 460 years (A.D. 180-641); the second and smaller part, and much less detailed, is a summary history of about 800 years (A.D. 641-1453).

Gibbon felt that during the century before A.D. 180, the Roman Empire peaked in its official competence and public content. Gibbon born before the freedom and prosperity of modern times, felt that this period of the Roman Empire represented civilization's highest achievements. He wrote:

> If a man were called upon to fix the period in the history of world during which the condition of the human race was most happy and prosperous, he would, without hesitation, name that which elapsed from the death of Domitian [A.D. 96] to the accession of Commodus [A.D.180]. The vast extent of the Roman Empire was governed by absolute power, under the guidance of leaders of virtue and wisdom. The armies were

restrained by the firm but gentle hand of four successive emperors whose characters and authority commanded involuntary respect. The forms of the civil administration were carefully preserved by Nerva, Trajan, Hadrian, and the Antonines, who delighted in the image of liberty, were pleased with considering themselves as the accountable ministers of the laws.[13]

However, great as this peace and happiness was, Gibbon observed that it hinged on the "instability of a happiness which must depend on the character of a single man. The fatal moment was perhaps approaching, when some licentious youth or some jealous tyrant would abuse ... that absolute power."[14] And so it finally happened that Marcus Aurelius allowed the Imperial Power to pass to his worthless son Commodus; and it is from this point in time that Gibbon begins to mark the decline of the empire. Gibbon felt that "civilization and progress" were the measure by which the happiness of men is secured and that an essential condition to that happiness was political freedom.

The fifteenth and sixteenth chapters of the *Decline and Fall* are considered the most famous. Here Gibbon traces the early progress of Christianity through the Roman Empire. Because these chapters discussed Christianity, notwithstanding the approbation of the work as a whole, many labeled Gibbon a heretic. Gibbon, carefully, yet as openly as possible, depicted the rise of Christianity in its later adulterated and changed form as contributing to the decline of Rome. Since there were laws that could construe certain expressions to be hostile toward Christianity—which would result in a serious crime—Gibbon had to be cautious in his writings. The punishment for propounding "heretical" philosophies was up to three years imprisonment without bail. Out of this protective necessity we probably do not have Gibbon's complete insight into the state of Christianity during the Roman decline.

In spite of his insights in the corruption of religion, Gibbon's faith was never shaken. He wrote in a letter to Lord Sheffield, upon the death of his Aunt Catherine; "I will agree with my Lady, that the immortality of the soul is on some occasions a very comfortable doctrine."[15]

Gibbon implied in his history that somewhere during the first century the Christian church was pure and unchanged. But from that time on many changes and influences came into the church. "Since every friend to revelation ... is convinced of the cessation, of miraculous powers, it is evident that there must have been some period in which they were either suddenly or gradually withdrawn from the Christian Church." Gibbon offers three different times when this cessation could have occurred: (1) at the death of the apostles; (2) at the conversion of the Roman Empire to Christianity; or (3) upon the extinction of the Arian heresy.[16]

Gibbon quotes the historian Eusebius (cir. 280), called the Father of church history, who was chosen Bishop of Caesarea in 314 A.D. Eusebius took part in the Council of Nicaea wherein he led a minority group of "moderates." This minority party opposed discussing the nature of the Trinity and preferred the language of Scripture to that of theology in referring to the Godhead.[17]

> They presume to alter the holy Scriptures, to abandon the ancient rule of faith, and to form their opinions according to the subtile precepts of logic. The science of the church is neglected for the study of Geometry, and they lose sight of Heaven while they are employed in measuring the earth.... Their errors are derived from the abuse of the arts and sciences of the infidels, and they corrupt the simplicity of the Gospel by the refinement of human reason.[18]

Gibbon attributed a fanaticism arising among the Christians to be a resurgence of the Judaic origin of Christianity. He felt Nero's persecution of the Christians was really a persecution of the Jews.[19]

Although Gibbon's views on the Roman empire were astute he was unable to see the recurrence of history in the decline of his own country. The whole of his work on Rome documented historical facts that led to decline and dissolution of governments. Ironically, he continued in the lifestyle of all Europeans living under aristocracy. England was on the very door of her empire expiring, and yet he refused to accept the obvious collapse even after years of study.

On one occasion during the American Revolutionary War he

rejected an invitation to meet with Benjamin Franklin, replying with a card saying that though he respected the American envoy as a man and a philosopher, he could not reconcile it with his duty to his king to have any conversation with a "revolted" subject. Franklin replied that he had such high regard for the historian that if ever Gibbon should consider the decline and fall of the British Empire as a subject, Franklin would be happy to furnish him with some relevant materials![20]

Adam Smith ranked Gibbon "at the head of the whole literary tribe at present existing in Europe." His historical works were supported by other well known historians: Hume, Robertson, and Warton. Horace Walpole announced to William Mason on the publication of the History: "Lo, there is just appeared a truly classic work."[21]

After writing the last lines of his great work, and alone in his summer house garden, Gibbon took a walk in the moonlight and recorded: "I will not dissemble the first emotions of joy on the recovery of my freedom, and perhaps, the establishment of my fame. But my pride was soon humbled, and a sober melancholy was spread over my mind by the idea that I had taken an everlasting leave of an old and agreeable companion."[22] Such was the devotion Gibbon had to his work.

His work had become his life and in so doing he fulfilled his destiny. Of this destiny Gibbon states: "Without engaging in a metaphysical (spiritual) or rather verbal dispute, I know by experience that from my early youth I aspired to the character of an historian."[23] Sensing his foreordained mission, Gibbon's greatness was poured into his book.

As surely as Robert Browning determined in boyhood to give his life to poetry, so did Edward Gibbon determine to devote his to history.... By temperament he was born to record history. It is therefore ... no marvel that the end-product was the most magnificent single historical work in the English tongue.[24]

NOTES

[1] Saunders, Dero A., ed. *The Autobiography of Gibbon.* Comp. by Lord Sheffield New York.: Meridian. 1961 p. 61.

[2] Encylopedia Britannica. 11th ed. 1910, 11: 928.

[3] Saunders., p. 61.

[5] Saunders., p. 101.

[6] See ibid., p. 65.

[7] Ibid., p. 68.

[8] Encyclopedia Britannica, 11: 929.

[9] Fitzhug, Percy, and Harriet Fitzhug. *Biographical Dictionary.* New York: Grosset & Dunlap, 1935, p. 248.

[10] Durant and Durant, 10:798

[11] Saunders, p. 154.

[12] Encyclopedia Britannica, 11:935.

[13] Durant and Durant, p. 801.

[14] Ibid., p. 801.

[15] Prothero, Rowland E., Ed. *Private Letters of Edward Gibbon 1753-1794.* Introduction By The Earl Of Sheffield. London: John Murray, 1896, 2:145.

[16] See Gibbon, Sir Edward. *The Decline and Fall of The Roman Empire.* New York: Harcourt, Brace, 1960, 1:190.

[17] Gibbon, 1:118.

[18] See *The American People's Encyclopedia.* Chicago: Spencer Press Inc., 1948, 8:207

[19] See Durant and Durant, p. 802.

[20] See ibid., p. 802.

[21] Ibid., p. 805.

[22] Saunders, p. 195.

[23] Ibid., p. 137.

Johann Wolfgang von Goethe   *1749-1832*

> *"If man was of divine origin, so was also language...These two things, like soul and body, I could never separate...God had played the schoolmaster to the first men."*

TO THE ENDURING NAMES OF SHAKESPEARE, HOMER, AND DANTE, the student of history and literature must add the immortal name of the German-born poet, Goethe. Goethe's mind and soul were so elevated and sublime that few have been his equal. His reputation was established almost overnight, and he was well-known all over Europe. His talent and perceptions were revered and sought by all, from Napoleon to Sir Walter Scott.

From the time he was a young man, Goethe saw not only the weight and fetters of daily life, but he also saw events in daily life as part of a much larger and more important picture. "Every situation—nay, every moment is of infinite worth," he said, "for it is the representative of a whole eternity." [1]

Like Shakespeare and others, Goethe rooted himself in the unchanging principles of human nature. He was convinced that no matter how tempted and tried man may be, good will always triumph over evil. "I believe in God," Goethe told Eckermann, a close associate and secretary, "in Nature, and in the triumph of good over evil."[2] Upon completing his most enduring work, Faust (which took fifty years to complete), Goethe enlarged upon this belief: "In Faust himself there is an activity which becomes constantly higher and purer to the end, and from above there is eternal love coming to his aid. This harmonizes perfectly with our religious view, according to which we cannot obtain heavenly bliss through our own strength alone, but with the assistance of divine grace."[3]

Most histories describe Goethe as a philospher as well as a writer. However Goethe disdained philosophy of his day. Goethe agreed with the premise, "There is a point of view beyond the sphere of philosophy, namely, that of common sense.... I have always kept myself free from philosophy."[4] Goethe felt that the Germans had wasted their time and energy in trying to find the solutions to philosophical problems, while the English with their great practicality were winning the world.

As a young student he debated the issue of philosophy with a fellow boarder. His opponent had studied at the University of Jena and contended that religion and poetry found their basis in philosophy. Young Goethe stubbornly opposed this view. As a result of this encounter Goethe began an intense study of the history of philosophy. Among the ancients, he discovered a more pure philosophy than that of his day because, as he noted, it was there that he found poetry, religion, and philosophy all combined into one. In his studies of the ancients he always included the first five books of the Old Testament. Socrates he esteemed as well, proclaiming him an "excellent wise man."[5]

Historians record that Goethe denied being a Christian, giving as evidence Goethe's encounter with the noted Reverend Lavater. Lavater, who was as extreme as he was narrow in his view, challenged Goethe to declare whether or not he was a Christian. Not, Goethe replied, if he had to use Lavater's definition.[6] According to Christian belief, man was born evil and Goethe could not agree with this. To the end of his life he felt that man was essentially good and trying to overcome the evil in the world around him.

Goethe always worked to help others maintain the good in themselves and felt great disdain for those who criticized others. He felt that doing so only caused personal destruction and brought great pain to all involved. "For the point is," he said, "not to pull down, but to build up, and in this humanity finds pure joy."[7]

Goethe felt that man had a special relationship with deity, even when he was sometimes left to his own resources for his growth:

> For a time we may grow up under the protection of parents and relatives; we may lean for awhile upon our brothers and

sisters and friends, be supported by acquaintances and made happy by those we love; but, in the end man is always driven back upon himself; and it seems as if Divinity had taken a position toward men so as not always to respond to their reverence, trust and love, at least, not in the precise moment of need. Early enough, and by many a hard lesson, had I learned that at the most urgent crises, the call to us is, "Physician, heal thyself"; and how frequently had I been compelled to sigh out in pain, "I tread the wine-press alone!..." While then, I reflected upon this natural gift.[8]

Goethe often reflected upon those divine gifts given to man in varying degrees. Those he most often referred to as possessors of divine gifts were Friedrich Schiller, Lord Byron, Robert Burns, Walter Scott, Napoleon, and Shakespeare. Referring to *Hamlet*, Goethe described it "as a pure gift from above."[9] Goethe further felt that "every extraordinary man has a certain mission which he is called upon to accomplish."[10] He felt that he had received gifts from above. When people sought to tear him down, he saw it as a foolish attempt to amend the purpose God had laid out for him.

Although Goethe chose not to be aligned with the Christian sects of his day, religion was always important to him. Goethe spent fifty years studying church history, often in its original language. The Old Testament was an integral part of his way of thinking and he often stated that truly great genius and art was never achieved without being integrally connected to religion. In any art, he maintained, little can be achieved if it is divorced from serious and noble thought. Goethe had definite ideas about how this union could be brought about in literature. "If any man wish to write a clear style, let him be first clear in his thoughts; and if any would write in a noble style, let him first possess a noble soul."[11]

"What would be the use of poets," Goethe further noted, "if they only repeated the record of the historian? The poet must go further and give us, if possible, something higher and better."[12] And "Here is the grand point and our present poets should do like the ancients. They should not be always asking whether a subject has been used before, and look to south and north for unheard-of-adventures, which are often barbarous enough, and merely make an impression as incidents. But to make something of a simple subject by a masterly treatment requires intellect and great talent, and these we do not find."[13] He detested those poets who wrote only of the woes and miseries of this life and spoke only of the joys of an afterlife. "This is the real abuse of poetry, which was given to us to hide the little discords of life, and to make man contented with the world and his condition."[14] He cautioned readers of poetry and viewers of art not to dissect each phrase or each brush stroke, but to look upon the work as a whole, for therein lay its beauty.

Goethe's understanding of the ancients came through diligent study. Through them he sought for the truly enduring elements in life. Of the ancients he wrote: "People always talk of the study of the ancients; but what does that mean, except that it says, turn your attention to the real world, and try to express it, for that is what the ancients did when they were alive."[15]

Encouraging all to study the classics, Goethe said, "The antique is classic, not because it is old, but because it is strong, fresh, joyous, and healthy."[16] He added further to his definition of a classic when he said, "The point is for a work to be thoroughly good and then it is thoroughly sure to be classical."[17]

Goethe's own works fulfill his definition in every particular. It would be a shallow critic who limited Goethe in his expansive scope. Those of his contemporaries were often too close to see how great he truly was. Our distance by now should give us a view of him in his true proportions.

Johann Wolfgang Goethe was born in Frankfort, 28 August 1749. His father, Johann Kaspar von Goethe, a lawyer who inherited a family fortune, was a stern and self-righteous man, but thoroughly honest. Combined with these attributes was a sound knowledge and a deep appreciation for art and literature.

Conscious of his abilities and distrustful of the teachers of the day, Johann Kaspar undertook to instruct his two children, Johann Wolfgang and his sister, Cornelia, at home, using tutors only when absolutely necessary. Goethe recalls that because of his prodigious memory he learned easily without having to really apply himself. Grammar was distasteful to him, but he learned Italian easily just by listening to his sister's tutor. The book *Robinson Crusoe* led him to dream of adventure. By the age of ten his Latin was flawless.

In intelligence and dignity, Goethe's mother, Catherine Textor, was like her husband. However, in temperament she was merry, genial and whole hearted. She was one of those rare women who make the world a happier place just by their presence in it. Her good humor was contagious, and she saw only the sunny side of life.

Much of Goethe's personality came from his mother and much of his natural ability for deep insight from his maternal grandfather, who was the chief magistrate of Frankfurt. Goethe's intellectual foundation was firmly laid by his father who devoted his entire day to his children's education. Because their rigorous education often lasted from morning until evening, the children were only too glad to enjoy an evening visit with their mother, who was noted for her story-telling. Goethe would likewise entertain his friends with his own stories.

The elder Goethe, having spent some time in Italy, took great pains to have good art in the home. Goethe said that cleanliness and order prevailed throughout and his father maintained an excellent collection of books.

Goethe adored his grandparents. From his paternal grand-mother, who lived with them until her death, the children received a puppet theater. For many years Goethe and Cornelia wrote and produced puppet shows. From these simple beginnings came one of the world's greatest dramatists. The adoration Goethe felt for his maternal grandfather is evidenced in the following:

> The reverence we entertained for this venerable old man was raised to the highest degree by a conviction that he possessed the gift of prophecy, especially in matters that pertained to himself and his destiny. It is true he revealed himself to no one distinctly and minutely, except to my grandmother; yet we were all aware that he was informed of what was going to happen by significant dreams.[18]

Though Goethe was very circumspect about his own personal experiences, there is enough evidence in his multitude of writings to see that he was heir to his grandfather's gift of prophecy. He tells of his parting, he thought for the last time, from his girlfriend, Fredricka, who lived in the country: "I rode along," he recalled, "... and here one of the most singular forebodings took possession of me. I saw, not with the eyes of the body, but with those of the mind, my own figure coming toward me, on horseback, and on the same road, attired in a dress which I had never worn. "[19] Goethe shook himself free of the strange vision. Strangely, eight years later he found himself on the very same road, dressed as he had seen himself.

Goethe's father rigorously guarded his children's curriculum. However, Goethe and Cornelia were able to smuggle a copy of Klopstock's "Messiah." The elder Goethe had forbidden Klopstock's work in their home not because of the content, but because it was not in the traditional meter. The two children, memorized and acted out the entire poem in secret. One day while their father was being shaved, Cornelia secretly acted out part of the "Messiah." When she came to an especially dramatic part, she shouted out, causing her father to spill his wash basin, and he immediately confiscated the smuggled poem.

About the time of Goethe's seventh birthday, Europe was shaken by the outbreak of the Seven Year War. Goethe's maternal grandfather sided with Empress Theresa and the Austrians while his father was an enthusiastic follower of Frederick the Great. This difference of opinion led to serious family disagreements.

It was an especially bleak day for his father when the French, who were allies of the Austrians, occupied Frankfort. To his father's great horror, the head French officer, Thorane, chose the Goethe home for his headquarters. Thorane was a circumspect gentleman, highly cultured and educated. He and young Goethe soon became friends, and Goethe rapidly became fluent in French. Because of Thorane, Goethe had free admittance to all the French plays, an activity which opened many avenues in the young boy's mind. Thorane also brought in his own art and artist. Goethe was so taken by French culture that for a number of years his thinking showed a strong French influence. This influence persisted until he fell under the spell of Shakespeare, whom he felt revealed a higher and freer view of the world with intellectual enjoyments as true as they were poetical. He described "the influence this extraordinary mind" upon him.[20] "But we cannot talk about Shakespeare; everything is inadequate."[21]

By the time Goethe was twelve years old he had a good knowledge of seven languages—Latin, Italian, French, English, Greek, Hebrew, and of course, German. For one of his father's assignments he chose to form a dialogue of various correspondents from different parts of the world each letter was written in the correspondent's native tongue.

In his fifteenth year, he had his first romance. This became the first in a long line of girls and women who had a deep, almost mystical affect upon him. He held women in highest esteem, adoring their divine origin. Each one he fell in love with appeared as a character in one of his great plays. "My idea of women is not abstracted from the phenomena of actual life," he told Eckerman, "but has been born with me, or arisen with me, God knows how."[22] No poet was perhaps more susceptible to feminine influence than Goethe, and except for Shakespeare he did more for the position of women than had been done in the preceding four hundred years.

When Goethe turned sixteen, he bade his family farewell and set out for Leipsig, where he was to study law. Although the study of law was not to his liking, Goethe persisted. To complete his studies he wrote a dissertation, which filled two volumes. The elder Goethe was so pleased with his son's accomplishments that he tried to get the two volumes published, but not one publisher would publish it. Ironically, Goethe's father felt that he had failed, that all his efforts in educating this child had come to naught. But time and patience would prove that his efforts had contributed to the making of the greatest literary genius Germany had ever seen.

Goethe's first work of note was the historical play *Goetz von Berlichingen*. Because of this play the poetic value of the Middle Ages was rediscovered. As Goethe wrote more, he gave rise to the literary movement called *Sturm und Drang* (or "Storm and Stress"). This movement unlike the bloody French Revolution, was a revolution through literature. The School of Enlightenment had emphasized the rights of reason. *Sturm und Drang* clamored for the rights of the heart to be added to reason.

Goethe's works attracted the attention of the great Duke of Weimar, who sought out men such as Goethe, Herder, Wieland, Schiller, and others to be part of his little kingdom. Here the great minds and souls of German talent were allowed to flourish.

Goethe served the duke faithfully, watching over the theater at Weimar with particular care. In addition to his writings, he also worked to advance the University of Jena. Of education, he said: "They teach in academies far too many things, and far too much that is useless."[23] Basic to all education he felt was to have a soul that loves truth and receives it wherever it finds it.

Goethe was lived to the age of eighty-three, thus becoming the sage of all of Europe. He was preceded in death by his devoted wife Christiane and their only son. Goethe had no fear of death, though he felt deeply about those he lost. At the age of seventy-five while reflecting upon the possibility of dying he stated:

> One must, of course, think sometimes of death. But this thought never gives me the least uneasiness, for I am fully convinced that our spirit is a being of nature quite indestructible, and that its activity continues from eternity to eternity. It is like the sun, which seems to set only to our earthly eyes, but which, in reality, never sets, but shines on unceasingly.[24]

Schiller, Goethe's dear friend and fellow writer, wrote in tribute to the great master: "He stood beside me like my youth, making actual existence a dream to me, weaving the golden vapors of the dawn about the common realities of life. In the fire of his loving soul, even the plain, every-day objects of life became, to my astonishment, exalted."[25]

Although Goethe's sun upon this life has set, his work has radiated for nearly two centuries. In his last moments he was heard to utter these words: "More light!"[26]

NOTES

[1] Eckermann, Johann. *Conversation with Eckermann.* New York & London: M. Walter Dunne, 1901, p. 34.

[2] Ibid., p. 51

[3] Ibid., p. 374.

[4] Ibid., p. 293.

[5] Goethe J. W. *Truth and Fiction Relating to My Life.* Boston & New York: The C.C. Brainard Publishing Co., 1902, 1:235-36.

[6] Goethe, 2:240.

[7] Ibid,. 2:276.

[8] Eckerman, p. 253.

[9] Ibid,. p. 255.

[10] Eckerman, p. 65.

[11] Ibid., p. 176.

[12] Ibid., p. 177.

[13] Ibid. , p. 231.

[14] Ibid., p. 97.

[15] Ibid., p. 136.

[16] Ibid., p. 302.

[17] Ibid P 277.

[18] Goethe, 1:37.

[19] Goethe, 2:120.

[20] Goethe, 2:111.

[21] Eckerman p. 133.

[22] Ibid., p. 279.

[23] Ibid., p. 57.

[24] Ibid., p. 68.

[25] Boyesen Hjalmar H. *Goethe and Schiller: Their Lives and Works* . New York: Charles Scribner's & Sons, 1911, p. 118.

[26] Duykinck Evert. *Portrait Gallery of Eminent Men and Women.* New York: H.Johnson. 1873, p. 239.

Oliver Goldsmith 1763-1846

IRISH/ENGLISH POET, PLAYWRIGHT, NOVELIST

> *"Oh,... if you could but learn to commune with your own hearts and know what noble company you make them, you would little regard the elegance and splendour of the worthless."*

A PAUPER IN HIS TIME AND A BELOVED LEGEND IN OURS, HE WROTE a number of enduring literary works. Among his most noted works are the poem "The Deserted Village", the play *She Stoops to Conquer*, and the novel *The Vicar of Wakefield*. He portrays in the novel the strengths of home, a humorous view of life, and the highest and enduring principles of human relations. Also reflected in its pages are the virtues of benevolence and faith.

From his tragic life, Goldsmith wrote of the refining elements that come from tragedy. Outwardly he suffered; inwardly he was pressed to pure gold. Nothing could change the kindness and generosity of his heart. When Johann Herder recommended to Goethe *The Vicar of Wakefield*, Goethe pronounced it to be "the best which has ever been written."

[It] represents the reward of good will and perseverance in the right, strengthens an unconditional confidence in God, and attests the final triumph of good over evil.... Doctor Goldsmith, has without question, great insight into the moral world, into its strength and its infirmities; ... I was overpowered by the subject-matter.... The above work had left in me a great impression, for which I could not account; but properly speaking, I felt in harmony with that ironical tone of mind which elevates itself above every object, above fortune and misfortune, good and evil, death and life, and thus attains to the possession of a truly poetical world.[1]

Samuel Johnson said of Goldsmith: "He touched nothing that he did not adorn."[2]

Born in Ireland to a poor farmer, Goldsmith was the second son and one of eight children. He wrote of his father, who was local curate:

> His pleasure increased in proportion to the pleasure he gave; he loved all the world, and he fancied all the world loved him.... He undertook to instruct us himself, and took as much care to form our morals as to improve our understanding. We were told that universal benevolence was what first cemented society; we were taught to consider all the wants of mankind as our own; to regard the human face divine with affection and esteem.[3]

At three years of age Goldsmith was taught by a good woman, who taught the village children their letters and kept them out of harm's way. At seven he was sent to the village school. A loyal Irishman, the master of the school expounded Irish verse and folklore, which instilled in Goldsmith a passionate admiration of Irish music and his imagination filled with a store of superstitions and lore. As he grew older, he became a master storyteller, drawing on these early stories to entertain and captivate his audience.

During these school years, Goldsmith contracted smallpox. He survived the disease but was left with a more than usual severity of marks. His appearance was not helped by arms and legs which seemed too long for his small body. At the age of nine he entered a school for older boys, where he suffered greatly for his looks.

He was rather a dull student and remained so throughout his entire formal education, which included a degree from the university. Although his mother had observed flashes of genius in Goldsmith as a child his mediocre school performance seemed less than promising. It would be some time before he matured and gained experience enough to respond to his gifts.

Goldsmith's naive and trusting nature often put him in embarrassing situations. One day Goldsmith was returning to his father's home for a visit from school, which was about twenty miles away. The road was impassable to carriages, so Goldsmith procured a horse to make the trip and a friend loaned him a guinea for traveling expenses. He was now sixteen, he had a horse, and money in his pocket. He was, he thought, a man of the world. He was determined to play the part.

Instead of hurrying home for the night, he stopped in a nearby town. He detained the first person he saw and asked with as much dignity as he could muster where the best inn could be found. Unfortunately for Goldsmith, he had asked the town jokester. The man, amused at the youth's attempt of self-confidence, directed him to what was literally the "best house in the place," namely, the family mansion of a local wealthy landowner, Mr. Featherstone. Goldsmith went to the supposed inn, and in the words of Washington Irving "ordered his horse to be taken to the stable, walked into the parlor, seated himself by the fire, and demanded what he could have for supper." On ordinary occasions he was diffident and even awkward in his manners, but here he felt called upon to act the experienced traveler, an image which was not characteristic of his stature, for his air and carriage was by no means distinguished. The owner, a man of humor, indulged the youth's mistake, especially when he accidentally learned that this intruding guest was the son of an old acquaintance.

"Never was [a] schoolboy more elated. When supper was served, he most condescendingly insisted that the landlord, his wife and daughter should partake. His last flourish was on going to bed, when he gave especial orders to have a hot cake at breakfast."[4] One can only imagine his dismay the next morning when his true situation was revealed to him. Goldsmith dramatized this experience in his well known play *She Stoops to Conquer*.

As a young man Goldsmith attended Trinity College in Dublin, he worked as a sizar because he was too poor to pay his way. As a sizar he had to mop floors every morning, wash dishes, serve meals, and wear a short-sleeved black robe which separated him as a pauper from the other students. Perhaps to make up for his embarrassment, he became the "buffoon" of the class, and created much mischief.

His tutor was violent and unkind. As devoted to math as Goldsmith was to the classics, he abused him in the presence of the class as ignorant and stupid. He ridiculed Goldsmith as awkward, ugly, and at times he used personal violence.

Although Goldsmith was able to graduate with a B.A., he did not know what he wanted to do. A family council decided that with the help of a kind uncle, Thomas Contarine, who would make the appointment, Goldsmith should apply to the clergy. Doing so necessitated a waiting period of two years, during which Goldsmith helped his family and relatives on their farm. He wandered, fished, and frequented the local pubs, getting to know the personalities of those who lived in the area and storing them in his memory for later use in his writings. Finally the day came for Goldsmith's interview with the Bishop. However, Goldsmith, who had little sense of decorum for such situations, showed up in a pair of scarlet breeches. How much this influenced his being turned down for the ministry is not known, but it certainly must not have helped.

He next tried tutoring but that too came to a sad end. His father had died and his mother barely had enough to subsist on, so the relatives, mainly his brother and an uncle, collected enough money to help him secure passage to America. This endeavor, too, was ill-fated, for when the winds were favorable and the captain set sail, Goldsmith was left behind, sitting at the local inn.

He resolved to try his hand at law, and his patient and supportive uncle advanced him £50. Goldsmith returned to Dublin, but before he could enter school, he lost the money in a game of chance. Money and Goldsmith never stayed together long. If he did not lose it in a game, he would give it to some beggar or hungry child. He was always benevolent, often giving most of his own income to the poor.

His uncle now felt that he should try medicine. This dear uncle, who never lost faith in Goldsmith's unconnected genius, once again came to Goldsmith's aid, helping him go to Edinburgh to the university. He remained three years but left without obtaining a degree. Traveling to the continent, he supported himself with his flute. Playing it usually got him food and a bed for the night with the poor, but rarely with the rich. He observed the lack of freedom and the sure "badge of slavery of the people." This slavery he predicted was drawing to a rapid close. He prophetically wrote: "I cannot help fancying that the genius of Freedom has entered that kingdom in disguise."[5]

He returned to England with a Doctor's degree. There is some question as to how the degree was obtained for he had few medical skills. He was therefore unable to adequately practice medicine and sustained himself in the poorest manner with a variety of odd menial jobs. At times he sank into deep despair, but he had what he termed "a knack at hoping"[6] which would soon pull him up again.

He began doing hack work for a magazine just to eat. His writing eventually began to gain recognition. He was introduced to Samuel Johnson, who was then the first of the English writers, and Joshua Reynolds the first of the English painters and renewed his friendship with Edmund Burke who had been a classmate in Dublin. Goldsmith was one of the original members of the famous literary club. Through his works he rose to a place among the writers of the day that was second only to Johnson. As he had done in the past, Goldsmith shared his new found fortune with the poor. He was nearly evicted from his apartment for lack of payment because all his money had been given to the poor.

Goldsmith ranks with the best essayists England ever produced. His novels were unique and original. Particularly his novel *The Vicar of Wakefield* exemplifies Goldsmith's remark "reputation of books is raised not by their freedom from defect but the greatness of their beauties."[7]

Goldsmith's last and unfinished work was "Retaliation," a poem which was a literary portrait of his fellow club members. He took ill while working on a poem about Reynolds he had only partially finished. He did not recover and died on 4 April 1774. He had just turned forty-six. He was buried in a little churchyard near his home. No stone marked the spot. His funeral was private with mostly just family, attending. However, the way to the cemetery was lined with a number of poor and homeless people who had gathered to pay their last respects to the man who had been their benefactor.

The coffin was followed by Edmund Burke and Sir Joshua Reynolds. Burke, when he heard of Goldsmith's death, burst into a flood of tears. Reynolds was so moved upon receiving the news that he flung aside his brush and palette for the day.[8] Reynolds suggested that a monument honoring Goldsmith be placed in Westminster

Abbey. Johnson furnished the inscription. The great actor David Garrick wrote that Goldsmith: "wrote like an angel and talked like a poor Poll."[9] Johnson, in reflecting on his dear friend said: "Let not his frailties be remembered, he was a very great man."[10]

NOTES

[1] Goethe J. W. *Truth and Fiction Relating to My Life.* Boston, and New York: The C. T. Brainard Publishing Co., 1909, p. 37-38.

[2] Inglis, Rewey Belle; Cooper, Alice; Cecilia; Oppenheimer, Celia; Benet, William Rose. *Adventures in English Literature.* 4th ed. New York: Harcourt, Brace, 1949, p. 295.

[3] Irving, Washington. *Oliver Goldsmith.* New York: Maynard, Merrill, & Co., 1904 p. 25-26.

[4] Ibid., p. 34

[5] Ibid., p. 84.

[6] Ibid., p. 42.

[7] Hilles Frederick W. *The Works of Oliver Goldsmith.* Roslyn, New York: Black's Readers Service Company, 1955, p. xx.

[8] See Encyclopedia Britannica, 11th ed. 1910, 12:218.

[9] Fitzhugh, Harriet and Percy Fitzhugh. *Concise Biographical Dictionary.* New York: Groset & Dunlap, 1935, p. 256.

[10] Irving, p. 448.

Henry Grattan *1746-1820*

> *"I found Ireland on her knees... Ireland is now a nation!"*

BORN 3 JULY 1746 IN DUBLIN, THE FIRST CHILD AND ONLY SON born to James Grattan and Henrietta Marlay, Henry Grattan displayed as a child exceptional gifts of intellect and a strong character. An incident that demonstrates his strength of character occurred while Grattan was a boy. Like most of the children of Ireland, Grattan knew many of the Irish superstitions, and he felt the paralyzing fear that came with them. One night he decided to rid himself of this fear, so he went into a churchyard near his father's house, after the clock struck midnight where he remained until "every qualm of terror had subsided."[1] This he did for several nights.

His strength of character and intelligence made him a powerful force in a day when governments and men were ruled by bribes. Although Grattan is classified as one of the world's greatest orators, it was not an inborn gift. He struggled greatly as his voice was not distinctive, his figure was awkward, and his delivery seemed to repulse his audience. Grattan overcame all these shortcomings and was compared to the great Greek orator Demosthenes.

As a boy Henry attended a Mr. Ball's Academy. One day, Mr. Ball asked him to translate two lines into English from the Latin classic *Ovid*. He promptly gave an interpretation that his father had told him. As he finished Mr. Ball told him to go on his knees for making such a stupid blunder. That night sensitive young Henry reported to his father what had happened and he was soon sent to another school.[2]

From his early youth Henry loved practicing speeches. This habit sometimes got him into difficult situations. "On one occasion his landlady in England requested his friends to remove that mad young gentleman who was always talking to himself, or addressing an imaginary person called Mr. Speaker."[3]

Grattan and his father, who had been Dublin's recorder for many years, got along well until Henry began to have an opinion about politics. Grattan's father sat for a number of years in the Irish Parliament, an office that was often held by the good favor of a rich patron.

The other representative for their district was a Dr. Lucas, who had raised himself from near poverty and had gained his seat by truly representing the people. The election of these two men had been the first in thirty-three years as England had previously limited Ireland's elections to coincide with the crowning of a new king. (In contrast, the English Parliament held elections every seven years.) Thus it had been many years since there had been a change. Dr. Lucas believed as Jonathan Swift had written that "All government without the consent of the governed is the very definition of slavery."[4] Lucas worked for a number of years before he was able to obtain the votes necessary to change the frequency of the election. Lucas's bill was finally voted on by the Irish Parliament and approved by the English Privy Council.

Young Grattan greatly admired Dr. Lucas, much to his father's disgust, although, both father and son did agree that Ireland had a right to manage its own affairs, separate from England's domination. Their other political views were so different that their relationship became strained and eventually the father partially disinherited his son.

Grattan, upon finishing his early education, went on to distinguish himself at Trinity College in Dublin. There he began a lifelong study of classical literature and of the great orators of the past. After completing his education at Trinity, Grattan was accepted at Middle Temple in London to further his studies for the bar. In 1772 he was accepted to the bar, but he never seriously practiced law. While in England he received word that a sister to whom he was very close had died after a short illness. Grattan writes of this sister as one, "whom I loved extremely."[5] Her loss came as such a shock to him it made him terribly lonesome for home. A month later another sister married Gervase Bushe, a lawyer who was later to play an important role in the fight for independence with Grattan. Soon after these events Grattan retreated to the countryside for a time. There he sought solace and time to work out his thoughts and lay his future plans.

While England was engaged in war with the thirteen colonies, many troops were withdrawn from Ireland. In an effort to help maintain order in the country, local groups were organized into "volunteers." Grattan and others became noted officers in this militia. It was the recognition of this work that brought him into public service. In 1775, Lord Charlemont gave Grattan a seat in the Irish Parliament. (Seats in Parliament at that time were often bought or "owned" by large landowners.)

Grattan immediately joined with the national party whose main object was to set the Irish Parliament free from the Privy Council of England, thus giving Ireland jurisdiction over its own matters. The restrictive measures enforced by the Privy Council had been opposed by great men such as Molyneux, Swift, and Flood. But it was Grattan who was able to change this repressive legislation.

In 1780 Grattan gave his famous speech entitled "Liberty as an Inalienable Right." It has been said that no speech in Ireland was equal to it, nor probably was there a superior speech ever delivered in the English House of Commons. Other speeches may have matched it in argument and information, but in its fresh burst of energy and splendor of style it was a classic. In concluding his speech, Grattan pleaded with his fellow representatives of the people: "Do not tolerate that power which blasted you for a century, [England] that power which shattered your loom, banished your manufacturers,... stopped the growth of your people; do not, I say, be bribed ... and permit that power which has thus withered the land to remain in your country."

Hereafter, when these things shall be history, your age of thraldom and poverty, your sudden resurrection, commercial redress, and miraculous armament, shall the historian stop at liberty, and observe—that here the principal men among us fell into mimic trances of gratitude—they were awed by a weak ministry, and bribed by an empty treasury—and when liberty was within their grasp, and the temple opened her folding door, and the arms of the people clanged, and the zeal of the nation urged and encouraged them on, that they fell down, and were prostituted at the threshold?... I never will be satisfied so long as the meanest cottager in Ireland has a link of the British chain clanking to his rags; he may be naked, he shall not be in iron; and I do see the time is at hand the spirit is gone forth, the declaration is planted; and though great men shall apostatize, yet the cause will live; and though the public speaker should die, yet the immortal fire shall outlast the organ which conveyed it and the breath of liberty, like the word of the holy man will not die with the prophet, but survive him.[6]

So persuasive were Grattan's orations that he was able to bring about change that had not been possible before. Henry Grattan opened the door for Ireland, through which Daniel O'Connell later led the people.

Grattan had been a student of the American Revolution and knew the value of independence and a constitution. So on 16 April, 1782, amidst unprecedented popular support, Grattan lead the Irish Parliament to a declaration of Independence. In a rare move the English Privy Council voted its approval. However, their independence was not the complete and full independence that the colonies had gained. The Irish Parliament had always intended to remain loyal to the reigning monarch, and the declaration of Independence did not remove them from subjection to the King. Because of this entangling alliance, Grattan's attempts to put into action constitutional measures ran into problems. England felt that Ireland's constitution was weak and offered little security. England was also concerned over a possible rebellion as had recently occurred in France and the constitution of 1782 provided no safeguard against revolt.

England's worst fears were realized when the Protestants in the north and Catholics in the south formed an organization of "United Irishmen." The purpose of this organization was to promote revolutionary ideas such as were had in France. An invitation was extended to the revolutionaries in France to invade Ireland. However, weather prohibited the French landing. The disastrous "Rebellion of 1798" was sternly and cruelly repressed, and action was soon taken to do away with the Irish Parliament and constitution.

A plan was presented that would send elected officials straight to the English Parliament. Up to this time there had been a growing conciliation between the Protestants and the Catholics. But England began courting the Catholic support for union with promises of full Catholic emancipation. The Protestants of the north, who were called Orange men, were vehemently opposed to this action. (The position of the Protestants and the Catholics later reversed under Daniel O'Connell, when the Catholics then supported separation from England.)

Grattan's family was still in the north at this time and reports reached Grattan that the "Orange boys had got up" where his children were with their French tutor. The "Orange Boys" were against Grattan because even though he was a faithful Protestant, he always represented the Catholic bills for emancipation. It was not long before Grattan found that these reports of threat against his family were true and that a whole machinery of spies and informers was in operation about his home. His sons later recalled that there were rumors of attempts to find witnesses to testify against Grattan, but none could be found. Lord Dufferin, a relative of Mrs. Grattan suggested that since she had gone to England in the past for her health that it might be wise for her and the children to leave under this pretext in order to get Grattan away, for he was watched and in danger. But Grattan refused to budge. Their home was invaded by a regiment that called themselves the Ancient Britons, who were known for their brutality. Fortunately, Mrs. Grattan had received word that they were coming and departed for Wales where Grattan met them. These personal troubles were but a mere reflection of the country's turmoil that led to the devastating rebellion of 1798.

The disgust with which Grattan viewed the loss of Ireland's independence and the rebellion so affected his mental state that his body became diseased. Losing all his strength he was bedridden for some time. Grattan was not then a member of the Irish Parliament as he had fallen out of grace with the ruling classes because of his parliamentary reform proposals and his dogged support of Catholic emancipation. Dismissing him from the highest council, they removed his portrait from the Hall in Trinity College and the Merchant Guild of Dublin struck his name off their rolls.

When England threatened to bring the Irish Parliament into the English Parliament, the people of Ireland turned to Grattan for help. Grattan protested pointing to his feeble physical condition for he could not leave his bed. His wife reminded him that he was born to defend Ireland and ordered a sedan chair to carry him to Parliament. Wrapping himself in a blanket and placing two pistols under his belt (his life was still in grave danger), he kissed his wife and left his home not knowing whether he would return. On 15 January 1800 Grattan returned for the last part of the last session that the Irish Parliament would hold as a group under a constitution. It would be many years before they would meet so freely again.

He attended the session as a legal representative in a position his friends had obtained for him just a short time before the session began. When Grattan made his appearance "there was a moment's pause, an electric thrill passed through the House, and a long wild cheer burst from the galleries. Enfeebled by illness, Grattan's strength gave way when he rose to speak, he was given leave to address the House sitting."[7] He then gave a magnificent appeal that lasted over two hours. But despite all these efforts, he was unable to keep the vote from going in favor of union with the English Parliament.

Though Grattan strongly opposed the union with England, once it was done he informed his followers that since union was now law, he intended to follow it. Grattan remained active in public affairs and in 1805 was elected to the English Parliament from Ireland. He modestly took his seat on one of the back benches, until Fox brought him forward to a seat near his own, exclaiming, "This is no place for the Irish Demosthenes!"[8] Grattan's first speech was in defense of Catholic emancipation. It was "one of the most brilliant and eloquent ever pronounced within the walls of Parliament."[9]

Grattan's stand on the Catholic issue was a complicated one. Because he was a loyalist, supporting the law, he supported the king's right of veto over the selection of Catholic bishops. Because of this stand, Catholics sought a new defender. But Grattan never failed in continuing his defense in his speeches and in his votes for the Catholic right to emancipation.

Grattan died on 4 June 1820. He left behind a paper to be read in the House of Commons and in it he advised England to grant the Catholics their rights; even in death he was the defender of the rights of all men. No honor was denied him in his death. All the members of Parliament attended his services and he was buried in Westminster Abbey alongside Fox, the English statesman he most admired.

Sydney Smith wrote soon after the death of Grattan: "No government ever dismayed him. The world could not bribe him. He thought only of Ireland; lived for no other object; dedicated to her his beautiful fancy, his elegant wit, his manly courage, and all the splendour of his astonishing eloquence."[10]

NOTES

[1] Lecky, William Edward Hartpole. *The Leaders of Public Opinion of Ireland.* London: Otley & Co., 1981, p. 94.

[2] See Gwynn, Stephen. *Henry Grattan and His Times.* Westport, Conn.: Greenwood Press Publishers, n.d., p. 8.

[3] Lecky, p. 95.

[4] Gwynn, p. 9.

[5] Ibid., p. 17.

[6] Brewer, David J., ed. *The World's Best Orations.* New Jersey: Mini Print Corp. New Jersey 1970 p. 2329.

[7] Encyclopedia Britannica. 11th ed. 1911, 2: 380.

[8] Ibid., p. 380.

[9] Ibid.

[10] Ibid., p. 381.

Alexander von Humboldt

FATHER OF PHYSICAL GEOGRAPHY   *1769-1859*

"Science is the mind applied to nature."

ONE DAY JOHANN VON GOETHE WAS VISITING THE HUMBOLDT house for dinner. After an evening of observing and quizzing the young child, Alexander, Goethe concluded his visit by placing his hand on the boy's head. "My child," he said, "I believe you have a distinct talent for science." Then Goethe turned and urged Humboldt's father to guide Alexander into the field of natural history.[1] Humboldt not only became one of the great scientists of all time, but he also became, with the exception of Napoleon, the most famous man in Europe in his time. Humboldt is to physical science what Goethe is to literature, and interestingly enough both were Prussian.

Friedrich Heinrich Alexander Baron von Humboldt was born into Prussian nobility in Berlin on 14 September 1769. His father was Major George von Humboldt, who had served as an officer in the Seven Year War under Frederick the Great. Alexander's childhood was spent in the family castle of Tegel where he and his brother Wilhelm were privately tutored. Humboldt's childhood holds no record that he was promising in health or in intellect. In fact, his older brother Wilhelm seemed to draw all the attention. Wilhelm was very precocious and Alexander was of a more quiet nature.

Humboldt's mother's family were Huguenots, a group of people dedicated to what they believed. His father passed away when he was about ten years of age, and his education fell to his mother who was rather particular about his tutors. One of his early tutors was a young man named Joachim Campe, who wrote *Robinson der Jungere*, based on Daniel Defoe's *Robinson Crusoe*. Campe was particularly interested in the development of the mind and not just the rote memory that was the learning style of the day. Campe's instruction reinforced Humboldt's natural love for explorations. "From my earliest youth, I felt an ardent desire to travel into distant regions, seldom visited by Europeans."[2]

When Humboldt turned fourteen, the brothers moved to Berlin to further their education at the University. Their studies covered a wide range of subjects. Humboldt particularly enjoyed the study of botany. During this time Humboldt became acquainted with George Forster, who had accompanied the celebrated navigator Captain Cook around the world as one of the ship's naturalists. This acquaintance gave such dimension to Humboldt's life that it set him on a path which led to his leading one of the world's greatest scientific expeditions. Forster took Humboldt on an exciting tour of the Netherlands. They traveled through Paris where Humboldt, young and enthused with liberty, became deeply touched by the common people's desire for freedom.

Humboldt's mother directed his studies towards finance but he prepared himself to work in the mines as a minerologist. In 1792, at the age of 23, Humboldt entered the Prussian mining service and soon became a mining leader. Since the miners were having difficulty seeing in the candle light, Humboldt worked on a solution. Designing and conducting a number of dangerous experiments, he invented a safety lamp and a rescue apparatus for miners threatened with asphyxiation.

For Humboldt this was not only a time of work, but also a time of intense study and observation. He was a natural born empiricist; to measure and apply numbers with the facts, he felt, was the cornerstone of science. He believed in universal harmony and felt that nature gave him glimpses of that harmony. He wrote of how nature reveals her information:

> "The rolling rock leaves its scratches on the mountain; the river, its channels in the soil; the animal, its bones in the stratum; the fern and leaf, their modest epitaph in the coal. The fallen drop makes its sculpture in the mud or stone...."[3]

Humboldt expressed an almost desperate concern over science not moving forward fast enough. With regret he wrote "whilst the number of accurate instruments is daily increasing, we are still ignorant of the height of many mountains and elevated plains."[4] It was Humboldt, who, from the enormous amount of data gathered on his extensive travels, was able to determine the elevation of the continents.[5]

During his mother's life he remained devoted to her and honored her request to not travel. Her death, however, left him free to follow the bent of his genius. He soon departed for Paris where he met Aime Bonpland, who was to be his companion for the next six years. These two young scientists sought for passage with Napoleon's scientific voyage to Egypt. Circumstances derailed their travel and they ended up in Spain. The well-educated and gracious young Humboldt was immediately accepted into the courts of Spain.

The Spanish throne granted not only permission to Humboldt and Bonpland to travel to New Spain (America) but also granted letters of introduction to its numerous governors. In 1799, they landed in Venezuela, narrowly escaping a malignant fever that took a number of lives aboard ship. Together these knowledge-seekers made their way through pathless forest, searching caves and seeking the tops of mountain peaks. The following spring they canoed down the Amazon. passing through regions infested with jaguars, crocodiles, mosquitoes, and wild cannibal tribes.

They filled the canoes with botanical specimens. Humboldt filled volumes with notes of all his observations and mapped all the areas with a talent that far exceeded the tools and abilities of his day. From the Amazon they turned down the Rio Negro and into the channel of the Orinoco. On they sailed, taking a side trip through underground caverns while the roaring Orinoco flowed overhead. Nothing escaped Humboldt's notice. Based on his observations, a large collection of his maps of North and South America was published in 1827. The accuracy with which these maps were drawn astounds geographers today.

Humboldt and Bonpland traveled and studied for five years. On the eve of their return to Europe, they were invited to visit Washington, D.C., as guests of President Jefferson.[6] Humboldt met several times with Jefferson and his cabinet, sharing his travels and bringing them up to date on information of Mexico. His maps were of special interest as the United States was in the process of making the Louisiana Purchase from Napoleon III.

Humboldt was also the first who called for the construction of a connecting water way we now call the Panama Canal. For more that fifty years he urged this advancement.

While Columbus made the discovery of America, Humboldt made the scientific discovery of America. His expedition was one of the most fruitful scientific expeditions in history. The great South America liberator Simon Bolivar, who became closely acquainted with Humboldt, gave this tribute to the great scientist. "Humboldt has done more good for America than all her conquerors."[7] A natural diplomat, Humboldt was often called on to advise Bolivar and helped him to chart a moderate course.

After the expedition, Humboldt returned to Paris, the scientific center of Europe. Here he spent the next twenty years compiling his massive research. He had gathered some 60,000 plant specimens, 6,300 of which were hitherto unknown in Europe. His notes and observation extended into many scientific fields: magnetism, meteorology, climatology, geology, mineralogy, oceanography, zoology, etc. This large work he endearingly entitled *Cosmos*. Humboldt eventually exhausted his fortune in publishing these volumes.

Humboldt's research led him to significant geographical discoveries. In 1817 he was able to establish the existence of "Isothermal lines." Cartographers were surprised to see, on Humboldt's map, that London, though as far north as Labrador, had the same mean temperature as Cincinnati, which is as far south as Lisbon.[8] His investigations led him to the origin of tropical storms. He discovered that the earth's magnetic force decreases in intensity from the poles to the equator. This work was important for its influence on physical geography and for giving accuracy to the manner of representing natural phenomena. As a result, Humboldt is often called the "Father of Geography."

In cooperation with other noted scientists and under his gentle leadership, many scientific advancements took place in Paris. The great American naturalist Dr. Louis Agassiz spoke of Humboldt's work in these terms: "They have as completely changed the basis of physical science, as the revolution which took place in France about the same time has changed the social condition of that land."[9]

Humboldt can be considered one of the last scientists whose mind could incorporate all the scientific fields. The expansive nature of his works even moved his old friend and fellow countryman, Goethe, to say: "[Humboldt] is like a fountain with many pipes; you need only to get a vessel to hold under it, and on any side refreshing streams flow at a mere touch."[10]

In his sixtieth year, Humboldt made an expedition to the Riley Mountains at the request of the czar. In six months time the expedition covered a distance of 9614 miles. The central Asiatic Plateau was more accurately measured and based on Humboldt's own geological calculations, diamonds were found in the Riley Mountains.

Much of Humboldt's time in his later years was spent as Minister for the King of Prussia and in advancing the institution of higher learning in Prussia. Beside his many great scientific labors, Humboldt was an indefatigable humanitarian. He was particularly cognizant of struggling gifted youth, offering them encouragement, and recommendations to universities, kings, and even presidents. These young scholars regarded themselves as "his children." Among these young beneficiaries were Ferdinand Eisenstein, Hermann Karl Vogel, Justus von Liebig, Fritz Johann Muller, and Louis Agassiz.[11]

He was also personally responsible for anti-slavery legislation in Prussia and spoke often against anti-Semitism and racism wherever it was found.[12] It was the slavery issue that kept him from total respect for the United States. He said, "By asserting the unity of the human race we also oppose every distasteful assumption of higher and lower races of man. There are more adaptive, more highly educated and more spiritually enriched peoples, but there are none nobler than others. All are equally ordained to be free."[13]

To the end of his life Humboldt remained a student. "We used to see in the crowd of students," remarked a future author, "a small, white-haired, old and happy-looking man dressed in a long brown coat. This man was Alexander von Humboldt, the "father of modern science" who came to "go through again what he had neglected in his youth."[14]

As he approached his ninetieth year, Humboldt's health began to fade. One of his last visitors was the American poet Bayard Taylor. Humboldt asked him of his friend, Washington Irving. As Taylor rose to leave, Humboldt from his weakened condition, held out his hand for one last time to his departing visitor. It was the same hand that had clasped in friendship many of the leading personages of the century; Frederick the Great, Friedrich Schiller, Napoleon Bonaparte, William Pitt, Johann Goethe, Thomas Jefferson, Alexander Hamilton, Ludwig von Beethoven, and Sir Walter Scott.[15]

The friend of every cultivated man, Humboldt sought to lose no opportunity to do all the good of which he was capable. His influence on the progress of science is incalculable.

NOTES

[1] Thomas, Henry and Dana Lee Thomas, *Living Biographies of Great Scientists*. Nelson Doubleday, Inc., New York, 1941, p.99.

[2] Ibid., p. 469.

[3] Thomas, p. 100.

[4] Ibid., p. 100.

[5] Proceedings of the American Academy of Arts and Sciences. Eulogy of Alexander Von Humboldt by Professor Agassiz, 24 May 1859.

[6] Fischer, Emil-Haberlandt Gottlieb. *Dictionary of Scientific Biography*. Ed. Charles Coulston Gillispie. New York: Charles Scribner's Sons, 1959, 5:551.

[7] Ibid., p. 551.

[8] Durant, Will and Ariel Durant. *The Age of Napoleon*. New York: Simon and Schuster, 1975, 10:609.

[9] Proceedings, p. 31.

[10] Thomas, p. 107.

[11] Fischer, p. 553.

[12] Ibid., p. 553.

[13] Ibid., p. 553.

[14] Thomas, p. 110.

[15] Ibid., p. 111.

Washington Irving

1783-1859

> *"Many a man of passable information at the present day reads scarcely anything but reviews, and before long a man of erudition will be little better than a mere walking catalogue."*

BORN AT THE END OF THE REVOLUTIONARY WAR, WASHINGTON Irving has been referred to as the Washington of American literature. He was born in New York on 3 April 1783, the eighth son and the youngest of eleven children. During the war New York had been devastated by the British, and Irving's family had been driven to New Jersey because they were loyal to the colonies. His father and mother did what they could for the prisoners held in the holds of the British ships, often taking food off their own table to furnish the prisoners with clothes, blankets, and other necessities. This they did at the peril of their own lives. Though British themselves, these acts did not endear the Irvings to the British.

The new baby boy was not baptized until after George Washington had retaken the city. At his mother's request he was christened Washington Irving. "Washington's work is ended, and the child shall be named after him." she said.[1]

In New York, in 1789, George Washington received the oath of office as president of the United States. Young Irving, age six, witnessed Washington as he was driven through the street on his way to his inauguration. Cannons roared, bells pealed, and the crowd shouted acclaim and cheered their hero. Everyone sensed that this occasion marked the real birth of the new nation. New York remained the nation's capitol for a number of years.

Irving in his later years recalls:

I remember George Washington perfectly. There was some occasion when he appeared in a public procession; my nurse, a good old Scotch woman, was very anxious for me to see him, and held me up in her arms as he rode past. This, however, did not satisfy her; so the next day when walking with me in Broadway, she espied him in a shop, she seized my hand, and darting, exclaimed in her bland Scotch, "Please, your excellency, here's a bairn that's called after ye!" General Washington then turned his benevolent face full upon me, smiled, laid his hand upon my head, and gave me his blessing, which... I have reason to believe has attended me through life. I was but five years old, yet I can feel that hand upon my head even now.[2]

Historians acquainted with this occasion have written that it was fitting that the father of the country bless the life of the future father of the country's literature.

Because Irving was not as robust as his older brothers, not as much was expected of him. The older brothers and sister doted over their younger brother, who repaid them generously with his warm heart and quick sense of humor. The father, William Irving, was a very strict Presbyterian. The family attended three sermons on Sundays and the children studied catechism on Thursday afternoon. It is little wonder that the Irving children's favorite game was to play church, preaching, and taking the sacrament.

At an early age Irving began to wander through the nearby streets. He had a natural love of rambling and was willing to listen to any stories told along the way. He observed the custom in the different hamlets, enjoying visits with those who had a life-time of experience. He became familiar with the Hudson River and was the first to describe its beauty. He made friends with the Dutch, who introduced him to Sleepy Hollow and the majestic Highlands beyond. The Catskill Mountains had a most bewitching effect on his lively boyhood imagination. Irving describes himself as a saunterer and a dreamer. And rightly so, for Irving was not of the colonial or revolutionary period; he was of the new independent era when the government was assured and dreams could become a reality.

In 1787, Irving entered kindergarten but did not find books and study very pleasant. Learning seemed to come hard to him.

Irving, however, was a favorite of the headmaster, who often called him "General." It was here, in the Romaine school, that he discovered his taste for the theater. At the age of eleven he performed in his first play. When it came time for the little star to make his grand entry, he was chewing on sticky honey cake. There was no time to swallow it or get rid of it. He found himself on stage before an audience, unable to speak, his mouth gummed up with cake. There was nothing else to do but put his finger in his mouth, hook the offending piece, and take it out, much to the delight of the audience.

At thirteen he wrote his first play in which the neighborhood children performed. His thirst for the theater was insatiable. His father was much against the theater, believing that in some way pleasure was bad. So, often young Irving would go out his bedroom window after prayers and down the roof of the coal shed, and attend the last acts of the play at the nearby theater. He returned to his room as quietly as he had slipped out.

Even though study was difficult, Irving loved reading, particularly adventure books. Among these were *Robinson Crusoe* and *Robin Hood.* His father permitted no reading after the children were in bed. But these adventures held such a fascination for him that he used stubs of candles to read by. Even at school he was found under his desk reading, instead of doing his work.

He also loved to wander down to the wharfs and watch the ships come in. He decided that he would become a sailor and go to sea. There was, however, one small problem: his distaste for living on salt pork. Rather than give up his plan, he began to practice eating salt pork and sleeping on the floor. It soon became evident that such measures were of no help. He gave up the idea entirely.

Because Irving wanted to see places outside New York, his brothers and sisters convinced their father to let him go up the Hudson to visit his oldest sister Ann. This visit was the beginning of his almost continual wanderings. He began to study law out of necessity, but his heart was not in it. He studied in the law office of Judge Josiah Hoffman and became an intimate friend of the family.

Not long after this his brothers and sisters, who were concerned for his health, sent him to England. He attended the theaters throughout England and toured Europe for two years. In Paris he was invited to a gathering put on by Mme. de Stael, where he met the great Alexander von Humboldt. In Italy, he saw the fleet of Lord Horatio Nelson sweeping by the port on its way to the great naval battle of Trafalgar. In Spain, he almost took up art as a profession. Upon his return to the states he began to write using the name of "Jonathan Oldstyle." His brother William published his work in a periodical called the *Salmagundi*. These writings do not contain the polish of his later work but they were brighter and livelier than anything that had yet been published in America.

Irving fell deeply in love with the daughter of Judge Hoffman and they became engaged. Although he was still studying law his heart was not in it. He wrote:

> In the midst of this struggle and anxiety she was taken ill with a cold. Nothing was thought of it at first; but she grew rapidly worse... I cannot tell you what I suffered... I saw her fade rapidly away; beautiful, and more beautiful and more angelic to the last... For three days and nights I did not leave the house, and scarcely slept. I was by her when she died.[3]

In his sorrow he wrote his brother, Peter; "May her gentle spirit have found that heaven to which it ever seemed to appertain! She was too spotless for this contaminated world."[4] Irving never married.

In his grief, Irving immersed himself in the work he had already begun: *Knickerbocker's History of New York*. It was to become the forerunner of American literary humor. The poor Dutch were not accustomed to such gentle ribbing and Irving sent them a letter of explanation.

Not long after, because of his knowledge and acquaintances at the Capitol, his brother sent him to lobby on behalf of the merchants in New York. This occupation was great medicine for his sorrowful heart. While in Washington, Irving attended the balls given by Dolly Madison and became good friends with the first Lady.

When the dreadful news reached Irving that the British had captured the nation's capitol in the war of 1812, he was sailing on a steamboat. He had been against the war but when the announcement was made on the boat, he overheard a snide remark about what President "Jimmy Madison" would say now. Irving sprang to his feet and said: "Sir! do you seize on such a disaster only for a sneer? Let me tell you, sir, it is not a question now about 'Jimmy' Madison or 'Jimmy Armstrong' or any other 'Jimmy.' The pride and honor of the nation are wounded, the country is insulted and disgraced by the barbarous success, and every loyal citizen should feel ignominy."[5] The whole cabin broke in applause. Irving volunteered his services to the governor and became a colonel.

When the war was over, he set sail for Europe. He intended to help his brother's business in London. But the business failed, providentially causing Irving to return to writing for maintenance. His fame had already preceeded him to England, and he was invited to Abbotsford in Scotland to stay as a guest of Sir Walter Scott. Scott delighted in the writings of this young American. Concerning the occasion Scott relates; "He [Irving] is one of the best and pleasantest acquaintances, that I have made this many a day."[6]

Irving chose the pen name of "Geoffrey Crayon" and made notes of all he heard and saw as he traveled. Using his notes he wrote his immortal *Sketch Book*. This work thrust him into instant stardom. The reviews were enthusiastic on both sides of the the Atlantic. This publication not only established him as America's first man of letters but also gave him financial independence. It was in this book which held the account of Rip Van Winkle, "The Legend of Sleepy Hollow" and "The Mutability of Literature," among many delightful others. Tales of this kind were until then unknown in English literature. The tradition of Christmas feasting experienced a revival as a result of one of the stories in the book.

It was this *Sketch Book* that caused Americans traveling to England to seek out and visit Westminster Abbey and other English places of note. It also helped Americans who had been estranged from the land of their heritage to feel more warmth toward it. The English writer William Thackeray called him: "the first ambassador whom the New World of Letters sent to the old."[7] Praising him for his constant good will to the mother country, Lord Byron wrote: "Irving['s] ... writings are my delight." Mary Mitford wrote: "Few, very few, can show a long succession of volumes so pure, so graceful and so varied." The comments of noted people of Europe continued. The great Shakespearean actress, Mrs. Sarah Siddons told Irving that he made her weep, and her actor brother John Kemble shared her admiration for the young American author.[8]

In 1826, Irving received an appointment from the U.S. government to go to Spain. Martin Fernandez de Navarrete asked him to translate the documents he had gathered on Columbus. Irving's interest was so sparked by these documents that he decided to write a biography of Columbus. It was only fitting that the man who took the new world to the old world should write the biography of the man who opened the way to the new world. *The Life of Columbus* was followed by *Companions of Columbus* and *A Chronicle of the Conquest of Granada*. Then Irving wrote the Alhambra, which is refered to by the historian Prescott as "the Spanish Sketch Book." For all this work he was elected to the Spanish Royal Academy of History.

After a seventeen-year absence, Irving returned to America. He was given a hero's welcome. He dined with President Jackson and became an unofficial adviser on foreign affairs. He settled in at his home, Sunnyside, in the state of New York, and wrote the biography of Oliver Goldsmith.

In 1842, at the urging of then Secretary of State, Daniel Webster, President Tyler appointed Irving as minister to Spain. He was well-known and well-received in Madrid. Spain was in tremendous turmoil during this time but Irving skillfully maneuvered among all factions. His correspondence and dispatches to Webster revealed his work. He championed Spain's possession of Cuba against English and French threats. He also promoted American trade interests in Cuba. After four years he returned again to America. Spain regretted the loss of her great defender.

On his return, Irving fulfilled his life's dream of writing the biography of George Washington. He had taken notes on the man for twenty-five years. So much of his life went into this work that after he finished the first two volumes he was heard to remark that if he could only live to finish it, he would be willing to die the next moment. Irving greatly suffered as he continued his work on the next volumes. He finished the fifth volume on 15 March 1859, then collapsed. His strength failed him but he had finished his work, and finally on 28 November 1859, he died.

From the stories he learned as a young boy, we have the story of George Washington and the cherry tree and others. The conscience of a historian and the love of legend combined to create stories full of humor and vividness. He lifted American literature and sent it on the road to greatness.

NOTES

1 Matthew Brander. *An Introduction to the Study of American Literature.* New York: American Book Company, 1918 p. 41.

2 Wood, James Playsted. *Sunnyside, A Life of Washington Irving.* Pantheon Books, n.d., p. 11.

3 Irving Pierre E. *The Life and Letters of Washington Irving.* London: H. G Bohn, 1864, p. 128-29.

4 Ibid., p. 127.

5 Wright, Mabie Hamilton, and Hale Edward Everett. *Men and Women of Achievement: Self-Help.* Philadelphia: The After School Club, 1909, 9:161.

6 Congressional Record, Entered According To Act Of Congress, In The Year 1860, By William Cullen Bryant, In The Clerk' Office Of The District Court Of The United States, For The Southern District Of New York *On The Life, Character, And Genius Of Washington Irving* p. 21.

7 Mathew, p. 49.

8 See iid.

Thomas Jonathan "Stonewall" Jackson

AMERICAN CONFEDERATE GENERAL   *1824-1863*

"Duty is ours, consequences are God's."

A NUMBER OF YEARS AFTER THE CIVIL WAR, TWO MEN, A MR. ST. John and General Thomas Jordan, found themselves at the foot of the mountains in a wild and lonely place near the Shenandoah Valley. Lost and hungry they approached a crude shack, hoping to find an "invite" for supper.

At last they met a rough gnarly woodsman, who rough as he was, invited them to share his food. To the traveler's astonishment, this rough backwoodsman rapped on the table and bowed his head in prayer. And such a prayer! Said Mr. St. John:

> Never did I hear a petition that more evidently came from the heart. It was so simple, so reverent, so full of humility and penitence, as well as of thankfulness. We sat in silence, and as soon as we recovered ourselves I whispered to General Jordan, "Who can he be?" To which he answered, "I don't know, but he must be one of Stonewall Jackson's old soldiers." [When asked, he responded,] "Oh yes, I was out with old Stonewall."[1]

General Jackson trained his troops not only in methods of war but also in the art of prayer. Jackson wrote to his wife, "My prayer is that it may be an army of the living God, as well as of its country."[2] From the very beginning of the war he asked the Confederate government to provide good chaplains. Under his leadership, Jackson caused that his chaplain, Reverend Lacy, preach every Sabbath when the troops were in camp. All were welcomed to come and worship, though no order was given. Through the constant attendance of General Jackson and frequent appearances of General Lee, these religious gatherings drew vast crowds of soldiers. The soldiers became impressed by Jackson's devotion and his great desire to lead them not only to do their duty in battle but also to follow the great Captain of their salvation.

Thomas Jonathan Jackson's ancestors came to America from Scotland. Not finding the coastal towns to their liking, his great-grandparents settled in the wild country of the Appalachian Valley. His great-grandfather and all of his sons bore arms in the Revolutionary War. They maintained a warm feeling of clanship and developed a capacity for hard work.

Jackson was born in Clarksburg, Virginia on 21 January 1824. (Clarksburg is now in West Virginia). He was but three years old when his father died. Since Jackson's father had been an officer in the Freemasons, they built a one-room log cabin for the family to live in.

Here, in this one-room cabin, Jackson's mother taught a little school and took in sewing in an effort to support her family. In 1830, Mrs. Jackson remarried, this time to a Mr. Woodson. Mr. Woodson's income was inadequate to support the little family that included not only Jackson but his older brother, Warren, and younger sister, Laura. Jackson and his brother were sent to live with relatives. It was a heart-breaking separation. His mother placed him on a horse to leave for his uncle's home, then "bidding him goodbye, her yearning heart called him back once more and, clasping him to her bosom, she gave vent to her feelings in a flood of tears. That parting he never forgot; nor could he speak of it in after-years but with the utmost tenderness."[3]

The health of Jackson's mother was not robust; she lived but a year after her remarriage. In the last moments of her life she sent for her two fatherless boys and at her bedside she gave them her farewell blessing. Jackson said later that his mother lovingly bade them farewell.

Major General Fitzhugh Lee, C.S.A., stated: "Great soldiers have been molded into shape by the watchful care of noble mothers.... [Jackson's] future career was sustained by the dying prayers of his mother."[4] Jackson named his only surviving child, born during the war, Julia, in memory of his mother.

Thomas and his sister, Laura, lived with their grandmother Jackson, passing many happy days together. Laura followed him everywhere, and they spent many hours making maple sugar together. Laura recalled that no matter what he undertook, whether of work or play he "never gave up." His brother Warren was of a an unruly nature. After Grandmother Jackson died, Laura had to go live with other relatives. This parting was difficult for the young children. Jackson and Warren stayed with Uncle Cumins, a bachelor.

When Jackson was twelve years old and Warren fourteen, the older brother convinced the younger to leave his kindly Uncle Cumins and accompany him down the Mississippi River to seek their fortune. The trip was a terrible struggle and after near starvation they returned to their relatives in the most pitiful condition. They had contracted fever and chills from having lived on an island. This incident deeply affected both boys' health. Warren never did recover, and in his nineteenth year he died of consumption. Before his death, he called for his sister and brother to come to his bedside. "They found that this long illness, with the influence of his sainted mother, had changed the ungoverned boy to such gentleness and submission, that he no longer wished to live, but was able to depart in perfect peace."[5] Jackson's personal motto was: "You may be whatever you resolve to be."

With the help of friends and the influence of his uncle, young Jackson was able to procure the position of constable when he was but seventeen years old. In those days the office of constable was not an easy job, for collecting debts, as the job entailed, was a thankless task. The day after a debtor did not show at an arranged meeting the same man rode into town on a new horse. While the horse could be used to pay the debt, the law stated that a man's horse could not be taken from him while he was on it. Jackson waited until the man had dismounted, then approached him about his breach of payment and took the reins. The man immediately remounted. Holding onto the bridle, Jackson led the horse to a nearby stable and told the man to either "get off or be knocked off." The man dismounted. [6]

Jackson dreamed of attending West Point and pursuing a military career, a dream which was unexpectedly realized just before his nineteenth birthday. An opening for his district occurred at West Point. Learning of this opportunity, Jackson worked hard to obtain the nomination. The recommendation came from his state representative, who in turn requested the Secretary of War to make the nomination. Jackson's lack of adequate education was his greatest obstacle. To this he countered that his determination would make up for his missing education. It was the Secretary of War who finally stated: "Sir, you have a good name. Go to West Point, and the first man who insults you, knock him down and have it charged to my account."[7]

Jackson's reputation as a "peculiar" country boy was immediately established when he stepped on to West Point's parade grounds in his home spun Virginia wools. Making him seem even more peculiar was his poor health. Due to a disorder of the stomach, he sat "bolt straight" in his chair through each class. So branded, he was often taunted by his classmates.

Being ridiculed was just the beginning of Jackson's troubles at West Point. His meager education, as had been predicted, was a great disadvantage. Afraid he might not make it through his first year, he spent many late nights studying, and that first year he finished fifty-first in a class of over eighty. The next year he climbed to thirtieth, his junior year he finished twentieth, and his senior year he graduated seventeenth. Some of his friends speculated that had there been one more year he would have graduated first in his class.

After graduating, he entered the Mexican War as a second lieutenant in the First Artillery. His bravery in this war won him recognition and advancement. At Vera Cruz he won the rank of first lieutenant, and for gallant conduct at Contreras and Chapultepec he was brevetted captain and major, a rank he attained after less than a year's service. While in Mexico, Jackson was promoted more frequently than any officer of the United States Army.

It was in Mexico that Jackson began to search for a spiritual basis to his life. Under the guidance of Colonel Frank Taylor, he was exposed to theological discussions and fervent prayers. He studied thoroughly the Catholic Church, and gained many spiritual insights from the clergy with whom he studied.

Returning home to Virginia, he left the army to be a professor at the Military Academy. Once he was settled there, Jackson renewed his investigation into religion. He visited all the local sects and became a great student of the Bible. Convinced of the need of baptism, he eventually joined the Presbyterian church, although he did not accept all of Presbyterian theology. In particular, the doctrines of predestination and infant baptism seemed unacceptable to him. He felt that he never found the completely true church.[8]

In 1853, he met and married Elinor Junkin, the daughter of Reverend Dr. George Junkin. Those who knew her referred to her as a "beautiful type of Christian womanhood." This marriage brought him great happiness. But his joy was not to last. Within fourteen months Elinor died in giving birth to a child also born dead. But his resignation to God's will was unshaken. In a letter to his aunt he wrote of his wife: "God's promises change not. She was a child of God, and as such she is enjoying Him forever."[9]

In an attempt to alleviate his grief he left on an extended tour of Europe. On this tour he studied the strategies of Napoleon and stand where the actual battles took place. "Napoleon," he said, "was the first to show what an army could be made to accomplish."[10] Here he may have come to understand the great power of being a military strategist as compared to a mere military tactician, an understanding that later affected his great successes in battle.

On the return trip his thoughts turned to a minister's daughter, Mary Anna Morrison, whom he had once met. Not long after he returned to the states, he traveled to see her, and soon they were married. This union soon produced an additional tragedy for Jackson; their first baby, a daughter, lived only a few weeks.

In 1861, the Civil War began, and Jackson entered the Confederate Army as a commissioned officer. Napoleon once said: "In war men are nothing; it is the man who is everything. The general is the head, the whole of an army."[11] A look at history shows the truth of this statement: history focuses not upon the great armies, but upon the great leaders—Ceasar, Hannibal, Alexander the Great, Frederick the Great, George Washington. Jackson became such a leader. It was at the first battle of Manassas that Jackson earned the title of "Stonewall." The tide of the battle had turned against the

South and General Barnard F. Bee rode to consult with General Jackson. Jackson reaffirmed to the general his intent to not give way. Inspired by Jackson, General Bee rode back to his troops and shouted, "Look yonder! There is Jackson and his brigade standing like a stone wall. Let us determine to die here and we will rally behind them."[12] Jackson's strategy was to march many miles, strike rapidly with great energy, and surprise the enemy at its flanks. A fierce, sudden attack, he felt shortened the conflict thereby saving additional lives.

One of his biographers writes of his military action:

> In thirty-two days he had marched nearly four hundred miles, skirmishing almost daily; fought five battles; defeated three armies, two of which were completely routed; captured about twenty pieces of artillery, some four thousand prisoners, an immense quantity of stores, and had done all this with a loss of less than one thousand men killed, wounded and missing.[13]

It was the element of secrecy that made Jackson's surprise attacks so effective. Often the only information his staff received was to "march at dawn." These scant orders avoided any possibility of "leaks" to the enemy. These early morning marches often appeared to be a retreat, but were really marches of many miles to arrive undetected in the rear flanks of the enemy.

Jackson's only defeat came from following orders from his superiors. So effective was Jackson, that at the time of his death he was the most trusted leader in the Confederacy, and the most dreaded by the Union. After each victory he would write in his report, "God blessed our arms with victory."[14] Jackson's men often joked that when the tent flap went down, the general was wrestling with the Lord or that he was always praying when he was not fighting. He inspired his soldiers to feats of bravery, while sitting on his horse as they marched by with heads bowed in prayer and one hand raised to heaven. So noble and pure was this saintly soldier, that it seemed no request of the divine would be denied him.

Jackson's troops, the "Stonewall Brigade," were the first to build a log chapel formally dedicated to the service of God. Other brigades soon followed their example. Protected against the rigors of winter by the cabins, soldiers frequently met during the week for spiritual rejuvenation. It was in this setting that Jackson's men were often led by him in humble and earnest prayer. It was by his example that many of his troops learned, for the first time, how to approach their Maker. There have been great men who have had the spirit of prayer, but few have had Jackson's gift of prayer. The gift of praying in public, however, had not always been his. When asked by a minister in the early years of his married life, to pray publicly, he failed miserably, embarrassing not only himself but the congregation. He was not asked to pray again.

After a few weeks Jackson had approached his minister, who admitted a reluctance to place his good member in further torment. Jackson commented, "Yes, but my comfort or discomfort is not the question: if it is my duty to lead in prayer, then I must preserve in it until I learn to do it aright; and I wish you to discard all consideration for my feelings."[15] Such perseverance was rewarded. Those who heard him pray in later years felt that when he opened his mouth he took them with him into the presence of the Lord. General J. B. Gordon described the effect his devotion had upon his men: "[These were] men grown old in sin, and who never blanched in the presence of the foe, are made to tremble under a sense of guilt, here in the forest and fields, are being converted to God."[16]

As the Civil War loomed overhead Jackson asked: "Should Christians be disturbed? It [the Civil War] can come only by God's permission, and will only be permitted if for His people's good; for does He not say, 'All things work together for the good of them that love God?'"[17] Although war seemed inevitable, he felt it might be averted and proposed: "Do you not think that all the Christian people of the land could be induced to unite in a concert of prayer to avert so great an evil?"[18] Apparently, there was no "uniting" in prayer.

Nevertheless, the war did "unite" people together as the wealthy Southerners and well-born privates shouldered their muskets together with those not born to the Southern "aristocracy"; they ate together, fought together, and died together. By the winter of 1863, two years into the war, class distinction among the armies of the South had all but vanished.[19] The magnanimous example of

Christian generals like "Stonewall" Jackson, Robert E. Lee, "Jed" Stuart, and others did much in replacing a class aristocracy with brotherhood. God raised these great men up not to divide the union but to reconcile the South.

Jackson supported a "states united" philosophy, rather the concept of a "united states." He was devoted to his native state of Virginia. When Virginia seceded, Jackson went with his state. However, his choice of going with the South should not be misinterpreted to read that he condoned the degradation of any race, especially the blacks. In the autumn of 1855, and in total disregard for the "opinions of the world," Jackson opened a Sunday School for the black people of the area. This black Sunday School grew rapidly and was well attended. Jackson used his money to support the school, and he and his wife were the main teachers. The school eventually grew large enough to involve twelve more teachers. The Sunday School remained successful until 1861, when the war broke out. In writing to a friend, Jackson said: "My Heavenly Father has condescended to use me as an instrument in getting up a large Sabbath-school for Negroes here."[20] He felt their souls were as important in the sight of God as were any man's.

Long after the war had ended, those who had been part of Jackson's Sunday School held him in highest esteem. The Negro Baptist Church of Lexington gave the first contributions for a large bronze statute of Jackson. This monument stands over his grave today.[21]

Jackson loved the Sabbath because it was the Lord's day. For years he had lobbied the government to not deliver the mail on Sunday. Jackson felt that since the Creator had set apart this day for his day, and commanded it be kept holy, it was wrong for individuals or governments to desecrate it.

It was on a Sabbath that Jackson's Creator called him home. On 2 May 1863, while engaged in reconnoitering at the battle of Chancellorville, Jackson's own men mistook him for the enemy and critically shot him several times. Fearing that the knowledge of his fall would create severe reversals for his men, the leaders concealed his identity as he was carried back through his own lines. He lingered two weeks and then died. The South was lost without him.

General Lee had lost his "right arm." This tragic turn of events might be summed up in words offered by a priest, one of Jackson's chaplains, at the unveiling of the Jackson monument in New Orleans. With these simple words he prayed: "When in thine inscrutable decree it was ordained that the Confederacy should fail, it became necessary for thee to remove thy servant Stonewall Jackson."[22]

Before the battle at Chancellorville, Jackson expressed to a friend that "he knew and was assured of the love of Christ to his soul." He said further, "Nothing earthly can mar my happiness. I know that heaven is in store for me."[23] Perhaps it had been a premonition of things to come. The South had lost its great warrior and with him went their strength to continue. The love of his staff and men is reflected in the intense feeling of a young staff officer who said, "God knows I would have died for him!"[24] Jackson's wife and baby daughter, whom he had seen only once, stayed with him during his last days. She reported that General Lee stopped by to relate that the whole army was praying for his recovery and exclaimed with deep feeling: "Surely ... God will not take him from us, now." He continued, "When a suitable occasion offers give him my love and tell him that I wrestled in prayer for him last night as I never prayed, I believe, for myself." Here his voice became choked with emotion, and he turned away to hide his intense feeling.[25]

When death was imminent, Mrs. Jackson received permission from the doctors to inform her husband. He had often said that although he was willing and ready to die at any moment, he preferred to have some notice in order to prepare to enter into the presence of his Maker and Redeemer. When his wife asked him if he was willing for God to do with him according to His own will, he calmly replied: "Yes, I prefer it, I prefer it."[26] From that moment he sank rapidly into unconsciousness. All at once he spoke out, to some unseen person, very cheerfully and distinctly, his last mortal words: "Let us cross over the river, and rest under the shade of the trees."[27] An officer who served with Jackson stated simply:

> No general made fewer mistakes. No general so persistently outwitted his opponents. No general better understood the use of ground or value of time. No general was more highly

endowed with courage, both physical and moral, and none ever secured to a greater degree the trust and affection of his troops. And yet, so upright was his life, so profound his faith, so exquisite his tenderness, that Jackson's many victories are almost his least claim to be ranked amongst the world's true heroes.[28]

It has been said that while Jackson was eminent for many things, he was preeminent for his trust in God. He lived to fulfill all that God had given him to do. He has left us a life of faith that strengthens our own.

NOTES

[1] Henderson, G. F. R. *Stonewall Jackson and the American Civil War.* New York: A Da Capo Press, 1943, p. 714.

[2] Richards, Warren J. *God Blessed our Arms with Victory: The Religious Stonewall Jackson.* New York: Vantage Press, 1986, p. 76.

[3] Jackson, Mary Anna. *Memoirs of Stonewall Jackson.* n.p.: Morningside Bookshop. Original 1895). Reprint, 1976, p. 16.

[4] Ibid., p. 604.

[5] Ibid., p. 24.

[6] Jackson, p. 28-29.

[7] Henderson, p. 9.

[8] See Richards, p. 36.

[9] Ibid., p. 84.

[10] Ibid., p. 591.

[11] Henderson, p. 598.

[12] Richards., p. 57.

[13] Jackson, p. 470.

[14] Richards, Title page.

[15] Ibid., p. 61-62.

[16] Ibid., p. 387.

[17] Jackson, p. 142.

[18] Ibid., p. 141.

[19] See Henderson, p. 605.

[20] Jackson., p. 60.

[21] See ibid., p. 478.

[22] Henderson, p. 603.

[23] Jackson, p. 394.

[24] Ibid., p. 305.

[25] Jackson, p. 454.

26 Ibid., p. 455.
27 Ibid., p. 457.
28 Ibid., p. 600.

Samuel Johnson 1709-1784

ENGLISH MORALIST, WRITER, LEXICOGRAPHER

> *"The natural flights of the human mind are not from pleasure to pleasure, but from hope to hope."*

THOMAS MACAULAY WROTE IN THE 1800S THAT JOHNSON WAS "more intimately known to posterity than other men are known to their contemporaries."[1] He produced the first English dictionary, using writers from the Elizabethan era as a measuring rod. His hope was to stabilize the English language, giving it order and consistency. His work was not limited to defining and describing words. He was also widely known and influential as a moralist.

Louis Kronenbrerger described Johnson as "a scarred and sick and deeply melancholy man... He had a larger nature, a truer benignity, a profounder humanness than any other English writer of his age."[2] As a child he contracted scrofulous, a tuberculosis of the lymph system, which left him scarred. His body was large boned and ungainly. Because of his childhood disease, he had a number of nervous ticks and starts. And since the disease had left him near blind, he squinted. Throughout his life, he was in poor health, though strong and muscular. All of these elements combined often left him at the mercy of others' startled reactions or silent stares. Notwithstanding these great handicaps, Johnson became the intellectual star of the century. Dr. William Adams told Johnson's biographer, James Boswell, that once people were able to get past his grotesqueness that he "was caressed and loved by all about him, was a gay and frolicksome fellow."[3]

Samuel Johnson was born in Lichfield, England, on 18 September 1709. Lichfield produced a number of eminent individuals around this time—David Garrick and Maria Edgeworth among them. A couple who married later in life, his father, Michael Johnson, was twelve years older than his mother, who was 37 when Samuel was born.

Samuel was born almost dead, after a long and arduous labor. When he finally began to breath, the male midwife said, "Here is a brave boy."[4]

According to custom the new baby be placed for ten weeks with a wet nurse. Sarah Ford could not stand this separation, so, everyday she walked down the street to visit him. Conscious that she was breaking the prevailing mores and that the neighbors would laugh at her if they saw her, Sarah tried to vary her walks or purposely leave something at the nurses that she would have to retrieve the next day.

Once home, Samuel contracted scrofulous, leaving his body diseased and distorted. In spite of this shaky beginning, Johnson showed early the strength of his intellect. He remembers with fondness sleeping in his mother's bed and listening to her teach him of heaven and of hell. She was a very religion person and she was very tender and attentive. Despite her limited knowledge, she was bright and intelligent.

She began teaching him his letters when he was three. While he was still a child in "petticoats" (about three), Sarah put the common prayer-book into his hands, pointed to the prayer for the day, and said, "Sam, you must get this by heart." She started up stairs, but in minutes he was following her. "What's the matter?" she asked. "I can say it," he replied. He had not had time to read the prayer more than twice, but recited the entire prayer from memory.[5] When he was an adult, a friend recited a lengthy poem to him. Johnson, hearing the poem once, repeated it entirely from memory. "Had he not been eminent for more solid and brilliant qualities, mankind would have united to extol his extraordinary memory."[6]

Dr. Samuel Swinfen, one of Johnson's godfathers, stated that he "never knew any child reared with so much difficulty."[7] But Sarah rose to the occasion. Johnson began school at the age of four with widow Dame Oliver who had a school just down the street. Johnson loved learning and attending school. In grammar school he made several good friends, but was seldom invited to their homes because, according to an old history of Lichfield, it was thought that he had "the appearance of idiocy, and the sons of the gentleman in the town were reprimanded for bringing home that disagreeable driveller." But at least one Lichfield parent saw through the scars and overhearing some children speaking contemptuously of the large, rawboned youth as "the great boy," she said, "You call him the great boy, but take my word for it, he will one day prove a great man."[8] Johnson's rising above the taunts of childhood bespeaks of an inner depth that few men have been able to find.

Johnson remained in Lichfield until his nineteenth year when he entered Oxford. A lack of funds prevented him from remaining the last year to obtain his degree. He returned to Lichfield and married the widow Mrs. Elizabeth Porter, who was nearly twice his age. But their marriage proved a happy one, as Elizabeth was a great support to Johnson.

Johnson felt he needed a new environment, so he and his good friend and student David Garrick left for London to seek their fortunes. He and Garrick carried a letter of introduction by Mr. Gilbert Walmesly, a neighbor and a man of culture and sophistication who had often invited the two prodigies to his home to visit.

Mrs. Johnson, or Tetty, as Johnson called her, remained behind until he could send for her. London was not without its struggles and he often had to walk the streets at night for want of a place to sleep. At times his imposing figure kept him from harm.

It took him about a year to find employment that provided a steady income, writing for the *Gentleman's Magazine.* He sent for Tetty and they began their time in London. Johnson loved London and felt that when a man was tired of London, he was tired of life.

Johnson's first recognition came with his *Life of Richard Savage.* As Johnson and his writings became known, there gathered around him a group of intellectuals. He loved to gather in the local inn or pub just for the pleasure of conversation. Intolerant of idle chatter, he loved true intellectual banter. The club provided a place for enlightenment and ideas among the still almost barbaric conditions of the day. Education and freedom were greatly lacking. Sewers ran in an open ditch in the middle of the road. A man could be hung for over a hundred crimes, even the simple act of chopping down a tree. In their literary club, these men found great solace in mingling with minds that were reaching beyond the present situation.

The famous club included Samuel Johnson; David Garrick; Edmund Burke, the great statesman; Oliver Goldsmith, author; Sir Joshua Reynolds, artist and founder of the Royal Academy of Art; Bennet Langton, professor of ancient literature; Tophan Beauclerk, a descendent of Charles II; Thomas Percy, a clergyman; Sir William Jones, a lawyer and student of oriental literature; Sir Edward Gibbon, the great historian; Adam Smith, author of *The Wealth of Nations;* Richard Sheridan, actor and parliamentarian; and Edmund Malone, a noted Shakespearean scholar.

The impact that this club and this group of men had on the western world cannot be measured. What we think, what we study, our very freedoms and forms of government reflect their influence. The framers of the U.S. Constitution studied Gibbon's *Decline and Fall of the Roman Empire* and Adam Smith's *Wealth of Nations,* men both influenced by Johnson. "Johnson knew more books than any man alive" said Adam Smith.[9]

Johnson also compiled, corrected, and annotated the plays of Shakespeare. His literary work in Shakespeare and David Garrick's Shakespearean acting began a new wave of attention to Shakespeare that has not ceased.

An extremely religious, man Johnson was adamant in condemning sin, yet remaining compassionate toward the sinner. Once he picked up a sick and dying prostitute, carried her home, nursed her back to health, and "endeavored to put her in a virtuous way of living."[10] Johnson kept his own *Prayers and Meditations* filling two volumes. On 3 April 1753, he wrote: "O God, who hast hitherto supported me, enable me to proceed in this labor, and in the whole task of my present state; that when I shall render up, at the last day, an account of the talent committed to me, I may receive pardon, for the sake of Jesus Christ. Amen."[11]

On his last visit to Lichfield, Johnson disappeared for a whole day. His friends asked where he had been and he related how fifty years before, his father had asked him to go into the market and attend his book stall. Johnson had refused his father. Now fifty years later he had gone to the market, and with his hat in his hand, stood the day long in an attempt to atone for his sin.

Johnson lived during the time literature reached its turning point. It had ceased to flourish under the patronage of the social elect, and had yet to flourish under the patronage of the public. Johnson and his club were a catalyst for that change. They aroused the public and helped them begin their role of support.

While Johnson enjoyed intellectual banter, which he used to start a debate or conversation, he was very serious about moral views. Upon his death bed, he requested that his physician be honest with him. When the physician told him he was near death, he said, "I will take no more physic, nor even my opiates; for I have prayed that I may render up my soul to God unclouded."[12] It has been said that this unclouded soul was not different from other that of others; it was greater.

NOTES

1 Greenough Chester, ed. *Macaulay's Life of Johnson.* New York: Henry Holt , 1912, p. xxxiv.

2 Kunitz, Stanley J. and Howard Haycraft. *Biographical Dictionary.* New York: Wilson Co., 1952, p. 295.

3 Krutch, Joseph Wood. *Samuel Johnson.* New York: Henry Holt, 1944, p. 18.

4 Krutch, Joseph Wood. *Samuel Johnson.* New York: Henry Holt, 1944, p. 6.

5 Boswell, James. *Life of Dr. Johnson.* New York: Doubleday, 1946, p. 5.

6 Krutch p. 457.

7 Ibid p. 6.

8 Bate, Jackson *Samuel Johnson.* New York: Harcourt, Brace, Jovanovich, n.d., p. 23.

9 Ibid., p. 23.

10 Durant Will, and Ariel Durant. *The Story of Civilization.* New York: Simon & Schuster, 1967, p. 10:830.

11 Krutch, p. 89.

12 Krutch, p. 553.

Pablo Benito Juarez

MEXICAN PRESIDENT, STATESMAN   *1806-1872*

"... as men we are nothing, principles are everything."

IN 1806 AND 1809 TWO BOYS WERE BORN ON THE BORDERS OF the wilderness in extreme poverty, one in America and one in Mexico. Both were deprived at an early age of the tender love of a mother. They also shared an unquenchable thirst for knowledge. Although their youth was greatly disadvantaged, they gave much personal time and effort to learning. They loved their respective countries and became disciples of freedom. The only major difference between them was that one was tall and lanky, the other short and dark. They each experienced many defeats and setbacks throughout their lives, yet each was elected to the presidency of their countries. They presided and preserved their respective country through devastating civil wars, putting their lives in continual danger. Because of their devotion to principles, history was changed not only in their own countries, but throughout the entire world as well. These two boys were Abraham Lincoln and Benito Juarez.

Juarez and Lincoln had great admiration and respect for one another. Juarez was born by the providence of God to establish religious freedom and the sovereignty of Mexico, freeing it from any European nation. His life began on 21 March 1806, near the village of Ixtlan, high in the mountains above the city Oaxaca. He was a full blooded Zapotec Indian. "I had the misfortune," he wrote, "not to have known my parents, Marcelino Juarez and Brigido Garcia, Indians of the primitive race of the country, for I was hardly three years old when they died, leaving me and my sisters, Maria Josefa and Rosa, to the care of our paternal grandparents, Pedro Juarez and Justa Lopez, Indians also of the Zapotec nation."[1] A few years later his grandparents died, his sisters married, and he was left under the care of an uncle.

In this remote mountain village he did not become familiar with or speak Spanish until about the age of twelve.

> In some idle moments my uncle taught me to read and impressed on me how useful and helpful it was to learn the Spanish tongue.... These promptings ... awoke in me a vehement desire to learn, so much so indeed that when my uncle called me to take my lesson, I myself brought him the whip to punish me if I did not know it.[2]

Life in this mountain village was so strenuous that there was very little time for studies, and there was no school. Anxiously, Juarez awaited the time he could go to Oaxaca and advance his education. When the time came he sadly departed from his uncle, and left to satisfy his desire for more education.

Arriving in Oaxaca, he found shelter as a "house boy" in the home of Don Antonio Salanueva, a lay member of the Third Order of Saint Francis. Salanueva often read the scriptures to young Juarez, and he was opened minded enough to support Juarez's education by paying his tuition for higher education.

In his attempts to gain an education Juarez experienced severe discrimination. Although it had been three hundred years since the conquest of Mexico by Spain, the treatment of the Indians remained cruel. In school, he and the other "poor" boys, mostly of Indian descent, were not allowed to sit inside the classroom. They had to sit in an outer room where an assistant treated them harshly. Juarez soon realized that he could learn more on his own and save his patron's tuition. He left the school and developed a plan to further his education. He worked late into the night reviewing old lessons by the light of a stump of resin which a woman in the next courtyard loaned him. Although he mastered his studies, he longed for more knowledge.

Because he was a poor Indian youth, the only educational opportunity opened to him was the seminary, which he was much disinclined to enter; however, because any education was better than no education, in 1821, he reluctantly entered the seminary.

His education there, as he had suspected it would be, was

narrow and limited. But Juarez did not give up. He had a sense of the future and believed miracles had happened before and would again, so he remained in the seminary until Providence could intervene. Such patience was characteristic with him.

Providence did respond. In 1810, Mexico had begun its weaning process from Spain. Gradually, new educational opportunities began to open up outside the control of the clergy. In 1827, a Civil College, based on a liberal education, was opened in Oaxaca. Juarez was not long in leaving the seminary to take advantage of this new and open education. Here, too, Juarez found persecution, particularly from the clergy who referred to the college students and professors as "heretic." So great was the pressure on the students and their families that many left the college. Others remained under the threat of excommunication. Perhaps, it was now a blessing that he had no family who would have to suffer with him in his struggle for progress. In 1831, he entered a law practice and, in 1833, was elected to the state legislature.

During this time, Mexico produced a number of great men who made significant contributions, many among Juarez's circle of friends. Among these men were Father Hildalgo and Jose-Maria Morelos, whose efforts led in 1824 to the first constitution, originally patterned after the constitution of the United States. Unfortunately the church and the military, wielding heavy political power deleted many good principles and rights. Having to compromise, as our founders did on the slavery issue, these men voted religious freedom out of this constitution.

The authoritarian traditions of the church and the army made them answerable to no laws or courts but their own. In these conditions democracy was impossible. The control these two entities held during the next half century resulted in anarchy, revolution, and civil war.

As a young college student, Juarez was well aware of his country's struggle for freedom as well as the Indians' struggle to overcome the caste system the Spaniards had established. At this time, Juarez met Miguel Mendez, a "liberal" or pro-reform instructor. At a meeting of like-minded persons, Mendez singled out Juarez and prophetically declared: "And this one [Juarez], so serious and reserved, this one will be a great politician. He will rise higher than any of us, and he will be one of our great men and the glory of our country."[3]

It was about this time, 1829, that the well-known General Santa Anna was entertained one evening at the new Institute where Juarez was studying. This was the first time Santa Anna saw Juarez and all that he remembered about Juarez was that he was barefoot and waiting on tables. To see greatness in meekness was not one of Santa Anna's abilities. "He [Santa Anna] was a fortune-hunter, not a fortune-teller; and being one of the coming men of the country himself, he saw only the feet."[4]

In 1841 Juarez was appointed to the bench, and in 1843, he entered into a marriage that was to provide him a never-failing source of devotion and strength. His wife, Margarita Mazza, of Italian descent, was a tireless, devoted supporter of the role he was to play in the destiny of Mexico and to the establishment of freedom. She bore him ten children. She never failed him, nor did he fail her.[5]

About 1844, Juarez accepted the position as secretary to the governor. However, when it came time to sign an order from the governor to the courts, directing them to prosecute those who refused to pay ecclesiastical tithes, Juarez resigned. By 1846, he was elected a representative from the district of Oaxaca to the National Congress. Even as a newcomer he began pushing for freedom of religion. Juarez did not remain long in the capital. In 1847, he became the governor of Oaxaca. This position marked the beginning of his destiny.

Juarez was a good governor. His top priority was education. Remembering his lineage, he said: "As a son of the people, I will not forget them; on the contrary, I will uphold their rights, I will see to it that they become educated.... Education is the primary base of people's prosperity and at the same time the surest means for making abuses of power impossible."[6] Juarez built over two hundred schools, and he encouraged the education of girls. "To form women with all the qualifications required by their necessary and lofty mission," he said, "is to form the fertile seed of social regeneration and improvement."[7]

Juarez's administration was an example to the country of what could be done with thrift and honesty. When he assumed office in 1847, the resources of the state were exhausted, a shortfall that resulted from the cost of several local revolts. When he retired in 1852, the deficit had been almost eliminated.

The oath of the governor's office bound Juarez to defend and preserve the Catholic religion. Juarez, true to this pledge, began his work of reform by cultivating the church in the areas of its original purpose and functions. He called upon church leadership to help during a cholera epidemic, and they established hospitals and provided nursing. He asked the church to bless and dedicate a newly built roadway and harbor which had been erected to stimulate the economy. Priests rallied, mobilizing their communities to help build badly needed roads. Juarez's efforts were not only beneficial to the government, but also to the church, which regained its "moral prestige" by coming out of its magistrative pursuits and doing good.[8]

During these years, Santa Anna used intrigue to become president of Mexico. Each of the five times he fell from being dictator/president, he fled the country. One time his flight took him southward towards Oaxaca. The former barefoot servant, Juarez, who was now governor, closed Oaxaca's borders to the deposed despot. However, in 1853, Santa Anna, through his covert activities, came again into power. As president, Santa Anna's first order of business was to rid the country of certain "undesirables." Benito Juarez's name was at the top of the list, and he, along with other reformers, was arrested and deported on a ship. They landed in Havana and eventually made their way to New Orleans. This small group of reformers in New Orleans began to mold the future of Mexico.

Most of the deposed reformers in New Orleans were anxious and impatient to return to Mexico and establish a lasting constitution. However, Juarez was calm and at ease, always studying, mostly constitutional law. One day he was invited by an American court to sit in on a case involving a land claim in California, a proud day for his friends, one of whom fondly reported that "his opinion was unanimously approved by the members of the court, he was enthusiastically praised and showered with a thousand attentions to which he was justly entitled."[9]

When revolution broke out again in Mexico, the little group of reformers had high hopes. Juarez was very concerned that in attempting to place reformers in office, the country did not have enough patriotism and enlighrampling on some of freedom's precious principles.

The new revolutionary armies sent for the deported Juarez, Ocampo, and the others to join them and be their leaders. Juarez landed secretly in Acapulco. Arriving in the camp of General Alvarez, he was greeted by the general's son, a colonel. The colonel who did not recognize him in his shabby and bedraggled state, demanded, "What do you want?"

In his unassuming way, Juarez responded, "Knowing that men are fighting for freedom here, I came to see in what way I could be useful." The men of the camp found a pair of trousers and a cotton blanket for him. It was not until three days later, when a letter arrived addressed to Benito Juarez, that they discovered his true identity. When the colonel questioned his reason for not announcing his identity, he merely replied: "Why should I? What does it matter?"[10]

When this revolution was successfully concluded and the reform government took over, Juarez was chosen to direct the ministry of justice and public education. The new president, Comonfort, proved to be weak and capitulated to the power of the clergy. Most of the cabinet resigned. But Juarez determined to remain in hope of even the slightest opportunity to effect change. Patient, as always, Juarez managed to have a new law passed that abolished the special judicial protection of the clergy and the military. This law became known as the *Ley Juarez*. It became the cornerstone of other freedoms, and in 1857 a new constitution was written. Juarez and his friends were able to establish most of the constitutional articles they wanted. This new constitution established freedom of religion, and freed Mexico from church control. All Mexicans were now free to gather for meetings, and free to speak and write what they wanted. The constitution also upheld the right to be tried in a public court of law.

The new constitution almost immediately ran into problems. The church forbade the faithful to swear allegiance to the constitution on threat of excommunication among those who did. Church officials were divided—those of the clergy who were preoccupied with power and dominion on one side, and those who were devoted to being servants of God and providing what was best for his children, on the other. As results of this division a new revolution began.

Another election was held, and this time Juarez was elected president of the Supreme Court, which, according to the new constitution, placed him next in line to succeed the president. The president eventually weakened to the opposition and had Juarez as well as other reformers in office placed under arrest. However, a *coup* took place, and Juarez escaped and made his way across the country walking alone until he arrived at Guanajuato. He and other deposed reformers reorganized the government according to the constitution with Juarez assuming the presidency.

There were many who saw this situation as hopeless. They reasoned that the old establishment—the church and the military— had plenty of money and the guns. Those who gave up hope did not know the strength of the "little Indian" from Ixtlan. This new anti-constitution revolution began a hunt for all the reformers and attempted to eliminate their supporters.

Once when Juarez and his cabinet were meeting in Guadalajara, the soldiers inside the palace suddenly turned traitor. Juarez and the others were locked up. Loyal soldiers outside the walls attempted to break in, but the traitors inside decided to kill the prisoners. One of the cabinet members, a great man and poet by the name of Guillermo Prieto, wrote of that event in his diary:

> The terrible column halted, with loaded guns, opposite the door. We distinctly heard, "Shoulder arms! Present arms! Ready Aim!" At the word "Aim!" Juarez grasped the latch of the door, flung back his head and waited. The fierce faces of the soldiers, their position ... my love for Juarez—what it was that made me do it, I know not. Swift as thought I seized Juarez by the shirt and thrust him behind me. I covered him with my body, and flung out my arms. Drowning the word

"Fire!" which rang out at that moment, I cried, "Down with those guns! Brave men are not murderers." An old man lowered his rifle and the others did the same. The soldiers wept, swearing they would not kill us, and vanished as if by magic.[11]

This anti-constitution revolution lasted three years. At the end of that time the constitutional government of Juarez returned to full power. This return was accomplished without any foreign aid or involvement. Throughout the revolution Juarez stubbornly refused to seek help from foreign powers. He felt the Mexican people could and should reclaim their liberty on their own.

A short time after the constitutionalists were back in power Juarez's good friend, Melchor Ocampo, often called "the author of reform," resigned because of critics' opposition to some of his efforts. He returned to his home in the country to retire. But there were yet in the countryside bandits from the revolt seeking to undermine the constitutional government.

These revolutionaries sought out the ranch of Ocampo and killed him. His death was a terrible loss for Juarez and the constitutional movement. But even in his own personal sorrow, Juarez's first thought was for justice. He ordered the prison guards doubled. Soon the people of the city began filling the streets seeking revenge and demanding that political prisoners be executed on the spot. Juarez would not permit this, ensuring the accused a public trial. Those who had sacrificed Ocampo were murderers, but Juarez was leading a people into a new and enlightened era. Upon this principle stood Juarez and his legacy—that government and law are a sacred trust. Even murderers must be treated as the law required.

Not long after Ocampos's death, the great patriot General Santos Degollado, whose untiring efforts had placed Juarez's constitutional government back in power, was also killed. Degollado's replacement, a young officer by the name of Leandro Valle, who had seen the new potential of his country, led the army to put down these insurrections. But he too was killed.

The loss of three top advisors by such tragic events would have shaken any government. Juarez declared a state of emergency and of necessity governed by decree. During this same time Spain, France, and England were demanding payment on the foreign debt that the anti-constitutional revolutionists had borrowed in their attempt to destroy Juarez's constitutional government. On 17 July, Juarez issued a decree suspending temporarily the payment of these debts. The three countries did not accept Juarez's explanation for the delay. They joined their military forces and proceeded to Mexico to force payment. Arriving in Vera Cruz, England and Spain became aware that it was the intent of France not only to force payment but to conquer Mexico. They wanted no part of such a scheme and returned to their own lands. However, the French, at the time ruled by Napoleon III, set about to expand the empire.

Napoleon III was so confident of his army's ability to succeed that he began looking for a monarch to rule the new empire. His choice fell on Maximilian, the great grandson of Empress Maria Theresa of Austria. By now the mighty French army had pushed Juarez and his army out of the capitol and as far north as Monterey. Maximilian wanted to rule Mexico only if the people of Mexico voted that they wished to have him as their emperor. While the people voted their acceptance of him, the vote of allegiance had been taken, unknown to Maximilian, at the point of a French bayonet. The results of this vote were delivered to Maximilian by those Mexicans whom Juarez had exiled when he returned to power. They deluded Maximilian into believing that Juarez was a tyrant and that the people of Mexico were begging for a benevolent monarch to rule them.

Maximilian and Princess Carlota arrived in Mexico with the best of intentions, but they were seriously deceived. No country that has once set its hand upon freedom will voluntarily return to servitude. Maximilian did all in his power to become one with Mexico, and as long as the mighty French army gave him support, his position was secure.

The French Empire in Mexico might have lasted much longer, had it not been for the personality of one man—Benito Juarez. The French army had done all in its power to either capture Juarez or push him over the border so that they could say that Juarez no longer had any claim to authority in the country. They did manage to push

Juarez as far north as El Paso, but he never left Mexico. He was willing to lose his life before crossing the border. "Show me the highest, most inaccessible, and driest mountain," he told his friends, "and I will go to the top of it and die there of hunger and thirst, wrapped in the flag of the Republic, but without leaving the national territory. That never!"[12]

During this time his life was always in peril, and on at least four occasions he was saved by divine intervention. On one occasion the enemy came within shooting distance of the famous black carriage, which had become the mark of Juarez. They filled the back of it with bullet holes. But there were no bullet holes in Juarez. Another time the town in which Juarez was staying received a surprise attack from the French soldiers. The soldiers searched the town and spied Juarez's black carriage a short distance out of town. The soldiers gave chase and caught the carriage, dragged the driver from his seat, and ripped open the door only to discover that for once Juarez had changed his method of traveling.

This incident was actually the last time the French sought Juarez. With the American Civil War, the threatening neighbor to the north during the days of Manifest Destiny had now become a fellow ally. Secretary of State William Seward had steadfastly refused to recognize Maximilian as the head of Mexico. In recognition of Juarez and his position as president of Mexico, Juarez's wife and his faithful representative Matias Ramirez, both of whom had been living in Washington for safety, were guests at a reception held in their honor by the president of the United States.

Now that the war was over, Secretary of State Seward began pressuring France to remove her troops from the American continent. Seward reinforced this diplomacy by placing the well trained U.S. troops under General Sherman along the Mexican border in a state of readiness. In France, Napoleon III had nearly drained his country's coffers in this imperialistic pursuit. All these events culminated in the almost immediate and complete recall of the French troops. As the French troops diminished, the territory Juarez actually controlled increased until Maximilian maintained control only of the capitol itself. Trapped with a few loyal troops at Queretaro, Maximillian surrendered.

Once again in control of the country, Juarez was flooded with pleas from heads of state and royalty from around the world to spare Maximilian's life. But Juarez had "met the orphans and widows of the patriots; he had seen the torn-up fields, the ruined towns, the wounded men. The pardon of Maximilian would cause the civil war to continue."[13] Juarez had to make it clear that no foreign intervention was ever again to be waged. Maximilian had to suffer for the sins of others. His death was the resounding signal to all Europe that the Americas were permanently off limits.

After the exodus of the French, Juarez was promptly re-elected as president. His tenacity and endurance had withstood and won against the great power of France and her armies. Mexico had produced at a critical time its own David to fight Goliath.

As President Juarez set out to make his vision of what the country could be in reality, one of the first freedoms that Juarez restored was freedom of the press. This powerful shaper of public opinion was immediately turned with full force against Juarez. But, like Jefferson, he refused to respond or curtail this liberty. He also reestablished religious liberty.

He began an intensive program of road building, and continued construction of the Mexico City-Vera Cruz railroad. Just as in his days as governor of Oaxaca, Juarez put his energies into building up a national education system.

In 1870, the Prussian army under Otto Bismark crushed the army of France. The fall of Napoleon III was due in large measure to the defeat he suffered in Mexico. Juarez was one of the first heads of state to sign a message of sympathy to the French people. He even gathered six hundred of his army and sent them to help the French in their struggle for freedom. Before they could arrive, an armistice was signed. Juarez was always the defender of liberty, even if it was the liberty of an old enemy. Like Lincoln, to whom he is often compared, Juarez was a true emancipator.

In 1869, Secretary of State William Seward visited Mexico. At a state dinner in a tribute to his host, Seward placed Juarez in the limelight of the American greats, comparing him with Washington, Lincoln, and Bolivar. Later, at a public gathering in Puebla, Seward described Juarez as the greatest man he had ever known. The most fitting tribute of all, however, is not to compare Juarez with others but to compare him with himself—great against ignorance, humble among greats. He is numbered among those apostles of freedom who suffered great persecution for the sake of principle and future.

ADDITIONAL READING

Viva Juarez! by Charles Allen Smart. Philadelphia: Lippincott Co., 1963. Written in story form. Interesting to read and a great book.

NOTES

[1] Roeder, Ralph. *Juarez and His Mexico.* n.p.: Viking Press 1947, p. 5.

[2] Ibid., p. 6.

[3] Ibid., p. 49.

[4] Ibid., p.

[5] Blancke, Wendell. *Juarez and His Mexico.* Washington, D.C.: Praeger Publishers, 1971, p. 40. This is an excellent book on the life of Juarez well researched, written with the best of Juarez in mind and well done for children.

[6] Ibid., p. 48.

[7] Roeder, p. 78.

[8] Ibid., p. 81.

[9] Ibid,. p. 112.

[10] Ibid., p. 116.

[11] Clarke, James Mitchell. "The People of Mexico, A History for Children." California State Department of Education: Sacramento, Calif., 1957, p. 303. Excellent and well written for children.

[12] Roeder, p. 602.

[13] Johnson, Ada. "The Great Figures of the French Intervention." Masters thesis, University of Arizona, 1942.

John Phillip Kemble

> *"As far as diligence and assiduity are claims to merit,*
> *I trust I shall not be found deficient."*

THE LATE 1700S SAW A WONDROUS REVIVAL OF SHAKESPEARE. John Kemble and his sister Sarah, who became Sarah Siddons and a great Shakespearean actress, were instrumental in this revival. These two, along with Dr. Samuel Johnson and actor David Garrick, did much to bring respect to the theater and to Shakespeare.

John Kemble returned Shakespeare to the original scripts and sought for accuracy in costume and scenery. During most of the 1700s theater was in a state of disrepute. Plays, even the remnants of Shakespeare, were mediocre. Theatrical costume were merely that of the contemporary fashion of the day. An actor playing a soldier of the crusade wore the uniform of a British general. Leading ladies in adaptations of Greek tragedies wore their hair powdered and dressed in richly trimmed dresses with large hoops. Historical application and research to period drama were largely unknown.

James Boaden, Kemble's close friend and biographer, wrote:

[Kemble] saw that much was yet to be done in the representations of his plays[that he produced], and determined, when he should acquire the necessary power, to bend every nerve to make them perfect, beyond all previous example. To do this, he was first himself to study the antiquities of his own and other countries; to be acquainted with their architecture, their dress, their weapons, their manners; and he by degrees, assembled about him the artists who could best carry his designs into effect.

To be critically exact was the great ambition of his life.[1]

Kemble studied all the branches of his art and read with infinite pains everything that related to his profession. He called it the archeology of drama.

Kemble turned what was then a questionable profession into an honored art of the highest scholarship. He brought to drama the respect that had been missing for more than a century, finishing the work David Garrick had begun. Through his attention to detail and his return to the original scripts of Shakespeare, theater began to enjoy one of its highest peaks of all time. It was on the vast ground of that poet that Kemble made his stand, says Boaden.

John Philip Kemble was born on 1 February 1757, at Prescot in Lancashire. His father, Roger Kemble, was manager of a provincial company. His mother, Sarah Ward, was a daughter of the previous company manager. In 1746, Sarah's father, gave a benefit play in the town hall of Stratford-upon-Avon, for the sole purpose of restoring the monument of Shakespeare in the church there.[2] John's parents and grandparents had an appreciation for Shakespeare even before the Shakespearean revival. It was into this multi-generational theatrical family that John Kemble and Sarah Kemble Siddons were born. Their unique background enabled these two children to do a great work for the fame of the world's greatest dramatic poet.

Kemble's parents had an impeccable reputation and high standards for which they were widely respected. Because theater was not a respectable occupation, they did not consider it as a choice for their children's career. Because he was a Catholic, Mr. Kemble sent John to the Roman Catholic seminary in Staffordshire. Here John distinguished himself, did well in his studies, and was very diligent in all his courses. At the conclusion of his courses at the seminary, he was sent to Douay, a Catholic school in France maintained by British Catholics.

At Douay Kemble received a classical education, of which he always spoke with admiration and gratitude. He became proficient in Greek and Latin and began to feel that the English translations of the Greek tragedies were not accurate enough. He read widely from the lives of the saints to the writings of the fathers of the church. This study of the classical and sacred literature caused him to consider studying for the ministry.

An incident during this time illustrates both the depth of his intellect and of his commitment to people. His class, because of some indiscretions had been placed under severe restrictions. To redeem the class, a student was to recite two books of Homer by heart. Kemble quietly and modestly volunteered to accept the task on behalf of the class. Using his keen ability for detail and an uncommon memory, Kemble was able to memorize 1500 lines to free his class. This act endeared him to the whole class.[3]

Like the great historian Sir Edwards Gibbon, Kemble felt from an early age that his life was destined for a mighty work, and for him it was to be the theater. Kemble returned from his studies to enter the stage, much to his father's discomfort. He began his debut by traveling with a troupe of players. At one point, between billings, Kemble and a fellow actor named Watson were reduced to searching out turnips in a field to keep from starving. While they were relishing in their modest feast they hit upon a novel idea to improve their finances. They planned for Kemble to act the part of a Methodist preacher and for Watson to act as clerk. As they neared the town of Tewkesbury, they drew together in a field a numerous congregation. Kemble preached with such pathos and conviction and with so much effect, that the pair were soon rewarded with a large collection for their labors.[4]

In 1778, Kemble's artistic talents began to flourish and establish his reputation. He had begun writing a play, a tragedy called *Belisarius*, which received some note. In 1780 he wrote a comedy, *The Female Officer*. On the first night of the performance he noticed the dragoon of Lord Percy, later known as the Duke of Northumberland, in the audience. He decided that several of his soldiers should have a part in the play. The head officer turned him down but, undaunted, he sought for an audience with Lord Percy. He gained that audience, and after explaining his need, Lord Percy granted the favor.

During the early 1780s, he delivered lectures in Edinburgh on the sacred and profane oratories. These were well received. Then in 1783, he joined his now famous sister, Sarah, on stage. Because her reputation drew large crowds, he was able to perform before many people, and his reputation grew.

David Garrick knew talent when he saw it. After viewing their performance, he convinced Kemble and his sister to leave the Covent Garden theater and perform in the famed Drury Lane theater. The brother and sister were widely acclaimed, particularly for their Shakespearean roles.

In 1788, Kemble became manager of Drury Lane, which left him free to choose scripts, actors, and, to design scenery. One of his first productions was *Henry VIII*, which had not been produced for over fifty years. Kemble made major changes. Although star roles had been held only by those actors who had seniority, he opened up roles to new and budding artists. He prohibited the sitting on the stage by the audience, and began for the first time the selling of tickets in advance of the performance. Under his tutelage and his sister's acting, Drury Lane flourished. But money problems arose when Sheridan, the owner, did not pay his actors according to contract. Kemble often had to pay the angered actors out of his own pocket.

In 1796, a Shakespearean forgery appeared in the country, and Sheridan, the owner of Drury Lane, in order to make monetary gains, bought the rights to the play. Sarah withdrew from the cast. Kemble refused to bill the play as written by Shakespeare. On opening night, the audience, by the end of the second act, could see that the play was not of Shakespearean quality. They began to make noise. Kemble ended the evening as only a perfectionist of Shakespeare could end it, by quoting the line: "And when this solemn mockery is ended."5 Finally, in 1802, the Kembles left Drury Lane, unable to work any longer under its present ownership.

Through a friend Kemble was able to negotiate with Covent Garden for one-sixth of the theater and the position as manager. In this new position he was able to let Shakespearean drama reign supreme. Kemble became the intellectual master of his art, and entry into the new century went well for him. His education and refined manners made him a sought after guest in the finest homes in London. Much of his popularity was due to the shrewd public relations of his devoted wife, Priscilla Hopkins, who performed her part well in the advancement of the theater. Even the Prince of Wales was fond of Kemble.

In 1808, tragedy struck. Covent Gardens caught fire and burned to the ground. Kemble's hopes, dreams and finances all seemed to have disappeared. He was devastated; the loss was enormous! Twenty-two lives were lost. Scenery that had been so painstakingly researched and made, dresses, stage-jewelry, uniforms—all were totally burned. The theater had possessed Handel's giant organ and a huge musical library, including irreplaceable scores of Handel. Kemble's own extensive library of antiquity was lost.

Fortunately, Kemble had insurance on the building. It was not long before subscriptions began coming in to help rebuild the theater. Lord Percy himself gave £10,000.[6] With this money and the insurance payment Covent Garden was rebuilt in grand style. Its seating capacity was enlarged to accommodate 2800 people. Such massive improvements left Kemble terribly in debt. To offset this debt he had to raise ticket prices. The public was angry. Playing to a full house on opening night, Sarah entered to perform and was shouted down with a loud chant: "Over-priced, over-priced."

This went on for three months until Kemble gave in and reduced the prices. In order to meet his debt, he began to produce extravagant plays to keep the theater full. It was a sorrowful turn for him from devotion to true theater.

In 1817, he played Coriolanus, giving his last performance before the most distinguished audience ever gathered in London. He retired to a country villa in Lausanne with his wife, where he spent much of his time gardening. Although he looked healthy, his health began to show the great strain it had been under for many years. During his last years, he studied his Bible every day and pondered greatly upon it. One visitor noted that the Bible study made him begin to look like Isaiah.[7] Kemble died in February of 1823. He was sixty-six years old. He had helped bring the world of theater and the works of Shakespeare to heights never known before.

NOTES

[1] Manvell, Roger. *Sarah Siddons: Portrait of An Actress.* New York: G. P. Putnam's Sons, 1971, p. 158.

[2] Boaden, James. *Memoirs of the Life of John Philip Kemble, Esq.* New York: Robert H. Small, Wilder & Campbelll, 1825, p. 2.

3 Ibid., p. 6.

4 Duyckinck, Evert. *Portrait Gallery of Eminent Men and Women.* New York: H. J. Johnson, 1873, p. 242.

5 Manvell, p. 198.

6 French, Yvonne. *Mrs. Siddons, Tragic Actress.* London: Derek Verschoyle, n.d., p. 224-25.

7 Baker, Herschel. *John Philip Kemble.* New York: Greenwood Press, 1942, p. 347.

Baron Justus von Liebig

FATHER OF ORGANIC CHEMISTRY

1808-1873

"Perfect agriculture is the true foundation of all trade and industry—it is the foundation of the riches of the states."

PRUSSIAN-BORN JUSTUS VON LIEBIG WAS THE GREATEST CHEMIST OF the nineteenth century. He presented a body of knowledge to the world that revolutionized not only chemistry but other laboratory sciences as well. His experimental method revolutionized science. Utilizing his procedures, an experiment could be tested, repeated, measured, and analyzed with consistent results. Although others had worked with elements of this method, Liebig brought them all together in a workable approach to scientific problems.

Scientific exploration before Liebig's time was known as the philosophical approach. This approach consisted of thinking about a scientific question in order to come up with a solution. The underlying attitude of this approach was that those who worked with their hands were inferior to those who worked with their minds. One early philosophical professor, for example, observed that "the influence of the moon upon the rain is clear, for as soon as the moon is visible the thunderstorm ceases."[1]

Before Liebig established his chemical courses in 1824, there were no universities in which students could practice in a laboratory and do their own scientific research and discovery. Students were permitted only to attend university lectures, perhaps watching the professor perform experiments at the front of the class. Liebig's first goal as a professor was to change this classroom format. He wanted to establish a laboratory large enough to accommodate his students. Because of this plan, the teachers at the University of Giessen objected strongly to Liebig's appointment, which had been made without their consent. But Liebig persisted, and finally, by the sheer force of his determination, a small room in an unused police station was turned over to him to use as a laboratory. The university, however, saw no reason to bear the necessary cost. Liebig was forced to borrow money in order to set up the laboratory, a debt which took him ten long years to pay off.

Like Louis Agassiz, Liebig felt that the discovery method was essential to the learning process. Students soon began coming from all over the world to learn in Liebig's laboratory. One of Liebig's American pupils, S. W. Johnson, later a professor of agricultural chemistry at Yale, gave this account of Liebig's teachings:

> It was in that spirit that Baron Liebig instructed the students who gathered in his laboratory from all quarters of the globe to learn the art of making *discoveries* in science.... It was not the novelty or the glory of discovery, but the genuiness of discovery that was regarded as of first importance.... He encouraged, but he criticized. He asked questions, suggested doubts, raised objections[2]

Like Agassiz, Liebig soon had more students than he could accommodate. Students came from America, England, France, and other countries. Many of Liebig's students and his students' students later became famous in their own right. In a lineal academic descent at least thirty-four of Liebig's academic descendants have received Nobel Prizes. Had Nobel Prizes been given before 1901, there may have been even more of Liebig's students who received the award. It has often been noted that although students often differed from their teachers and did not follow exactly in their master's footsteps, "they had learned the *principles* involved in exploring new regions, so they themselves became pioneers."[3]

Like Michael Faraday, in England Liebig felt no need to confine his knowledge to a university setting. He shared his knowledge with others through public lectures and demonstrations. All were welcome, an attitude that was particularly pleasing to women, who usually were not able to attend universities. During one of these lectures, which was attended by the royal family, Leibig burned carbon disulfied in nitric oxide and accidently caused an explosion. When the smoke settled he noticed blood trickling from the Royal couple's faces. He was mortified, but grateful that they had received only some minor scratches.[4]

A key to Liebig's unique approach to teaching and science can be found in his early childhood. Justus Liebig was born 12 May 1803 at Darmstadt, Germany. His parents, Georg and Marie Moserin Karoline, were devoted to their son and loved learning. His father sold paint and varnishes, which he manufactured according to the elements of the day. The elder Liebig would often send his young son to the Royal library to check out different books on chemistry. Justus Liebig read any books he could find in the chemistry section.

In spite of his love of learning, Liebig didn't do well in school. He struggled with the lecture system that was prominent in that day. He had difficulty learning by lecture, but he had a photographic memory and remembered easily things he saw and read.

Liebig's school performance was so miserable that the headmaster made an example of his poor abilities and told him that he was the plague of his teachers and the sorrow of his parents. The headmaster ended his tirade against him by asking him what he thought would become of him. Liebig, mustering all the courage that he had and drawing on considerable knowledge from his library readings and experiments with his father, answered simply that he would someday be a chemist.

This comment sent the teacher and the other students into peels of raucous laughter. No one at that time even dreamed that chemistry would eventually exist as an entire subject by itself and that Liebig himself would play a prominent role in its future development.[5]

Because at the age of fifteen Liebig was still failing in school, his father removed him and placed him in a nearby town as an apprentice pharmacist. There he remained for about ten months and learned all the chemicals in the shop. One night when Liebig was attempting one of his own experiments in his attic room, his experiment went awry and blew out the bedroom windows.[6] The druggist decided that it was safer for Liebig to be with parents and sent him home. Liebig's parents continued to place their confidence in their son. They sent Liebig out again, this time to work with a soapmaker. He was soon producing perfumed soap for his father's paint shop.

Through careful observation he learned much of the trade of the tanner, the smith, and the brass founder. He learned so much this way that he could have began an apprenticeship with any one with advanced knowledge. However, he did not want to work in a shop; he wanted to discover and to learn. Liebig convinced his father to let him enroll in the University of Bonn. Here, he worked hard to overcome the shortfalls of his studies from his elementary years. He soon found that it was virtually impossible to study chemistry in the university, and persuaded his father to let him go to Paris, where the great minds in science had accumulated in centers established during the progressive era of Napoleon. He desired in particular to study the experiments of Joseph-Louis Gay-Lussac, a well-known French chemist and physicist.

After about a year of study, Liebig was given the honor of reading a paper on his analysis of certain explosive compounds. Afterwards an older gentleman came up to Liebig, complimented him on his presentation, and invited him to dinner the following Sunday. Liebig was so flustered by such attention that he failed to get the man's name. On Sunday Liebig was the most unhappy young gentleman of Paris. He walked the streets of Paris in despair.

The next day a friend asked, "What on earth did you mean by not coming to dine with von Humboldt yesterday? He invited Gay-Lussac and a number of other chemists to meet you."[7]

Distraught, Liebig hurried off to Humboldt's residence to apologize. When the great man heard Liebig's pitiful story, he was amused and arranged a second dinner with Gay-Lussac and Liebig. Gay-Lussac was struck with the quickness of Liebig's mind and invited him to use his private laboratory. Here Liebig was able to fulfill his dreams of working in a laboratory, and he began his career as a pioneer in science. Modern sciences owes much to these early men of science like Humboldt and Gay-Lussac who opened the way for young scientists to flourish. They became mentors to many of the fathers of scientific disciplines.

A year after Humboldt introduced Liebig to Gay-Lussac, he also secured for Liebig the post of assistant professor of chemistry at the University of Giessen, although no chair of chemistry even existed. It was not long before Liebig became a full professor and, through sheer determination, established his laboratories. Liebig's department at Giessen became a center for budding young chemists of the nineteenth century. When President Abraham Lincoln created the United States Department of Agriculture in 1862, he appointed C. M. Wetherill, one of Liebig's students, to head the department.[8]

While Liebig was at the university, he became the first to provide the courtroom with a scientific analysis of evidence in order to help solve criminal murder cases. It was a popular defense of the time to claim that the deceased had died of spontaneous combustion created by over-drinking. Liebig dispelled this popular defense with his analysis of the corpse in the courtroom.

Liebig remained at Giessen for twenty-eight years, becoming the greatest chemist of the nineteenth century. He took the lead in four important areas: organic chemistry; chemistry tas it related to agriculture; agriculture as it related to physics; and pedagogy. He was an outstanding teacher, and his influence was not only felt through the university and local lectures but also through his prolific writings. His first letters, revealing insights about the practical relations of the sciences to the arts and to other departments, were written with great clearness.

Liebig is perhaps best known for his work in agriculture. He showed that plants robbed the soil of its nutrients, which needed to be replaced with manure and other organic matter. He also noted, after examining plant ash, that certain elements were lacking even after fertilizers were added. In 1845, he began working on producing chemical fertilizers to supplement natural organic fertilizers. He succeeded but cautioned that chemical fertilizers should be considered only as a supplement to organic fertilizers. In Liebig's day nine farmers could feed themselves, and with their combined surplus, they could feed one city family. As a result of his work, by 1865, one farmer could feed twenty-seven people.

Liebig accepted no credit for originality. He felt that the knowledge he worked with had existed for years. His contribution was to give that knowledge more light, so it could be seen better. He described the facts he worked with as a room full of furniture and other objects which have always been there, but which were not always visible or useful to those in the room. Many people who were familiar with certain objects totally missed others. Liebig felt that he had brought more light into the room, therefore more objects were seen and could be used.[9]

Liebig was known not only for his excellent scholarship, but also for his generous disposition to his students and others. An incident that occurred when he was about fifty illustrates his character. He and his friends were on a walk through the mountains to another village, when they came upon an elderly soldier. The man was poverty stricken and enfeebled by disease. As Liebig's company came near, the old man told his sad tale. Liebig, whose heart and purse were often readily open, gathered with his friends a little stock of money for the old soldier.

They then passed on to the next village, where they stopped at an inn to dine and rest. When all had feasted they settled down for an afternoon nap.

After half an hour his friends awoke to find Liebig gone. Upon inquiring of the landlords to his whereabouts, they discovered that after they had gone to sleep, Liebig asked for directions to a pharmacy. When he was told that there was none in that village, but there was one in the next, Liebig began hiking to the next village. The inquiring friends immediately set out to find Liebig, who they presently saw near the knoll of a hill. Liebig explained to his friends that he had noticed that the old soldier had showed signs of a low grade fever, and he desired to obtain some quinine for him.[10]

Liebig's compassion, however, did not always extend to other scientists, of whom he was often critical when they disagreed on theories. But he soon apologized if he was in the wrong. Liebig sometimes combined his attacks with humor. "Imagine yourself," he would say, "in the year 1900, when we shall both have been decomposed again into carbonic acid, water and ammonia, and the lime of our bones belongs perhaps to the very dog who then dishonors our grave. Who then will care whether we lived at peace or in strife?"[11]

Because of him millions now live on increased production of the soil. To better the world was Liebig's hope. He said, "If I can impress the farmer with the principles of plant nutrition, soil fertility, and the causes of soil exhaustion, one of the tasks of my life will have been accomplished."[12]

What Newton was to mathematics and astronomy, Liebig has been to organic chemistry. Said Theodor von Bishcoff:

> I do not think I am mistaken ... that there are not many among the younger [generation] ... who know, or have even a distant notion how great—or, rather, I should say, how immense—the influence of Liebig's researches, writings, and teachings has been. They care but little for him to whom science, and with science they themselves, are indebted for their present position.[13]

NOTES

[1] Cannon, Grant. *Great Men of Modern Agriculture*. New York: Macmillan, 1963, p. 151.

[2] Moulton, Ray Forest. *Liebig and After Liebig A Century of Progress in Agricultural Chemistry*. American Association for the Advancement of Science, Washington, D. C., 1942, p. 7.

[3] Krebs, Hans. *Reminiscences and Reflections*. Oxford: Clarendon Press, 1981, p. 177.

[4] See Twigg, C. A. And M. V. "Centenary of the Death of Justus von Liebig." *Journal of Chemical Education*. Vol. 50 Number 4, April 1973, p. 273.

[5] See Shenstone, W. A. F.I.C. *Justus Von Liebig: His Life and Work, 1803 1873*. New York: Macmillan, 1895, p. 12-13.

[6] Cannon, p. 151.

[7] Ibid., p. 152.

[8] See ibid., p. 154.

[9] Farber, Eduard. *Great Chemist*. New York and London: Interscience Publishers, 1961, p. 547.

[10] Shenstone, p. 205-206.

[11] Moulton, p. 3.

[12] Cannon, p. 159.

[13] Shenstone, p. 152.

David Livingstone

SCOTTISH MISSIONARY, PHYSICIAN   1813-1873

> *"Had I a thousand lives, they would be dedicated to him who loved us and gave himself for us."*

IN 1850, DAVID LIVINGSTONE WROTE HIS SISTER FROM THE DEPTHS of Africa. "I am a missionary heart and soul. God had an only son, and he was missionary and a physician. A poor imitation of Him I am or rather wish to be. In this service I hope to live; in it I wish to die."[1] David Livingstone's wish was granted. He lived and died as a missionary in the heart of Africa.

Livingstone was also one of greatest explorers the world has ever known. He traveled over one-third of the continent of Africa. Due to his explorations the maps of Africa were redrawn. He was the first cartographer to traverse that great continent from the Atlantic to the Indian Ocean. He was the first white man to view the magnificent Victoria waterfalls, which he named after his British Queen. The publication of Livingstone's many writings, describing the horrors of slave trade, helped to bring it to an end.

Livingstone's time in Africa (encompassing most of his adult life) can be divided into two periods: First, his missionary work, and second his exploration and discoveries in Africa. During this time he moved his family to remote villages where no "civilized" family had ever lived. He was often chastised for risking his family in such barbaric circumstances. Livingstone was torn by his desire to have his family with him and the great drive that was in him to reach the innermost parts of Africa. Upon the advice of his father-in-law, he brought his family closer to civilization.

David Livingstone was born 10 March 1813, in the village of Blantyre Works, in Lanarkshire, Scotland. "His parents were typical examples of all that is best among the humbler families of Scotland."[2] Livingstone wrote of his early life:

My own inclination would lead me to say as little as possible about myself. My great grandfather fell at Culloden, my grandfather used to tell us national stories, and my grandmother sang Gaelic songs. To my father and the other children [grandfather's] dying injunction was, "Now, in my lifetime I have searched most carefully through all the traditions I could find of our family, and I never could discover that there was a dishonest man among our forefathers. If, therefore, any of you or any of your children should take to dishonest ways, it will not be because it runs in your blood, it does not belong to you. I leave this precept with you—be honest."[3]

Livingstone recalled listening to this same grandfather who had a "neverending stock of stories, many of which were wonderfully like those I have since heard while sitting by the African evening fires." His grandfather "could give the particulars of the lives of his ancestors for six generations."[4] Of his own father, Livingstone wrote that "by his kindliness of manner and winning ways he made the heartstrings of his children twine round him as firmly as if he had possessed, and could have bestowed upon them every worldly advantage." He describes his mother like other poor Scottish women: an "anxious housewife striving to make both ends meet."[5]

Because of the family's limited circumstances, Livingstone left school and went to work at the age of ten. He was a "piecer" in a local cotton mill, working from six in the morning until eight o'clock at night. With part of his first week's wage he bought a book, *Rudiments of Latin,* which he propped up on the machine in front of him and read while he worked. He was able to tune out the noise of the factory and concentrate on the words in front of him. This talent of concentration stayed with him throughout his life. He was able to read among children playing or natives dancing. He began to obtain other books, mainly scientific works and travel books.

His father was somewhat disappointed that his son didn't peruse "dry doctrinal" religious texts, as Livingstone called them. However, his failure to read such text did not affect his deeply religious motives. Having been raised to love truth and light,

Livingstone gave his life to Christian ideals. "In the glow of love which Christianity inspires, I soon resolved to devote my life to the alleviation of human misery."[6] He first planned to be a medical missionary in China, an effort he began while he was still working in the factory. About this time some friends encouraged him to join the London Missionary Society. He was much inclined to do so, for the group were non-sectarian and their sole purpose was to bring the gospel of Christ to the "heathen." With the society's help, which was difficult for him to accept, Livingstone pursued his medical degree and finished theological training. He was admitted to pastoral office in 1840. His great desire to work as a medical missionary in China was thwarted when the Opium Wars started.

The London Missionary Society also had a base of operation under Robert Moffat in Africa, and despite Livingstone's disappointment, the society was able to convince him to go to Africa. China's closing was providential, for he did more for the continent of Africa than perhaps any other man up to that time.

After a voyage of three months, Livingstone landed at Capetown, Africa. He proceeded around the bay on the east coast and headed into the interior some seven hundred miles north, where he joined the Reverend Robert Moffat in his work. Here Livingstone worked and lived as a bachelor for four years. Much of his time was spent traveling northward looking for a suitable outpost for a mission. He selected a sight two hundred miles north of Moffat's station. He then married Moffat's daughter, Mary, and they settled on this new northern station.

While there, Livingstone was attacked by a lion, which crushed his left arm. The injured arm was never set right and, due to another injury, he could not support the barrel of a gun with his left hand. He describes the experience as follows:

> Settling among the Mabotsa tribe, I found that they were troubled with attacks from lions, so one day I went with my gun into the bush and shot one, but the wounded beast sprang upon me, and felled me to the ground. While perfectly conscious, I lost all sense of fear or feeling, and narrowly escaped with my life. Besides crunching the bone into splinters, he left eleven teeth wounds on the upper part of my arm.

I attached myself to the tribe called Bakwains, whose chief, Sechele, a most intelligent man, became my fast friend, and a convert to Christianity. The Bakwains had many excellent qualities which might have been developed by association with European nations. An adverse influence, however, is exercised by the Boers, for, while claiming for themselves the title of Christians, they treat these natives as black property, and their system of domestic slavery and robbery is a disgrace to the white man. For my defense of the rights of Sechele and the Bakwains, I was treated as coniving at their resistance, and my house was destroyed, my library, the solace of our solitude, torn to pieces, my stock of medicines smashed, and our furniture and clothing sold at public auction to pay the expenses of the foray.

In traveling we sometimes suffered from a scarcity of meat, and the natives to show their sympathy for the children, often gave them caterpillars to eat; but one of the dishes they most enjoyed was cooked *mathametlo*, a large frog.[7]

Tales such as this was sent back to England, which made Livingstone an instant hero.

In 1849, Livingstone crossed the Kalahari desert, the first ever to write a detailed account of the region. During the next few years, he took his wife and three children into an unexplored region ending up near the Zambezi River. However, since the children were growing up, the need for further education caused them to return to Capetown in 1852 and subsequently to England. Livingstone remained behind.

He spent the next four years in exploration, always looking for missionary outposts and carefully logging the latitude and longitude, the astronomical readings, and noting the plants and the animals. He wrote voluminously and accurately on all aspects of his observations.

Even languages made their way into his records, and he struggled to create a written language from a verbal one. He recorded: "When I heard the new language ... I felt that if I could be permitted to reduce their language to writing and perhaps translate the Scriptures into it, I might be able to say that I had not lived in vain."[8] Although he was never able to make such a translation, he laid a foundation for others who did.

Livingstone soon realized that most of the natives' culture were so far removed from the gospel that there would be few conversions at that time. In his journal he described some barbaric practices: a child who cut the upper before the lower incisors was put to death; hands were cut off for the slightest indiscretion; and slave trading operated within some tribes. Tribes stole children from adjacent tribes and sold them for clothing. Livingstone wrote: "Who will stop the stream of human blood which has flowed for age .... if we with our great instrument, the gospel, do not?"[9]

Livingstone realized that he and others of his time were laying a foundation, pioneering, and opening new ground. He could see that the fundamentals of human kindness and other basic elements of civilized life had to be taught before the principles of Christian living could be adapted. In his private journal Livingstone wrote:

> We work towards another state of things. Future missionaries will be rewarded by conversions for every sermon. We are their pioneers and helpers. Let them not forget the watchmen of the night, we who worked when all was gloom and no evidence of success in the way of conversion cheered our path. They will doubtless have more light than we, but we served our master earnestly and proclaimed the same gospel as they will do.[10]

He did all he could to give any light possible. He was often known to beg the tribes not to fight on the Sabbath, and out of respect for Livingstone they usually agreed.

Some of this time and effort Livingstone spent trying to teach reading. He felt that reading exposed people to civilization and Christianity. He also shared gardening techniques and new plant seeds with the natives, which they easily adopted.

In 1856, Livingstone, very emaciated and sickly, arrived at a Portuguese settlement. After a sixteen-year absence he returned to England to a hero's welcome. While in England he wrote *Missionary*

Travels and Researches in South Africa. A year later he returned to Africa as Consul for the British government. On this trip he experienced the terrible loss of his wife. His two sons, because of health reasons, were compelled to return to England. Livingstone returned to England in 1864.

However, it was not long before he was prompted to return to a work that was not yet complete. He had two main objectives: to suppress slavery by means of civilizing influences and to ascertain the African watershed. This trek was one of extreme hardship, disease, and desertion. It was seven years before Livingstone saw another white man. A disgruntled native started rumors that Livingstone was dead. When word of his supposed death reached England, the *New York Herald* financed and outfitted H. M. Stanley to go in search of the great explorer.

Stanley eventually came face to face with a very sick Livingstone. After moments of silent staring, Stanley spoke the now famous words, "Dr. Livingstone, I presume." Stanley nursed the ill and aging Livingstone back to health and urged him to return home with him. But Livingstone felt that his mission was not done. Stanley returned to England and Livingstone continued his explorations. However, his dysentery returned, and he finally had to consent to be carried on a litter in order to further his explorations.

On 30 April 1873, he wound his watch before retiring. Minutes later one of the natives returned to find "the great master," as they called him, kneeling beside his bed in the act of prayer. But Livingstone was dead. His last effort in a sick and emaciated body was to kneel humbly before entering the presence of his heavenly king.[11] His faithful men preserved his body as best they could. As he had requested, Livingstone's heart was removed from his body and buried in Africa.

The natives revered him as a superior being, a man who was kind and gentle. The motto of his life was "fear God and work hard."[12] Livingstone said, "The earth shall be filled with the knowledge of the glory of the Lord.... The poor Bushmen ... shall see his glory, and the dwellers in the wilderness shall bow before Him. The obstacles to the coming of the Kingdom are mighty, but come it will."[13] H. M. Stanley wrote in euology of him: "Britain

.... excelled herself ... when she produced the strong and perseverant Scotsman, Livingstone."[14]

NOTES

[1] Livingstone, David. *Livingstone's Private Journals, 1851-1853.* Berkeley: University of California Press, 1960, p. xxii.

[2] Encyclopedia Britannica. 11th ed. 1910, p. 16:816.

[3] Murray, George. *The Popular Educator.* No. 8. World's Greatest Literature Series, p. 667.

[4] Duyckinck, Evert A. *Portrait Gallery of Eminent Men and Women.* New York: H. J. Johnson. 1873, p. 605.

[5] Ibid., p. 606.

[6] Ibid., p. 607.

[7] Murray, p. 668.

[8] Livingstone, p. xx.

[9] Ibid., p. 201.

[10] Ibid., p. 168.

[11] Chambliss, Rev. J. E. *The Lives and Labors of Livingstone.* Boston: Hubbard Co., 1875, p. 750-51.

[12] Encyclopedia Britannica, 16:816.

[13] Livingstone, p. 167.

[14] Encyclopedia Britannica, 16:815.

Thomas Babington Macaulay   *1800-1859*

ENGLISH HISTORIAN, ESSAYIST, POLITICIAN

"Our civil and religious liberties have been bought with a fearful price."

THOMAS MACAULAY WAS KNOWN IN HIS CENTURY FOR HIS literary works, his character and principles, and his quick grasp of public questions. While in India he supported freedom of the press and established the legal equality of Europeans and natives; he also instigated a system of national education. He helped millions of Indians who had suffered for generations under the corrupt policies of the East Indies Company and tried to undo much of the wrongs perpetrated upon India.

Macaulay's first public speech was against the slave trade. He worked for the Reform Bill, which gave better representation in the Parliament for all the people. He became Secretary of War and later paymaster-general. Once he lost an election because he supported a grant for a Catholic school in Ireland. He helped to abolish an obsolete commission on which he sat and for which he was paid. When it came time to vote on the slave trade bill he resigned from his party in order to vote his conscious.

Notwithstanding Macaulay's great work in the advancement of good government, his first and final love and devotion was to literature. His most compelling work is his History of England. Though this history has been surpassed by later works (mostly because Macaulay allowed his partisan view to color his history) his work achieved the distinction of making history as attractive as fiction, for he wrote about people. William Makepeace Thackeray said that "[Macaulay] reads twenty books to write one sentence; he travels one hundred miles to make a line of description."[1]

Thomas Babington Macaulay was born 25 October 1800 His grandparents had been Scottish ministers, and his grandfather had hosted Samuel Johnson on his trip to Scotland. His father, Zachary Macaulay, was a quiet man of very strong political convictions. On a brief trip to Jamaica in his youth, Zachary had become acquainted with the cruelties of the slave-trade, and so he spent his life in the work of an abolitionist. As a young man he became the governor of Sierra Leone, and with the help of a number of Christians he established the capital as a free city for those natives in the neighboring states. He endured much hardship, especially when a French garrison attacked the city. As is the nature of revolutions, all that was sacred and of use was destroyed. A revolutionist announced to Zachary that "the National Convention have decreed that there is no Sunday, and that the Bible is all a lie."[2] These stories and others were often repeated to young Macaulay and greatly influenced his later beliefs and actions.

Macaulay's mother was Selina Mills, a former pupil of the great English moralist, Hannah More. Macaulay claimed that he inherited his jovial nature from his mother. The early education of the future statesman and historian was personally superintended by his mother. He first demonstrated his vivacious character and vitality for life in his affections for her. Mrs. Macaulay told friends that his sensibilities and affections were developed at a young age and she detected that he was no ordinary baby. He was always moved with tenderness towards his mother. He cried for joy at her return after having been gone but a short while. Like Johnson's mother, Macaulay's mother taught her son to read by the time we was three, and from then on he read incessantly. His favorite reading place was on the rug in front of the fireplace with his book on the ground and a piece of bread-and-butter in his hand. He did not particularly care for toys, but loved taking his daily walk.

Hannah More was fond of relating that one day she knocked at the door and little Macaulay answered. He told her that his parents were out but that he could bring her a glass of old spirits. This comment greatly startled the good lady, so she questioned the little child as to what he knew about old spirits. The little boy merely shrugged his shoulders and said that Robinson Crusoe often drank some.[3]

His mother told how Thomas, when he was eight years old,

took it into his head to write a compendium of universal history ... and he really contrived to give a tolerably connected view of the leading events from the creation to the present time, filling about a quire of paper.... He told me one day that he had been writing a paper ... to persuade the people of Travancore to embrace the Christian religion. On reading it, I found it to contain a very clear idea of the leading facts and doctrines of that religion, with some strong arguments for its adoption. He was so fired with reading Scott's "Lay" and "Marmion," the former of which he got entirely by heart, and the latter almost entirely, by heart ... he determined on writing himself a poem in six cantos which he called "The Battle of Cheviot". ...I make no doubt he would have finished his design, but as he was proceeding with it the thought struck him of writing an heroic poem to be called "Olaus the Great" ... after the manner of Virgil.... He has composed I know not how many hymns.[4]

Hannah More often took the boy to her home, where she shared many educational ideas with him. He basked in the conversation of the adult ladies of the house, who were some of the grandest ladies in all the land. Each day Hannah would end the discussion with a lesson from the Bible.

Such a beginning in letters could not help but flourish in his adult life. Macaulay's first work of note was an essay on the works of Milton published in the *Edinburgh Review*. He was instantly famous. This sudden fame seems to have two causes. First, there had been no new contributors to the *Review* for several decades and they were in great need of new talent. Second, this particular essay filled a great vacuum in the area of literary criticism. Other essays soon followed. He wrote a critique on Croker's review of Boswell's *Life of Johnson*, as well as essays on Warren Hastings and Frederick the Great. In addition to literary criticism he also wrote poetry and historical and biographical essays. He wrote sometimes two articles a month.

Of Macaulay, Elizabeth Barrett Browning wrote to a friend, "You are very right in admiring Macaulay; he has a noble, clear, metallic note in his soul, and makes us ready by it for battle. I very much admire Mr. Macaulay, and could scarcely read his ballads and keep lying down. They seemed to draw me up to my feet as the mesmeric powers are said to do."[5] His writings were full of life, brimming with description and beautiful reflections. However, he could introduce a point so sharply and suddenly that the reader sometimes felt a debate was to take place. Lord Melbourne was quoted as saying, "I wish I were as cocksure of any one thing as Macaulay is of everything."[6]

In spite of these literary excesses, Macaulay was always found on the side of justice and fairness for the underling and for the oppressed. In his private life Macaulay was beyond reproach. A fellow writer, Sydney Smith, characterized Macaulay by saying:

> There are no limits to his knowledge, on small subjects as well as great; he is like a book in breeches.... But what is far better and more important than all this is, that I believe Macaulay to be incorruptible.
>
> You might lay ribbons, stars, garters, wealth, title, before him in vain. He has an honest, genuine love of his country; and the world could not bribe him to neglect her interests.[7]

The genuineness of Macaulay's character is evidenced by the love and care he gave his family. When he first entered Parliament, the business House of Babington and Macaulay, which his father owned failed. Macaulay's father was unable to pay the debt so his son Thomas took over and became the soul support of his family eventually paying off all his father's debt.

His interaction with his family went beyond merely supporting them. He was a great friend and playmate, and all his brothers and sisters deeply loved him. The instant his father left the house, wild pandemonium began. Macaulay would play he was a tiger, hiding growling in such a terrible manner his siblings screamed with mocked fright. Another popular activity was to play fire. They piled all the furniture in the middle of the room, heaping books, and clothing, with rugs on top. Then Macaulay would rescue his mother, if she appeared, carrying her to safety. Their play was always followed by a pillow fight.[8]

Because he never married, he lived a great part of his life in his sister Hannah's home. He was so loved by her children that she complained that he sometimes got in the way of her discipline.

When he died he was found by his sister and nephew sitting with his head bent forward on his chest. A magazine lay open on his lap. He was buried in Westminster Abbey along with the other great literary giants. It could be said of Macaulay that "where much is given much is expected." He fulfilled that expectation.

NOTES

1 Lord, John. *Beacon Lights of History*. New York: James Clarke & Co. 1896, 13: 268-69.

2 Trevelyan, George *The Life and Letters of Lord Macaulay*. New York: Harper, 1875 , 2:33.

3 Ibid ., p. 40.

4 Ibid., p. 42.

5 Letter of Elizabeth Barrett Browning as found in Thomas Ward's *The English Poets*. New York: Macmillan, 1894, 1:166.

6 Encyclopedia Britannica. 11th ed. 1911, 17:196.

7 Lord, 13: 262.

8 Hubbard, Elbert. *Little Journeys to the Homes of the Great*. New York: Wm. L. Wise & Co., 1916, p. 179.

Lord Horatio Nelson

BRITISH NAVAL HERO *1758-1805*

"I have done my duty, thank God for that!"

HORATIO NELSON WAS BORN 29 SEPTEMBER 1758 IN THE OLD parsonage at Burham Thorpe, the sixth of eleven children. His parents who were devoted to each other and their God. There are few facts about Nelson's early childhood; however his father, the good Reverend, was a strict disciplinarian. His mother died while he was only nine years old, but her devotion affected him deeply. She passed away the day after Christmas. Her death left her husband with eight children, the youngest only ten months old.

She appears to have influenced his life's profession as Nelson's older sister wrote:

> Somehow, the Navy must always be interesting to me.
> I may say I suck'd it with my Mother's milk,
> for she was quite a heroine for the sailors.[1]

As a boy, Horatio exhibited qualities of leadership, daring and preseverance. He attended three different schools in and around his childhood area. At one school, North Walsham, where he boarded, some delicious pears grew beneath the boy's second story window. No one dared scale the wall for the pears, fearing a flogging from the master. Nelson lowered himself on several bedsheets tied together and claimed the pears. The headmaster, discovering that pears had been taken from the tree, offered a reward of five guineas to whoever could name the culprit. No one came forward to tell. Such was the loyalty that those in Nelson's presence felt for him.[2]

One day Horatio and his brother William attempted to go to school in a snowstorm that blocked the road. Unable to proceed, they returned home. The two brothers, reported to their father that the way was impossible to pass. Their father replied that they should try at least one more time. They departed to make their second attempt. After a period of time, William felt they had struggled long enough and should return home again. Horatio, however, insisted that they not retreat, reminding his brother that their father had left them "on honor" to try to get through.[3]

During the Christmas holiday of Nelson's twelfth year, he learned through an article in the paper that his uncle, Captain Maurice Suckling, was scheduled to go to sea again on the sixty-four gun ship, *Reasonable*. Nelson begged his brother to write to their father and tell him of his great desire to go to sea with his uncle. The Reverend, who was at Bath, was ill and still had seven children to provide for, so he readily gave his permission.

The letter was sent to Uncle Maurice, who responded with some surprise: "What has poor Horace [Horatio] done, who is so weak, that he above all the rest should be sent to rough it out at sea? But, let him come; and the first time we go into action, a cannonball may knock off his head, and provide for him at once."[4]

Nelson took a stagecoach to Chatham, but because of a mix-up in communications, there was no one to meet him upon his arrival. He finally identified the *Reasonable* in the bay, but could find no one to take him out to board it. A kindly officer befriended the lad and took him to his home to feed him. Then he made the necessary connections to get young Nelson to the ship. The *Reasonable* did not see much action on its voyage, and Captain Suckling knew that if his nephew was to have a chance to advance in the navy, he would need to gain more experience than the Royal Navy could offer at that time.

The captain was able to obtain a position for young Nelson as a "captain's servant" on a merchant vessel which was to set sail for the West Indies. From the West Indies, Nelson sailed to the Arctic and from there he was sent to the East Indies. While in the Arctic Nelson served under Captain Lutwidge, who later was fond of telling the following story about his famous former coxswain.

The ship became stuck in the ice and the crew grew bored. One night Nelson and a companion slipped overboard in the fog. As the fog thickened, Lutwidge grew worried about their safety. When the fog cleared in the early hours of the morning, the two wayward seamen could be seen at a distance, attacking a bear. Lutwidge sent up a call for them to return immediately to the ship. Nelson's companion urged him to obey, but Nelson was intent on getting the bear, and attacked the bear with the butt of his gun. Captain Lutwidge, knowing more than Nelson about the capabilities of polar bears, fired one of the ships guns and frightened the animal away.[5] Nelson regrettably returned to the ship empty-handed.

Finally, after freeing their ship from the ice, they sailed for the East Indies. It was in the East Indies that Nelson became ill and was sent home on a returning vessel to recuperate. It was on this ship, that he experienced a singular event that would shape his future. At the time he was just a boy of sixteen years. His poor state of health gave way to the weight of depression, and he felt totally alone. As he reached the extreme of his despair, he felt the following as related in his own words:

"After a long and gloomy reverie, in which I almost wished myself overboard, a sudden glow of patriotism was kindled within me, and presented my King and my Country, as my patrons. My mind exalted in the idea. 'Well then,' I exclaimed, 'I will be a hero, and confiding in providence, I will brave every danger." This impression was accompanied with "radiant orb," as he described it, which ever urged him onward.[6]

After some time, Nelson's health returned. Returning to sea, he rapidly advanced to the rank of captain and was sent to the West Indies. There he found trading going on with American merchant vessels, contrary to the British Navigation Act. As senior officer, Nelson began to enforce the Navigation Act, which distrubed those living on the islands, as the trade was their livelihood. Nelson stood firm in his duty, which eventually led to lawsuits against him. Although Nelson was exonerated in each case, his actions in the West Indies plagued him throughout much of his career.

While in the West Indies, Nelson visited the island of Nevis to met the governor. As Nelson waited in the study, the governor's five-year-old nephew, Josiah, wandered in. By the time the governor arrived, the "stern" supreme officer of the West Indies was engaged in serious play with Josiah under a table! Josiah's mother was Fanny Nisbet, an attractive widow, known as the most captivating and attractive young lady on the island. Nelson was not slow in his own observations. Within time they became engaged and were married. The couple returned to Burnham-Thorpe to live with Reverend Nelson in the parsonage. No children ever came from this marriage.

Once back in England, Nelson requested command of another ship. But because of the difficulties resulting from his strict enforcement of the law in the West Indies, the Admiralty was slow to hear his plea. It was not until England went to war with France, five long years later, that Nelson was given his desire.

The war put naval commanders in high demand, and Nelson was immediately sought after. The Royal Naval, forgiving all former disturbances, gave Nelson command of a sixty-four gun ship and orders to sail for the Mediterranean to join Lord Hood in an attempt to secure a position on the French coastline. Nelson was sent to take Bastia on the Island of Corsica. There he led two hundred seamen, who struggled to haul cannons onto the sand. During the battle that followed, a shot from town struck the battery near where Nelson was standing. It drove sand and gravel against his face and chest, bruising him severely and destroying the sight in one eye. [7]

In another battle off the coast of Spain, Nelson led his crew of boarders through the cabin window of a Spanish ship shouting, "Westminster Abbey or victory!"[8]

Later in the summer, Nelson led an attack off the Island of Teneriffe. A cannon ball shot during the attack so badly mangled his right arm that it had to be crudely amputated, and he was ordered home to recuperate. By this time he had seen four actions with the fleet of the enemy. Three of the actions included taking towns, serving ashore for four months with the army as "Colonel of the Marines," commanding batteries in two sieges, assisting in the capture of over seventy enemy vessels, and personally engaging the enemy 120 times, with severe wounds to his body.

His wounds, particularly the complications from the amputated arm, forced Nelson to return to England, where Fanny nursed her husband back to health. Because of his actions in battle, he soon became known throughout England as a great patriot. He was soon called up to London, where he was knighted for his action in the

Mediterranean and advanced to the rank of Rear Admiral. An incident at this occasion demonstrated Nelson's consideration for his subordinates. When the king said, "You have lost your right arm," Nelson replied, "But not my right hand." Nelson then turned to companion, Captain Berry, whom he then presented to the king.[9]

Like Napoleon, Nelson was a great master of the souls of men. He did much to make the strenuous duty more tolerable for men. He was free from any petty jealousy and at times had the cabin boys sit beside him at the Captain's table.

Nelson returned to the Mediterranean with orders to discover what had become of the French fleet, which seemed to have disappeared under the very nose of the British. During the trip his flag ship became dismantled in a storm. He recorded in his journal: "I ought not to call what has happened by the cold name of accident, but I firmly believe that it was the Almighty's goodness to check my consummate vanity."[10]

Nelson's fleet lost precious time in repairs. Failing to find the French fleet on the European coast, Nelson deduced that they had to have sailed to east, most probably to Egypt. He arrived in Egypt catching Napoleon's army aboard the ships of the French fleet. He immediately called for an attack although his fleet was outnumbered. By skillful maneuvers, the British soon had the upper hand. The battle began at sunset and raged until daybreak. It was a victory so decisive and so overwhelming that some recorded the battle not just as a victory, but as an actual conquest.

The fame of the battle spread throughout England. Nelson was called "Nelson of the Nile," and given the title of Baron. In spite of his fame and titles, Nelson remained concerned that the officers of the fleet also received due recognition. He went to great extent to seek the proper recognition for a Captain Troubridge, whose ship ran aground during the battle. He wrote to the Admirality:

> It was Troubridge who equipped the squadron so soon at Syracuse; it was Troubridge who exerted himself for me after the action; it was Troubridge who saved the Culloden, [the grounded ship] where none I know in the service would have attempted it.[11]

In the Battle of the Nile, Nelson received another severe injury. A piece of shrapnel struck him on the head creating a large bruise and cutting a sizable area of skin, which fell down over his eyes leaving him temporarily blind from the profuse bleeding. For many months he suffered from severe headaches, and some speculate that he never fully recovered from this injury.[12]

After Nelson's defeat of the French fleet in the Nile, in 1798, his father wrote the following:

> My great and good son went into the world without fortune, but with a breast replete with every moral and religious virtue; these have been his compass to steer by, and it had pleased God to be his shield in the day of battle, and to give success to his wishes to be of service to his country. His country seems sensible of his service but should he ever meet with ingratitude, his scars will plead his cause; for at the siege of Bastia he lost an eye; at Teneriffe an arm, on the memorable 14th day of February he received a severe blow on his body, which he still feels; and now a wound on his head.[13]

When Nelson arrived in the port at Naples, Italy, after his decisive victory, the elderly Sir William Hamilton and his beautiful young wife, along with the King of Naples, boarded his ship and called him their "deliverer and preserver."[14] The Hamiltons lavishly entertained and doted over Nelson, especially Lady Hamilton. Nelson's relationship with Lady Hamilton became much like that of the Biblical characters of Sampson and Delilah. She sought Nelson's help on their behalf, who was greatly flattered, and in return he supported the Royal Family in any way he could, including using his force to return them to power.[15]

Nelson made some decisions of sad consequence at this time. His loyalty to the royalty of Naples at times began to supersede his patronage to his own king. Nelson felt himself bound to the King and Queen of Naples. Similarly, his intimacy with Lady Hamilton, a close companion to the Queen of Naples, led to his separation from his devoted wife. An old friend, Lord Minto, said that in fulfilling his stewardship of naval activities Nelson was unsurpassed; but in other aspects of life he was but a "baby."[16]

It was years before he returned to England. Once he returned, he was then sent by the Admiralty as second in command on an expedition to Denmark. The Scandinavian powers were threatening England. Arriving in Danish waters, he led an advance squadron against the Danish capital, and fought the desperate battle of Copenhagen. The battle at first looked bleak for the British, and his commanding officer ordered a retreat. But Nelson, putting the glass to his blind eye, claimed that he could not see the order and continued to fight. With those under his command he nearly destroyed the Danish line of defenses. At this point Nelson sent a message to the Danes seeking a cease-fire and surrender on their part. The message said in part: "The brave Danes are the brothers, and should never be enemies of the English."[17]

At length a treaty was concluded. This British victory established the maritime superiority of England. In 1803, Nelson received the command of the Mediterranean fleet. Once during the campaign, while Nelson's fleet was driven to sea by a storm, the French Admiral, Villanueve, was able to join his fleet to that of the Spanish. Nelson chased these combined fleets to the West Indies and back. Villanueve secured his ships in a protected area along the shore line near Trafalgar, Spain. Nelson hid some of his ships, and Villeneuve, thinking Nelson had inferior numbers, was drawn out of port. At once Nelson's fleet bore down in two columns, with Nelson leading one and Collingswood the other. An immortal part of British glory is said to be Nelson's concluding message to the fleet: "England expects every man will do his duty!"[18]

In a horrendous battle that lasted twenty-four hours, the French were defeated and Napoleon's navy was virtually annihilated. But England had bought its victory at a dear price, for the valiant warrior who brought Napoleon to a stan still, was dead. As he lay dying in his comrade's arms, his last words were: "I have done my duty, thank God for that"[19]

Lord Horatio Nelson, the greatest Naval hero England has ever seen, performed a miracle on behalf of England's safety as wonderful as the mighty storm that destroyed the Spanish Armada. It was Nelson who set the outer limits of Napoleon's conquest, stopping him at the crossroads to the East, in India, then defeating his move toward England and beyond. Nelson's final recorded prayer stated: "May the Great God, whom I adore, enable me to fulfill the expectations of my country."[20] Nelson's prayer was answered.

NOTES

[1] Oman, Carola. *Nelson.* Conn.: Greenwood Press, n.d., p. 7.

[2] Ibid., p. 9.

[3] See ibid., p. 10.

[4] Ibid., p. 10-11.

[5] See Warner Oliver: *Victory: The Life of Lord Nelson.* Boston: Little Brown, n.d., p. 17.

[6] Encyclopedia Britannica. 11th ed. 1911, 19:353.

[7] Stephen, Sir Leslie, and Sir Sidney Lee. *The Dictionary of National Biography.* London: Oxford University Press, 1960, 14:193.

[8] Spofford A.R., Weitenkampf Frank, and J. P. Lamberton. *The Library of Historic Characters and Famous Events of All Nations.* Boston: J. B. Millet, 1902 6:368.

[9] Warner, p. 128.

[10] Encyclopedia Britannica, 19:354.

[11] Duyckinck, Evert A. *Portrait Gallery of Eminent Men and Women* . New York: Henry J. Johnson, 1873, p. 386.

[12] Stephen and Lee, 14:197.

[13] Warner, Oliver, ed. *Nelson's Last Diary.* Ohio: Kent State University Press, 1971., p. 12.

[14] Stephen and Lee, p. 197.

[15] See Duyckinck, p. 386. See also Encyclopedia Britannica, 19:355, and Spofford, p. 369.

[16] Encyclopedia Britiannica, 19: 355.

[17] Duycknick, p. 390.

[18] Spofford , p. 371.

[19] Encyclopedia Britiannica, 19:357.

[20] Warner, p. 23.

Daniel O'Connell

IRISH STATESMAN

1775-1847

> "My political creed is short and simple.
> It consists in believing that all men are entitled
> to civil and religious liberty."

IRELAND HAD BEEN RULED AND OPPRESSED BY ENGLAND FOR SEVEN hundred years before Daniel O'Connell was born. Daniel O'Connell, the Irish "liberator," did for the Irish people what no other leader had been able to do for hundreds of years.

Much of the oppression centered in religious intolerance and persecution. A large portion of the population were denied the rights of citizenship because they belonged to the Roman Catholic Church. The Catholics were hated because the Irish Catholics had defended the Catholic King James ll of England, who, in 1690, fled to Ireland to take his last great stand against William of Orange (III) in the Battle of Boyne. The Irish Catholics and James were soundly defeated, and the Protestant Irish Parliament passed the penal laws, penalizing Catholics for their support of James.

The penal laws prohibited Catholics from being legal guardians to their own children. They could not attend school, nor could the clergy hold school. A Catholic could not buy property and could hold only a thirty-two year lease. No Catholic could own a horse worth more than five pounds. If he owned a better horse, a Protestant could pay him five pounds and take it. When a father died, the property had to be divided equally among his sons, usually making it useless to anyone. Priests were required to register with the law, and friars were banned from the country. The ultimate insult was that the Catholics had to pay a tithe to the Church of England. The law was carefully designed to eventually cause the ruin of the Catholic church in Ireland.

But the Catholic Church did not die out, in part, because some "honest" Irish Protestants, as O'Connell called them, ignored the law. Daniel O'Connell's own uncle, nicknamed "Hunting Cap," was able to obtain much property and many leases by using his Protestant cousin's name to make the purchases. He also operated a large smuggling trade, a trade that was allowed to flourish because the county officials wanted the smuggled products as badly as anyone else. They, along with all Irelanders, were deeply affected by the trade restrictions England applied in order to protect its maritime trade. Ireland was treated in much the same manner as the American Colonies were, but the results were worse in Ireland because of her limited resources. To some, Ireland was one vast slave plantation.

The people as a whole had become apathetic as nothing they did seemed to make a difference. Even the great efforts of John Curran and the fight for Catholic Emancipation by the Protestant, Henry Grattan, failed to arouse the people. The people felt their only recourse was to fight, and fight they did, staging small rebellions that were always followed by swift and terrible reprisals.

Tens of thousands of the more educated people fled Ireland. Many of those who left Ireland had great influence on the world. England reaped the contributions of Oliver Goldsmith and Edmund Burke. In America four signers of the Declaration of Independence were born in Ireland and four others were descendants of Irish parentage. Ireland, however, was left bereft of educated leaders.

In spite of Ireland's gloomy situation, God does not forsake a country in search of liberty; often he sends choice people to further the cause of liberty. Daniel O'Connell was one of those men. He was born in 1775, one year before America declared her independence and the same year that the great Irish statesman, Henry Grattan, became leader of the Patriots Party. Grattan campaigned continually on two issues—independence for Ireland from England as commonwealth state and the emancipation of Catholics. He was tireless in pursuit of religious freedom. Because of Gratttan's efforts, by the time O'Connell reached the age at which he should attend regular school, he was able to attend the first legal school operated by Catholics.

Soon after his birth, O'Connell was "put out to nurse" with a peasant family by the name of Moran. Some historians believe this practice was designed to "toughen up" the sons of gentry. Families of France did the same thing, sending babies by the thousands to the countryside to wet-nurse as it was not stylish to keep and nurse one's child, who was usually returned at about four years of age.

The Moran family was both poor and good. Rocked and cradled in the arms of his foster mother, O'Connell learned the songs and stories of Ireland in Gaelic. Playing on the dung-smeared floor with his foster brothers, he came to have an intimate feeling of their hopes and fears and loves and hatreds. He did not know he was of different class and thought he was one of them.

When he returned to his family at the age of four, he wore as all peasant small boys in Kerry did, a *caulac* or girl's dress. (This was because the peasants thought that fairies were jealous of small boys and sometimes stole them away.[1] O'Connell's father was appalled to see his son in a dress and promptly replaced it with a suit. A short time later, O'Connell had disappeared. He was found tramping through the rugged terrain back to his foster home, wearing his *caulac*. Years later he often spoke of his foster parents with fondness and referred to them as parents. He careed for them in their old age.

Shortly after his return to his family, O'Connell was adopted by his rich widower uncle, "Hunting Cap," Maurice O'Connell of Derrynane, who sent him to the new Catholic school at Queenstown. He often played alone and was unflinching in the face of danger. One day O'Connell was attacked by a savage bull. Instead of running away, O'Connell stood his ground and threw a stone in the bull's face. This gave him time to climb over a ditch to safety.

Beagling, or hunting rabbit, became his favorite sport. In Kerry the sport was done on foot because of the rugged terrain and steep mountainside. "It was an incredibly tough sport requiring tremendous strength of wind and limb to follow hounds uphill, and reckless courage in bounding down after them in great leaps, like a boulder falling down the mountain, trusting to luck that one would land on sound ground and not on a stone or in a hole with a broken ankle."[2]

Another one of O'Connell's uncles was a colonel in the French army and persuaded "Hunting Cap" to send O'Connell and his brother Maurice to France to further their education. Because it was illegal for Catholic children to go abroad for schooling, O'Connell and his brother had to be smuggled aboard ship. Just one year later the Catholic Relief Bill of 1792 was passed, permitting Catholics some privileges, including the right to travel abroad.

The boys were enrolled in Saint-Omer, a Jesuit school. After some time "Hunting Cap" became concerned about whether he was getting his money's worth from the school. He wrote to the president, Dr. Stapleton, asking how the boys were doing. O'Connell's brother Maurice was commended with some qualifications, but of Daniel he wrote: "With respect to the elder, Daniel, I have but one sentence to write about him and that is, that I never was so much mistaken in my life as I shall be, unless he is destined to make a remarkable figure in society."[3]

Even though the boys were very happy at St. Omer's, the colonel insisted that the boys be transferred to Douay, another Jesuit school. However, the boys' stay at Douay was cut short by the rapid developments of the French Revolution. The boys received notice to return home and after some difficult delays and threats, they left on the same day that King Louis XVI was beheaded. They proceeded on their way with great difficulty. The mob rule of the French Revolution left a deep impression on O'Connell. The terror of mobocracy and the tyranny of rebellion and reprisals that he saw in his own land led him to be an advocate of change by peaceful means. The revolutions he led would not be accomplished with blood, but with the "moral force of public opinion."

Returning to Ireland, O'Connell was able to take advantage of another reform. For the first time Catholics were permitted to study to become lawyers. O'Connell entered law school. An incident that occurred while he was a student is indicative of his sense of helping others, although in this particular instance his help was less than helpful. One night O'Connell had an extra amount of Claret, a cheap Irish drink. He returned home late and saw a fire. The workmen were trying to get the water pipe opened. O'Connell, wanting to help, took up a pick and and broke open the valve.

Fired by honest zeal, he kept working away ... until he had

dug up half the street. A militia patrol arrived, but was unable to persuade him to desist from his excavations. 'I was rather an unruly customer,' he admitted, 'and one of the soldiers ran a bayonet at me which was intercepted by the cover of my hunting-watch. If I had not had the watch it would have been the end of the great Irish "Liberator"[4]

In O'Connell's day it was a strict tradition that marriages be arranged, usually to a material advantage. Uncle "Hunting Cap," at the close of O'Connell's law school began to actively make a match for his nephew. But O'Connell had other ideas. When his good friend introduced him to his sister-in-law, Mary O'Connell, Daniel's own distant cousin, he fell in love at first sight. Almost forty years later O'Connell described their engagement as follows:

> I said to her, "Are you engaged, Miss O'Connell?" She answered, "I am not." 'Then,' said I, "will you engage yourself to me?" "I will," was her reply. And I said I would devote my life to make her happy. She deserved that I should, she gave me thirty-four years of the purest happiness that man ever enjoyed.[5]

The marriage took place quietly for fear Uncle "Hunting Cap" would find out. But the marriage could not be hidden for long. Soon Mary became pregnant and "Hunting Cap" had to be told. In a flood of tears and rage, "Hunting Cap" disinherited O'Connell on the spot. But as O'Connell's fame grew, "Hunting Cap" softened and eventually restored O'Connell's inheritance. The marriage of Daniel and Mary was a good one, and she became a great source of his strength. Mary brought O'Connell to a spiritual depth that he had been lacking. Had it not been for his marriage to Mary he could never have been the great liberator of Ireland.

Mary bore O'Connell ten children, seven of whom lived. O'Connell was a good husband and a kind father. Mary encouraged him in his work. When O'Connell was in the English Parliament, his opponents attempted to "bribe" him to leave Parliament, promising him knighthood and peerage. But he refused. Mary wrote in response to his decision: "Thank God you have acted like yourself, and your wife and children have more reason to be proud of you now than they ever were.... You now stand firmly on the affections and on the love of your countrymen."[6]

With O'Connell's spiritual awakening came a deep desire to liberate his people, particularly from their own apathy. He was determined to take action against tyranny by staying within the law and using peaceful means. He knew the masses could have great power if they arose in unison to demand change. He appealed to the structure of the church to make contact with the people. The church responded by creating an association to work together for a common cause. Because it was unlawful for Catholics to gather in large meetings, O'Connell brought them together for suppers as it was not illegal to get together to eat. At these suppers, O'Connell rallied the people, and they began to speak with one voice.

O'Connell ran for Parliament and won, the first Catholic to sit in Parliament. The "Association" behind O'Connell had grown to nearly a million Irishmen, and as they pressed for demands, O'Connell won support in Parliament for many changes. Parliament passed O'Connell's reform bill, making life more tolerable in Ireland and also leaving the English in O'Connell's debt.[7]

O'Connell pushed for Irish independence, creating an Irish Parliament that was loyal to the King. In one of his speeches he said: "I demand, I respectfully insist on equal justice for Ireland, on the same principle by which it has been administered to Scotland and England. I will not take less. Refuse me that if you can."[8] He held rallies called "monster meetings" so large were the crowds. He traveled to every corner of Ireland, arousing the people by his impassioned oratory. His voice was so powerful that one could hear him a mile off, and it flowed as if it were coming through honey. It could be heard even by the vast multitude (said to number three-quarters of a million people) gathered at the ancient site of the Hill of Tara on 15 August 1843. These gatherings remained peaceful, through the sheer strength of O'Connell's personality, which restrained them from bursting forth in revolution.

The government officials understood O'Connell's position and eventually outlawed monster meetings and arrested and imprisoned O'Connell and his son. An appeal was immediately sought and granted after three months. This incident endeared the people even more to O'Connell. In his later years O'Connell planned for a very large meeting, and the law declared it illegal. O'Connell, abiding by his own rules, obeyed the order, an incident which increased O'Connell's popularity as a leader.

O'Connell devoted a lifetime of service to his country. He also linked the constitutional movement of Henry Grattan and Protestant patriots to the emancipated Catholics. In a few short years his dream of an independent Ireland would come true. Daniel O'Connell was a liberator, an emancipator, who "found the Irish peasants slaves and left them men."[9]

NOTES

[1] Trench, Charles Chenevix. *The Great Dan: A Biography of Daniel O' Connell.* London: Jonathan Cape, p. 13.

[2] Trench, p. 16.

[3] Duyckinck, Evert A. *Portrait Gallery of Eminent Men and Women.* New York: H. J. Johnson, 1873, p. 6.

[4] Trench, p. 51.

[5] Macdonagh, Oliver. *The Hereditary Bondsman Daniel O'Connell 1775-1829.* New York: St. Martin's Press, 1987, p. 71.

[6] Macdonagh, Oliver. *The Emancipist Daniel O'Connell, 1830-1847.* New York: St. Martin's Press, 1989, p. 43.

[7] See Duyckinck, p. 10.

[8] Copeland, Lewis, ed. *The World's Great Speeches.* New York: Dover Publication, 1958, p. 214.

[9] McCarthy, Joe. *Ireland.* New York: Time, Inc. 1964, p. 13.

George Peabody *1795-1869*

AMERICAN PHILANTHROPIST

> *"What I spent I had; what I kept I lost;*
> *what I gave away remains with me."*

THE UNITED STATES, FROM ITS EARLIEST BEGINNING, HAS BEEN rescued by men of wealth whose patriotic devotion has saved the country from certain financial ruin. During the Revolutionary War, financier and signer of the Declaration of Independence, Robert Morris, borrowed money on his own credit and continued the difficult task of managing finances throughout the war. The financial confidence of America during the War of 1812 was sustained by Stephen Gerard, an American financier who purchased much of the depreciated stock of the Bank of the United States in London, thereby bolstering confidence. In the dark days of the panic of 1837, George Peabody, an American merchant living in London, used his wealth to sustain the United States.

The country was in desperate financial straits, and the nation itself was near disgrace. Money was desperately needed but credit for the government was nowhere to be found. It had no funds to borrow at home and no foreign source was willing to give a loan under such dire circumstances. Peabody showed faith in his country by buying American bonds, even though he suffered a loss by doing so. His example was contagious and established confidence in the credibility of the bonds. When the crisis passed, the government wanted to honor Peabody for his valuable services, but he declined to accept any recognition. Peabody continued to transfer his business concerns to England, where he prospered exceedingly and grew very rich. Leaving his merchandise business he established the banking house of Peabody and Company.[1]

George Peabody was born in the south parish of Danvers, Massachusetts 18 February 1795. He was able to attend school only until he was eleven years old, when he went to work in a grocery store. The store owner was a kindly gentleman by the name of Proctor, who treated him with much parental kindness and direction. Peabody wrote of these early years:

> It was ... in a very humble house, in the south parish, that I was born, and from the common schools of that parish, such as they were in 1803 to 1807, I obtained the limited education my parents' means could afford; but to the principles there inculcated in childhood and early youth, I owe much of the foundations for such success as Heaven has been pleased to grant me during a long business life.[2]

Early on in his life two indispensable qualities began to stand out in his work habits: integrity and perseverance. When he first went to work, his employer, Mr. Proctor, often bragged about a former employee who could in one day make six dozen leather whips. Peabody, a young boy of tremendous drive and perseverance, secretly desired to compete with the former employee's record. One day when Mr. Proctor was gone, Peabody set to work and wove a large pile of eight dozen ropes. These he proudly displayed to his astonished employer upon his return.

During his tenth year, Peabody lived with his grandparents, who lived in Vermont. During his visit, his grandfather desired to have a hillside cleared, which was overgrown with Sumac trees. This hillside included many acres, and the trees numbered some hundreds. George undertook to cut them down, and his grandfather gave him a week for the task. George sallied forth one morning, axe in hand, and by the evening of the same day the task was accomplished. The sun went down, and left not a Sumac standing to exult over its fallen companions.[3] Another incident involved his collecting a bad debt for his grandfather by repeated appeals to the incorrigible debtor.

Peabody was employed in a dry goods store of his eldest brother. This employment was soon brought to an end by a devastating fire that caused the loss of the business by his brother. These were difficult times for merchants for England had placed embargoes on America and raided any ships she could find that carried supplies for her ports. These actions led to the War of 1812.

For some years Peabody worked at any position he could find. His father died when he was seventeen, so George left his native state in the company of his bankrupt uncle, hoping to better his lot elsewhere. They sailed by ship to the District of Columbia. Because of the uncle's previous bankruptcy, young Peabody's name was signed to all transactions. He was sharp enough to see one thing: business conducted in this manner left him in danger of being held responsible for all his uncle's debts. He thought it wise to change his occupation and not have his name used carelessly.

Soon after his arrival in Washington, D. C., the U.S. declared war on England. Young Peabody volunteered in an artillery company. He served at Fort Warburton on the Potomac. One of his companions while on duty was Francis Scott Key, the author of the U. S. national anthem, "The Stars Spangled Banner."[4]

The war over, the nineteen-year-old-Peabody obtained employment with a Mr. Riggs of Baltimore. Here he managed a dry goods store. Mr. Riggs had observed the young man and knew that in spite of his youth, George was a wise investment. "The boy was alert and careful in business, with sound judgment, knowing when to make a deal and when to avoid one, when to spend and when to save. He had abundance of energy, he was industrious, honest, courteous, and had no bad habits."[5]

Peabody proved worthy of his trust and soon the enterprise became Riggs and Peabody. Their business spread to the cities of Philadelphia and New York. The partnership lasted for fifteen years at which time Mr. Riggs retired from the company. The business had prospered under Peabody's wise management and when Mr. Riggs left, they had both achieved considerable wealth. Peabody became the senior partner and Mr. Riggs' nephew, the junior officer. The company now became know as Peabody, Riggs and Co.

Peabody traveled the coast extensively in his business dealings. He worked many long hours and industry and integrity as always seemed to be his strongest assets. In 1827, he visited England for the first time and established many sound business contacts. Then in 1837, Peabody retired from the firm of Peabody, Riggs and Co. and sensing new and growing business opportunities took up his permanent residence in England.

He became a noted merchant, exchanging goods between America and England. Money was made at both ends and Peabody's customers often left large sums of money with him in order to do future business. This practice eventually led to his going into the banking business. His bank was named simply George Peabody & Co. and dealt mainly in American securities. Through this banking establishment he became one of the richest men of his time. His bank was looked upon as one of the strongest in London and great amounts of money passed through its daily operations.

In spite of his great wealth, Mr. Peabody was a man of very modest ways. He dressed plainly, he was courteous and generous of heart. Having never married, he lived in an ordinary bachelor's apartment. Giving was early a part of his life. While yet a youth, he gave part of each pay check to support his mother and sister. In 1848, he helped the State of Maryland negotiate an important loan, which enabled the state to avoid an embarrassing financial situation.

On 4 July 1851, Peabody performed one of the greatest services a son of the republic and a grandson of Mother England could have rendered. He invited all the notables of England and the visitors from America to a grand celebration. The best entertainment was engaged at Peabody's own expense. The large hall was appropriately decorated with flags of the two great countries and portraits of Queen Victoria and of Washington. Among the guests was the Duke of Wellington. This event was referred to as the marking of a new era in the feelings between England and America. For many years thereafter Peabody held grand celebrations on the fourth of July.

About this time the World's fair was being held in London with emphasis on inventions and products. Congress did not have the funds to support an American exhibit. Peabody supplied the necessary contacts and money for the Americans to show their talents. This was the first occasion that the world was able to see the great things America could do, and Peabody gave her that opportunity. This World's Fair was acclaimed for heralding a new era of universal peace.

In 1852, Peabody's hometown of Danvers celebrated its centennial anniversary. Its most distinguished son, Peabody, was invited. Because he was unable to attend the celebrations Peabody wrote a gracious letter of thanks and then enclosed a donation of $20,000 dollars with an additional $50,000 dollars to come. This money was to be used exclusively by his request "for the promotion of knowledge and morality."[6] Eventually he gave this fund $200,000.

Peabody was wise enough to know that just giving money to the needy could lead to more harm than good. When he gave, he wisely stipulated how the money given was to be used. For instance, noting conditions of squalor that the poor of London lived in, he granted $2,500,000 for the tenant housing for these working poor.[7] Queen Victoria offered him a title of nobility for his generosity but Peabody turned down the offer. In his letter of response he wrote: "I have been actuated by a deep sense of gratitude to God, who has blessed me with prosperity."[8] He gave ten thousand dollars for an expedition to the Arctic Seas in search of Sir John Franklin who had failed to return. He gave $1,500,000 to found the Peabody Institute at Baltimore, which provided a free library, an academy of music, and an art gallery. Another $3,500,000 went to the South to help promote education after the devastation of the Civil War. In giving to the South he stated:

> With my advancing years my attachment to my native land has but become more devoted. My hope and faith in its successful and glorious future have grown brighter and stronger and now, looking forward beyond my stay on earth,... I see our country united and prosperous, emerging from the clouds which still surround her, taking a higher rank among the nations, and becoming richer and more powerful than ever before.... Her moral and mental development should keep pace with her material growth.[9]

He gave funds to the building of a memorial Congregational Church, as a tribute to his dear mother. In a grant to Phillips Academy he wrote to this institution: "Phillips Academy, which I am informed and believe, seeks to give ... not only the highest mental discipline ... but such a general training in manly virtues and in Christian morality and piety as all good men should approve ... I trust will ever remain, free from all sectarian influence."[10]

When the conductor of an English train overcharged him on purpose, he reported him and had the man discharged. "It was not that I could not afford to pay the shilling," he explained, "but the man was cheating many travelers to whom swindle would be oppressive."[11]

Peabody did not save his money to be divided upon his death; he gave it away during his lifetime. His acts of generosity are reflected in all that is great in America today. He sought to give dignity and restore hope through his wealth.

George Peabody died 4 November 1869. His body was laid in state in Westminster Abbey, and then was brought to America on a British royal man-of-war. Americans received their native son with highest respect and buried him with national honors.

NOTES

[1] See Encyclopedia Americana. 1949, 21: 438.

[2] See Duyckinck, Evert A. *Portrait Gallery of Eminent Men and Women.* New York: . J. Johnson, 1873, p. 291.

[3] See ibid., p. 292.

[4] See ibid., p. 293.

[5] Morris Charles. *Heroes of Progress in America.*   Philadelphia: Lippincott, 1919, p . 247.

[6] Duyckinck, p. 299.

[7] *Concise Dictionary of American Biography.* New York: Scribner & Son, n..d, p. 775.

[8] Duyckinck , p. 299.

[9] Ibid., p. 300.

[10] Ibid., p. 299.

[11] Morris, p.252.

Hiram Powers   *1805-1873*

AMERICAN SCULPTOR

> *"There should be a moral in every work of art."*

Hiram Powers was perhaps the most famous American sculptor of his day. After viewing some of Powers' works, John Quincy Adams wrote the poem entitled "To Hiram Powers":

"Sculptor! thy hand hath moulded into form
The haggard features of a time-worn face
And whosoever view thy work shall trace
An age of sorrow, and a life of storm!
Artist! May fortune smile upon thy hand!
Go forth, and rival Greece's art sublime;
Return, and bid the statesmen of the land
Live in the marble through all after-time!
O, snatch from heaven the fire Prometheus stole,
And give the sculptured block a living soul!"[1]

At the beginning of the nineteenth century, the great Italian sculptor, Antonio Canova, was the man most responsible for returning sculpture to the standard from which it had declined in both classical beauty and moderation.[2] The era of Canova, Thomas Jefferson is reported to have said, was without rival. The acknowledged heir to Canova's classical crown, Hiram Powers ushered in the neoclassical period. The great Danish sculptor Thorvaldsen said, "The entrance of Powers upon the field constituted a [new] era in art."[3] Powers became the first American artist to achieve international recognition and because of his reputation, he did much for elevating the artistic education of his countrymen.

Hyrum Powers was born at Woodstock, Vermont, 29 July, 1805. He was the last of eight children. The family was frugal, hardworking, and affectionate. Powers accounted it as a special blessing of his childhood to have been reared by honest and harmonious parents. The family struggled for existence on a poor farm, Hyrum's father signed a note for a friend who defaulted causing him to lose what little property they possessed. The family had to leave beautiful Vermont and move to Cincinnati. Powers' expressions about his childhood show that he held dear his recollections of Woodstock.

He wrote:

> Dreams often take me back to Woodstock and set me down upon the green hills, the rocks or up to the knees in [the] Queechy. The dear old church bell is ringing in the distance and the smell of orchards greets me. I shall never forget the morning I left. I sat in the hind end of the wagon and watched the village as it faded away ... When I looked backed on the church spire shooting up into the clear morning sky, and gazed on the hilltops I had wandered over for the last time, and the pure river, whose banks I should tread no more, I turned away my head and wept alone.[4]

Members of the family were often sick because of the swampy land on which they settled. Soon after the family arrived in Ohio the father became sick and died.

Hiram was sixteen years old when he left home. His total schooling amounted to about four years. He obtained a job in a hotel taking care of the newspapers in the reading room. Here he became an avid reader. His pay consisted only of room and board, but he was grateful to have food to eat. When his only set of clothes began to rot off his back, he found a paying job in a grocery store In his spare time he made models of animals and monsters in butter.

He soon became an apprentice in a clock and organ factory. He grew so knowledgeable about the factory machinery that he was able to improve its efficiency. He soon surpassed most of the other workers in talent and skill. Later he found a job in a museum where he used his talents in the repair and fabrication of wax figures. His genius began to show when he designed a mechanical organ that had life-sized figures which moved, sounded trumpets, and rang bells.

This innovation brought him to the attention of a noted English lady, Mrs. Frances Trollope, who was visiting Cincinnati. Together they designed for the museum a scene that was reminiscent of Dante's hell. They called it "The infernal Regions." The exhibit included smoke, lightening, clanging of chains, and other frightening sounds. He designed stalactites and stalagmites in a dark grotto. Wax figures that could be moved by a string were set up. He succeeded so well that he ended up inventing a whole series of automations. The museum became so popular that people had to stand in long lines in order to get in.

Powers remained at this job for seven years. During this time he met Elizabeth Gibson, who was to be the perfect companion for this budding artist. They married and she managed their household affairs in such a manner that the family never wanted.

Soon after his marriage Powers began to discover his real expertise. He had an opportunity to visit the studio of a German sculptor, where he saw for the first time a marble bust. He was fascinated and excited by it and asked many questions which gave him some general ideas about sculpturing. He borrowed a lump of clay and began to experiment. It was not long before he began taking orders for busts.

One of the orders came from a wealthy man named Nicholas Longworth. Longworth had ardently believed that the United States needed artists, particularly sculptors. He provided financial assistance for Powers to go to Washington, D. C., supplying him with letters of introduction to some of the leading men of the time. In time Powers created busts of a number of the most eminent men of the period—Chief Justice Marshall, Daniel Webster, John C. Calhoun, and even President Jackson. When the President came for his "sitting," he warned Powers to "make me as I am, Mr. Powers, and be true to nature always, and in everything. It's the only safe rule to follow."[5] The result was an exacting work in realism.

Powers realized that in his country he had progressed as far as he could, for America had yet to produce its own masters. With a loan from another wealthy businessman, John Smith Preston, he traveled to Italy to study. He was accompanied by his wife and two little children. Smallpox broke out on board ship, and Mrs. Powers came down with the disease. They stopped over in Paris for her to convalesce. Powers used this opportunity to visit the Louvre and other museums.

When the family arrived in Florence they were welcomed by another American sculptor, Horatio Greenough, who helped them get settled. Powers found a studio and began filling orders, mainly for busts of prominent Americans. These sculpture/portraits were dominated by a strong "naturalism." During this time he produced some 150 portrait busts.

After a few years in Italy, the great Thorvaldsen visited Powers' studio and remarked that the bust of Daniel Webster was the finest example of its type. Powers had just completed his ideal statue, a representation of Eve, and Thorvaldsen stopped momentarily in front of it Powers began to apologize, stating that it was his first full statue. But the noble old sculptor would not let him proceed with his apologies and gently said, "Any man might be proud of it as his last."[6]

When Mrs. Trollope, Powers' early mentor visited Powers at his studio, she discovered her protege struggling to advance his craft as he could not afford marble to carve the ideal figures he had been trying to do in his spare time. In time, however, Powers' reputation would grove and he would be able to accumulate enough money to carve his famous statue, *The Greek Slave.*

It has been said that *The Greek Slave* was the best-known American work of the mid-century and quite possibly the entire century.[7] Its first exhibition was at the 1845 World's Fair in the Crystal Palace in London. It had enormous impact on all classes of people. Two years later it toured the United States. For the first time one of America's own sons culturally affected the nation through "high art."

This particular statue reached into the very fiber of American life and thought. It touched deeply sensitive areas such as the role of women, attitudes towards sexuality, and growing feelings over the slavery issue. Powers described the moral of his *Greek Slave,* noting the Greek War for Independence had been over for about ten years, when he made his statute.

The Slave has been taken from one of the Greek islands by the Turks. Her father and mother, and perhaps all her kindred, have been destroyed by her foes, and she alone preserved as a treasure too valuable to be thrown away. She is now among barbarian strangers, under the pressure of a full recollection of the calamitous events which have brought her to her present state; and she stands exposed, [stripped of her clothes and possessions], to the gaze on the people she abhors, and awaits her fate with intense anxiety, tempered indeed by the support of her reliance upon the goodness of God. Gather all the afflictions together, and add to them the fortitude and resignation of a Christian, and no room will be left for shame. Such are the circumstances under which the Greek slave is supposed to stand.[8]

Powers further commented:

I hold that artists should do honor to their own times and their own religion instead of going back to mythology to illustrate, for the thousandth time, the incongruous absurdities and inconsistencies of idolatrous times, especially as our times and our religion are full of subjects equal in beauty, and have all the qualities necessary to a full development of art.[9]

He accomplished this ideal with *The Greek Slave* and other statues that followed. "It is an error to suppose that features are accidental [Powers said] and nature makes them up at haphazard; for the face is the true index of the soul, where everything is written had we the wisdom to read it."[10]

In 1839, Italy's Bartolini pronounced Powers the greatest portrait sculptor then living.[11] Although Powers remained in Italy and eventually died there, he was a patriotic and loyal son to the land of his birth. The son of a common American farmer, he gave to his homeland the virtues of art that lifts civilization.

Authors Note: Because our modern culture often tantalizes us with nudity, it is difficult today to distinguish between a great work of art representing the beauty of creation and the abomination of pornography. Dr. Arthur Henry King helps us with a simple rule of thumb. He writes: "To tell the difference, we need always to ask ourselves whether a picture enables us worshipfully to enjoy the wonder of creation or simply arouses lust. A completely unclothed figure may produce a feeling of reverence, while a partly clothed figure in a glossy magazine may be provocative or inane."[12]

NOTES

[1] Gardner, Albert TenEyck. *Yankee Stone Cutters.* New York: Columbia University Press, 1945, p. 1. Published for the Metropolitan Museum of Art, New York.

[2] See Lynes Russell. *The Art Makers.* New York: Atheneum, 1970, p. 145.

[3] Gardner, p. 5.

[4] Wunder, Richard. *Hiram Powers, Vermont Sculptor.* Vermont: The Countryman Press, 1974, p. 8.

[5] Ibid., p.12

[6] Duyckinck, Evert A. *Portrait Gallery of Eminent Men and Women.* New York: Henry J. Johnson, 1873 p. 527.

[7] Lynes, p. 140

[8] Thorp, Margaret Farrand. *The Literary Sculptors.* Durham, N. C.: Duke University Press, 1965, p. 117-18.

[9] Gardner, p.5.

[10] Ibid., p. 30.

[11] Craven Wayne. *Sculpture in America.* New York: Thomas Y. Crowell, 1834, p. 114.

[12] King, Arthur Henry. *The Abundance of the Heart.* Salt Lake City, Utah: Bookcraft, 1986, p. 212-16.

Sir Joshua Reynolds

ENGLISH PAINTER

1723-1792

"What we now call Genius, begins, not where rules, abstractly taken end, but where known vulgar and trite rules have no longer any place"

Notwithstanding the great achievements in literature through the 1700s, the arts in England in general had fallen to their lowest state. The tradition of Puritanism confused beautiful art with sensual art, thereby inhibiting the development of new talent. "The Puritan Reformation brought to England and Scotland a wave of intolerance, intense and bitter beyond even the developments in Germany and Holland. The rich medieval arts of Britain, painting, sculpture, and ornamentation, which had survived through the days of the Tudors and the Stuarts, were wiped out in a stroke. In the 1600's, English Parliament mandated the destruction of much artwork. A single entry in the records of 1643 states: we brake down 1000 pictures superstitious.'"[1] It was into this artistic climate that Sir Joshua Reynolds was born.

Joshua Reynolds was born in 1723. He was the son of the Reverend Samuel Reynolds and Theophila Potter, the seventh of eleven children. His father was a master of a grammar school but for some reason lost that position. Joshua became his only pupil, and he studied under his father's tutelage until he was seventeen. Although his father instructed him in the classics, Joshua gave no sign of classical interest. However, in his later years, after studious application, he became eminently distinguished as a classical scholar.

Young Joshua did not display any extraordinary skills, but was known from childhood to make little sketches. One day, when Joshua was about twelve, while listening to Reverend Smarts' sermon, Joshua made a sketch of the Reverend. Taking the sketch he proceeded to a boathouse, and there using sail canvas and marine paint, he painted his first portrait (still in existence today.) His father/schoolmaster once discovered his son's Latin exercise book elaborately "doodled," and wrote, commenting in the margin, "This is drawn by Joshua in school out of sheer idleness."[2] As the years continued Reynolds filled his leisure hours with his pencil.

Reynolds' father had set his mind on medicine as a career for his promising son and was about to apprentice him to the local apothecary. However, Reynolds' "genius for drawing" persuaded the father in the interest of his son to change his plans.

Hudson, a portrait artist of the time, came to pay a visit to a Mr. Cutliffe, a friend of Reynolds' father. Reynolds' father prevailed upon Mr. Cutcliffe to show Joshua's drawings to Hudson to ascertain if he would consider the lad for a pupil. "Everything jumped out in a strange, unexpected manner to a miracle,"[3] and he was accepted as an apprentice. Half of the tuition was paid by the good reverend and half was a loan by a kindly sister.

When Joshua first arrived in London, painting was mechanical. "The art," he said, "was at the lowest ebb: it could not indeed be lower."[4] Although Hudson's instructions were barely adequate, Joshua did not seem to care. He wrote his father saying, "While I am doing this [art] I am the happiest creature alive."[5] After two years of instruction, Joshua painted a portrait of an elderly lady with such artistic superiority that it aroused the jealousy of his master. They soon parted ways, for in truth such teachers as Hudson could teach Reynolds nothing further.

Reynolds spent the next few years in and around London, painting to make a living. When Reynolds was released from the "mechanical" productions of Hudson, he turned to paint nature with a new breath of life. In a rare twist of fate, Reynolds came in contact with "Commodore Keppel." Reynolds painted the commodore's portrait, which turned out to be the best he had ever done, and the two men became good friends. Keppel invited Reynolds to accompany him to the Mediterranean. Reynolds debarked from Keppel's ship at the Island Minorca, having painted enough portraits to finance his pilgrimage to Italy. He had long desired to study the great masters in Italy, for he felt that Italy was the mother and nurse of the arts.

Arriving in Rome, he was at last able to see the fine works of Raphael, and to his mortification he was unable to appreciate them. He began to see that the art of the great masters was not to be understood immediately, and that it took great study and time to fully perceive the profundity of their works. He later remarked, "Notwithstanding my disappointment ... I viewed them again and again; I even affected to feel their merits, and to admire them more than I really did. In a short time a new taste and new perceptions began to dawn upon me, and I was convinced that I had originally formed a false opinion of the perfection of art."6 Reynolds was especially inspired by the works of Michelangelo." I was let into the Capella Sistina in the morning," he states in his notebook, "and remained there the whole day."7 He spent a great amount time in the Vatican. Due to the dampness there he caught a cold that left him partially deaf the rest of his life.

One of Reynold's students later found a writing by Reynolds titled, "The Dream of a Painter." In the narration Reynolds told of having spent a day studying in the Vatican. He stopped to rest not realizing the lateness of the hour. "I was so entirely absorbed in thought," he wrote, "that whether I really slept or seemed to sleep, I will not determine; but me thought a form like that of an angel approached, and addressing me with mild air, said, 'You have enlisted under the banner of the arts, fine arts you call them, a noble and a bold resolution, where labor and study may be rewarded with immortality.'"8 Reynolds was taken on a tour by the angelic visitor. The description he gives of the vision is like Isaiah in style. The lives of the early masters of art were shown to him. (The whole of the vision cannot be related here, but interesting highlights will be attempted).

Leonardo da Vinci, with his patron, Francis the First of France, were presented to Reynolds. Leonardo was surrounded by ingenious contrivances which he himself designed. Reynolds angelic guide pointed out that Da Vinci had been "endowed with an ample capacity to embrace the whole circle of the sciences."9

The next scene approached with such majesty and brightness that Reynolds stated: "Its glory was too powerful to be viewed without pain, and turning from it to relieve my aching sight, I saw it no more." "You have had this transient view of Michelangelo Buonarotti," said his guide.[10]

Among other great artists shown to Reynolds in this vision were Raphael, from whom beauties instantly sprang and the orphaned Pierino del Vaga, who was placed in Raphael's care. Titian passed with Pordenone, the Bassanos, Girolamo, Mutiano, Giacomo, Palma and other artists bearing the train of his robe. Titian was also accompanied by Tintoretto and Paul Veronese. Preceding them went Bellino and Georgione, both bearing a light in each hand so luminous that the whole group shone with splendor. The vision followed with the unfortunate Correggio, Annibal and the disgrace of Guido Reni, Frederico Baroccio, Claude Gelee of Lorrain, Nicolo Poussin, Salvator Rosa, Vandervelde, and the duo Chevalier Adrian Bander Welf and Balthasar Denner. The strengths and weaknesses of each artist were revealed to Reynolds in this vision.

The last artist he saw had no name given, but his guide told him that this artist was an Englishman. Reynolds observed that this artist's

> manner at once distinguished him as a man of refined mind, his carriage was unassuming, gentle, and simple to the utmost degree; he appeared to be untouched by vanity, although attended by a great company of grave philosophers, divines, and poets, who all paid him homage, which he received with the humility and simplicity of a child.[11]

In his narration Reynolds did not attempt to name the artist either, however, reviewing Reynolds' life, it is obvious that the last artist was Reynolds himself. In his later years he lived to fulfill all the virtues extolled by the angel. His contemporaries confirmed these virtues. Dr. Samuel Johnson said of Reynolds, "There goes a man not to be spoiled by prosperity." Edmund Burke recorded of Reynolds that, "his native humility, modesty, and candor never forsook him."[12]

When Reynolds returned to England, he immediately made a name for himself by painting portraits. This he did in a "novel, simple and natural, yet so dignified" manner.[13] His master talent was painting the qualities of the sitter. This was particularly true of his portraitures of women. Reynolds often said that a writer has an entire book to tell his story, but an artist has but one page. He was intent on that one page, expressing the finest qualities of the individual being painted. It has been said that a painter cannot make his hero talk like a great man. He must make him look like a great man. Reynolds' portraits could be studied to help us understand what constitutes "dignity of appearance" in real life. "Polite behavior," he wrote, "and a refined address, like good pictures make the least show to ordinary eyes."[14]

Time has a way of savoring that which is most enduring. Reynolds great contribution to the world was not only in his actual paintings, even though he was the leading portrait artist of his day, but also in his contribution in promoting the dignity of art.

Because of his influence artists of the time began joining together for art exhibitions. These exhibitions eventually led to King George III, in 1765, granting a royal charter. By 1768, this organization became known as the Royal Academy. Reynolds, by acclamation, was elected its first president, a position he held for over twenty years. It was on the occasion of his first election that Reynolds was knighted. It was not only providential that the Academy came into being at this time because of the number of excellent artists (Gainsborough, Romney, etc.), but also because Reynolds felt a need to begin a repository for great examples of art. "These," he said of the collection of great art "are the materials on which genius is to work"[15] The Royal Academy exists today. It is world famous for its promotions of meritorious arts.

As part of his role as president of the academy, Reynolds annually addressed its members. These now famous discourses alone would have entitled him to literary fame. They were seen as the highlight of the season. In a land long starved for the uplifting touch of refining arts, these discourses were like manna from heaven.

These discourses were so eloquent that it has been said that they were written by the literary giant of the time, Samuel Johnson. However, Johnson was as ignorant of art as was the rest of England, so the plagiarism charge fell idle. In fact Johnson desired so much to have Reynolds as an acquaintance that he sat on Reynold's doorstep on three different occasions, trying to gain an audience with the great painter. Reynolds soon relented and there quickly developed a deep and abiding friendship. This friendship had a substantial effect upon England, and even today is looked upon as one of the cornerstones of English history.

Reynolds could recognize greatness wherever it was found, and he suggested that Dr. Johnson form the famous literary club. This club operated for more than half a century and its members were many of the most celebrated personalities of the late 1700s. To this club came the great tragedian actors Garrick and Kemble, the historian Gibbon, the great writer of comedy, Goldsmith, and others.

Reynolds was as great in character as he was in painting. Once his servant was mistakenly arrested and held overnight. Upon his return to Reynolds, the servant told him of a poor soul being held awaiting his death sentence. Reynolds promptly dispatched another servant, named Kirkly, to make inquiries.

He was soon admitted to the cell of the prisoner, where he beheld the most wretched spectacle that imagination can conceive—a poor forlorn criminal, without a friend on earth who could relieve or assist him, and reduced almost to a skeleton by famine and by filth, waiting till the dreadful morning should arrive when he was to be made an end of by violent death. Sir Joshua now ordered fresh clothing to be sent to him, and also that the servant should carry to him every day a sufficient supply of food from his own table."[16]

Another incident demonstrates Reynold's integrity. In a letter written to Dr. Beattie, he said:

I sit down to relieve my mind from great anxiety and uneasiness, and I am sorry when I say, that this proceeds from not answering your letter sooner. This seems very strange, you will say, since the cause may be so easily removed; but the truth of the matter is, I waited to be able to inform you, that your picture was finished, which, however, I cannot now do. I must confess to you, that when I sat down, I did intend to tell a sort of a white lie, that it was finished; but on recollecting that I was writing to the author of truth, about a picture of truth, I felt that I ought to say nothing but the truth. The truth then is, that the picture probably will be finished before you receive this letter; for there is not above a day's work remaining to be done.[17]

The painting was completed and delivered as promised.

When the famous author, Goldsmith, first published his poem "Deserted Village" he dedicated it to his friend Sir Joshua Reynolds. Goldsmith observed: "The only dedication I ever made was to my brother, because I loved him better than most other men. He is since dead. Permit me to inscribe this Poem to you ."[18]

In 1784, Sir Joshua displayed a new landmark of paintings. Of all his paintings the most famous and enduring was a portrait of Mrs. Sarah Siddons as *The Tragic Muse*. A contemporary wrote that it was "the finest picture, perhaps of the kind in the world."[19] As with other of Reynolds' paintings a poetic tribute was penned in honor of the "Muse."

The Muse

Thy pencil, Reynolds! innocently gay,
To virtue leads by pleasure's flowery way
But, for our love when grace and merit vie,
Th' instructive canvas moral worth excites,...
And REYNOLDS paints the lessons JOHNSON writes.
Should time, whose force our hopes in vain withstand,
Blast the nymph's face , and shake the painter's hand
Yet may these tints divide the fame they give,
And art and beauty bid each other live!

Author unknown

Sir Joshua Reynolds had the power of promoting moral values through art. He was always cautious to preserve an unblemished character and careful not to make any enemies. However, his friend Samuel Johnson was concerned about Reynolds' painting on the Sabbath and his dying request to Reynolds was that he give up this practice. Reynolds willingly acquiesced. "All this excellence had a firm foundation. He [Reynolds] was a man of sincere and ardent piety. [His] first care is to please God."[20]

Reynolds' famous yearly discourses at the Royal Academy yield many insights regarding art. His advice to budding artists was first, study the rules of art; second, study the great masters, (on this he put great emphasis); and third; forget the rules! He warned that our culture often makes it difficult to distinguish between that which is natural from that which is the result of education.

As did the great naturalist Louis Agazzis, Reynolds felt the works of genius and science, if founded upon truths in nature, would live forever. He warned artists to beware of not paying enough attention to the works of Nature and the great Master, Jesus Christ.

In his last "discourse" to the Academy, Reynolds reflected on his favorite master of art saying:

> I feel a self-congratulation in knowing myself capable of such sensations as he [the great master] intended to excite. I reflect, not without vanity, that these discourses bear testimony of my admiration of that truly divine man; and I should desire that the last words which I should pronounce in this Academy, and from the place, might be the name of Michelangelo.[21]

It might be noted here that Reynolds felt Raphael had more taste and fancy, but Michelangelo had more genius and strength. Raphael was supreme in art skills but Michelangelo was superior in portraying the sublime. Reynolds felt the inspiration for such divine art was supplied by the Creator himself.

He opposed the critic's "*good old rule*" that the first part of a critic's duty is to discover blemishes. Reynolds never tolerated the criticism of others while in his presence. He had a maxim that the arts, in their highest province, should not be addressed to the gross senses, but to that spark of divinity which we have within us. Reynolds lived this maxim in his personal life.

Reynolds was grateful for the good life the Creator had granted him. As he approached his last years he had a premonition that perhaps great physical suffering was yet in store for him. He often stated that he had been fortunate to have had good health and felt that he had not the right to complain of ill health in his remaining days. In his last few years he did suffer, for particularly disturbing was the loss of his eyesight.

Edmund Burke eulogized Reynolds, saying: "Sir Joshua Reynolds was, on very many accounts, one of the most memorable men of his time. He was the first Englishman who added the praise of the elegant arts to the other glories of his country. He was equal to the greatest masters of the renowned ages. In portrait he went beyond them."[23] He was born to dignify art, and through his life England breathed a new breath that only comes when art is restored to the dignity God intended it to have.

NOTES

[1] Cheney, Sheldon. *A World History of Art*. New York: Viking Press, 1947, p. 759.

[2] Leonard, Jonathan. *The World of Gainsborough, 1727-1788*. New York: Time-Life Books, 1969, p. 77.

[3] Evert A. Duyckinck. *Portrait Galley of Eminent Men and Women*. New York: Henry J. Johnson, 1873, p. 170.

[4] Ibid., p. 170.

[5] Ibid., p. 171.

[6] Ibid., p. 173.

[7] Ibid.

[9] Ibid., p. 6.

[10] Ibid.

[11] Ibid., p. 20.

[12] Duyckinck p. 177.

[13] Ibid., p. 174.

[14] Northcote, p. 197.

[15] Ibid., p. 88.

[16] Ibid. p. 100.

[17] Ibid., p. 165.

[18] Ibid., p. 100-101.

[19] Duyckinck, p. 179.

[20] Ibid., p. 181.

[21] Northcote, p. 288.

[23] Ibid., p. 296.

Johann Christoph Friedrich von Schiller

GERMAN POET, DRAMATIST, HISTORIAN *1759-1805*

> *"I loathe this ink-wasting century, when I read in my Plutarch of great men."*

IN THE LATER PART OF THE EIGHTEENTH CENTURY, EUROPE FELL under the spell of the pursuit of liberty and freedom, much of it springing from the results of the American revolution. Such success kindled in the people of Europe a desire for their own freedom.

This compelling spirit rumbled and boiled in France, finally giving way to a major eruption. So massive was its convulsions that it was some time before the effects of the French Revolution brought any benefits to its people.

Germany, unlike united France, was still in a semi-feudal state with powerful Dukes exercising great control over a small area and limited number of people. These conditions precluded revolt. Nevertheless, Germany's people felt the pull, and its revolution was carried out in their literature and dramas. The German literary revolution, or "The Storm and Stress" as it is often called, had its lead in author Friedrich Schiller.

Schiller is considered by modern Germans as their poet of liberty. His influence reached its zenith with the production of his drama *William Tell*. In this play Schiller unfurls freedom to the then awaiting world, establishing its standard on the most elevated peaks of Europe. As the story unfolded he aligned freedom with nature, clothing it in such eloquence that it would never again return to the oblivion from which he had plucked it. Though his life spanned but a brief forty-five years, Schiller attained great heights in the application of his intellectual and moral talents. In all his writings there is a profound reverence for all that is good. His histories came alive with great men and great deeds.

Schiller was born in Marbach on 10 November 1759, to Johann Kaspar Schiller and Elisabeth Dorothea Kodweis. Most of his childhood days were spent in the beautiful countryside of Lorch and Ludwigsburg. Born under one of the more restrictive dukes in Germany, the Duke of Wurtemburg, even as a child Schiller felt in a very personal way the loss of his freedoms. During the first four years of Schiller's life, his father was away at war on orders of the duke. Only on occasional leaves did Schiller see his father.

In his father's absence, Schiller's entire education and rearing fell to his mother. Those who knew her observed that she was deeply religious and had a great reverence and a love of nature. From her letters it can be observed that she was the most tender of mothers.[1] She read a good deal, and her favorite books were historical in nature. She particularly liked to study the biographies of famous men. Young Schiller adored his mother, and he attributes his own deep spiritual search and development to his mother.

He and his sister loved to hear her tell them Bible stories. Schiller's sister, Christophine, wrote in her memoirs:

> Once, when we two, as children, had set out walking with dear Mamma to see our grandparents, she took the way from Ludwigsburg to Marbach, which leads straight over the hill [a walk of some four miles]. It was a beautiful Easter Monday, and our Mother related to us the history of the two disciples to whom, on their journey to Emmaus, Jesus had joined himself. Her speech and narrative grew ever more inspired; and when we got upon the Hill, we were all so much affected that we knelt down and prayed. This hill became a Tabor to us.[2]

It was by these means—through Bible-passages, tales of history, and poems that their mother guided the soul of Germany's future voice of freedom. Because she also nourished his sense for the beauties of nature, he loved to be out in it. Nature became his refuge for inspiration during his writing years.

When their father was released from the army, he was

appointed steward of the duke's nurseries. The family moved from its beautiful countryside to Ludwigsburg. Because their father was in the duke's employ, the children were allowed to attend the theater free of charge. Schiller and his sister Christophine often reconstructed the plays at home, using paper-doll actors. Schiller considered his sister his truest friend, a faithful companion in his poetic dreams.

Schiller cherished the few years he was tutored under his father who, from his earliest years, had planned that his only son should go into the clergy. But these plans were shattered in Schiller's fourteenth year. The duke had established a military school for young boys, where under his personal direction future servants and directors of state would be trained. Knowing of young Schiller's abilities, the duke selected him for the school.

This was a devastating blow. How could the family contest such an action when their livelihood depended on the duke? In spite of the risks, Schiller's father approached the duke, seeking permission for their son to continue his studies for the church. The duke refused. Again the father approached the duke, but he would hear no objections. The duke did not simply request Schiller's attendance at his school; he ordered it.

Accordingly Schiller was sent to the institute. There, he studied not theology, as was his want, but law. The school was demanding with strict rules. The record is not clear as to whether families could visit the school. Thomas Carlyle wrote that visitations were limited to the sisters and the mothers on some Sundays.[3]

There were no vacations and few holidays. Each day the students spent long hours in class, and they were forbidden to read books inconsistent with their lessons. Schiller, responding to a divine edict within himself, devoured Plutarch and Shakespeare in secret.

In spite of its restrictions, the institute had one advantage. It had gathered the best and brightest, the most promising young men from all parts of Germany. One of Schiller's friends was Cuvier, the father of paleontology. Cuvier became the instructor of the eminent natural scientist, Louis Agassiz. Schiller's associations provided intellectual comradeship of the very best kind.

But his poetic soul chaffed against the rigidity and mourned the loss of freedom. Reading and writing poetry was strictly forbidden, but this restriction could not quench the poetic fire that was already smoldering within him. His disdain for the restrictions placed on him extended to the course of study chosen for him. He disliked law. His hatred for it grew to the point that he was allowed to abandon it and study medicine. Referring to law Schiller wrote, "Law has never yet made a great man, but liberty breeds colossuses and extremes."[4]

Schiller completed his studies, writing his final thesis in the field of medicine. However, the duke was displeased and retained him in the institute for another year. Schiller, now twenty years old, was still told what he was to wear, eat, and read and when he was to go to bed. To have been unjustly forced to remain in such circumstances filled him with a burning hatred of all tyranny and oppression, and he swore eternal enmity toward tyranny of every kind.[5]

It was in the depth of his soul that Schiller found a release for his long-suppressed rebellion. During these years he wrote a drama simply entitled *Robbers*. It was young, it was forceful, it was rebellious and with it Schiller began to ride the waves of the literary revolution. His duke, alarmed, forbade Schiller to ever write poetry again. He even imprisoned him for a short time. To all of this Schiller acquiesced for fear of retribution to his family.

After his release from the institute, the duke had him work as a doctor in the military. The duke's promises of good pay and status were not forth-coming, and once again the chains of oppression tried his determined soul. He had read records of the great deeds of heroes of the past, and he felt his soul akin to theirs and wanted to be like them. But to do so while in the power of the duke was impossible. He decided that the way to follow the yearnings of his spirit was to flee beyond the control of his duke.

One last time he went to his parents' home. His sister had told their mother of his intentions, but none dared tell his honorable father. As the evening progressed he and his mother were able to slip away unnoticed. Returning after nearly an hour, Striecher, Schiller's friend, noticed the wet red eyes of both, betraying the intense pain of parting once more.[6]

Schiller and his friend fled to Mannhem, hoping that the director of the theater there would give them a job. The director, Baron von Dalberg, was the first to produce *Robbers*, and they hoped he would be sympathetic towards them. Dalberg however, was unable to be of assistance at that time. Schiller had published *Robbers* with borrowed money, and was now deeply in debt and in desperate need of help. Baroness von Wolzogen, the mother of two of his former classmates, brought him under her roof with her family and did much to restore his confidence and self-esteem.

Finally, in 1783, his bargaining with Dalberg saw results, and he was appointed as theater-poet. Through this position he was able to make enough money to pay off a portion of his debts. However, because of illness, he was unable to finish his contract with the theater. An intermittent fever confined him to a sick bed, and although he eventually regained some health, he was never fully well again. Too ill to finish his contract, he was unable to pay his debts.

Shiller desperately needed help, and help came from Christian Korner, a man who became his close friend. He invited Schiller to come and live with them until his health improved, saying that he would "loan" Schiller money to live. Korner offered a loan because he knew that Schiller's integrity would not allow him to accept a dole. Under these blessed circumstances Schiller was once again able to concentrate on his works.

Although his writing was excellent it did not bring him enough income to sustain him. In 1784, Schiller was invited to read the first act of his *Don Carlos* to the Duke of Weimar. The Duke was the patron of some of the leading men in Germany, among whom were Goethe, the father of German literature, and Wieland, who translated Shakespeare into German. After hearing Schiller's presentation, the duke bestowed upon the young writer the title of court-councilor. Though this new title brought no new pecuniary advantage, it did much to establish Schiller's credibility with managers and theaters. In this position he felt secure for the first time since he had fled as a fugitive from the duke. Schiller now sought for a greater expanse in his writings. He strove to include history in his dramas, rather than using merely individual interest as had been done. Much of this influence must be attributed to Korner, who encouraged Schiller to build on a firm basis.[7]

The longing for a companion and a home of his own became a great desire. He began in earnest to look about him for both. His travels took him to the home of his dear friends the von Wolzogens. Schiller and Wilhem von Wolzogen made an excursion to a nearby village to visit the von Lengefelds, near relatives of Wilhem. The widow had two lovely daughters, Caroline and Charlotte.

It was Charlotte who stole Schiller's heart. Schiller felt that matrimony, along with its other benefits, ensured the full and free development of the intellectual powers. The two married and Lotte, as Schiller called his wife, was very devoted to him. It is probably from her and his queenly mother that Schiller obtained his noble conception of women and womanhood. Schiller revered, admired, and loved his wife as did all those who knew her.

During this time Schiller became acquainted with Goethe. Although their acquaintance was slow at first, the friendship soon blossomed into one that could rival Jonathan and David in its strength. Goethe used his influence to obtain for Schiller the position as a professor of history at the University of Jena. Schiller elevated Goethe's own spiritual nature to new heights.

Schiller's professorship was a resounding success. The university had difficulty in accommodating the large crowd of students that would gather for Schiller's lectures. He wrote to Lotte of his new position in his typical unassuming manner: "I shall appear ridiculous to myself. Many a student probably knows more history than the professor. However, I think in this case as Sancho Panza did about his vice-regency: when God gives an office to a man, He also gives intelligence to administer it."[8] Although his health was still poor, Schiller often wrote and lectured fourteen hours in a single day.

During this time Schiller completed his *History of the Revolt of the Netherlands* and *The History of the Thirty Years War*. If written today as Schiller wrote it, history would be a more popular subject. Schiller explained his ideas of history when he said: "History may be written with historic fidelity without being a strain on the reader's patience." He also said that "history may borrow something from a kindred art without necessarily becoming a romance."9 A fine example of this may be seen in his description of the "Death of Gustavas Adolphus."

Among Schiller's admirers were the Duke of Augustenborg and Count Schimmelmann, both of Denmark, who when they heard of the poet's illness granted him a three-year pension. This aid provided a welcome relief to Schiller's struggle against poverty.

Schiller's talents extended to a variety of literary forms, but the true home of his genius was the historical drama. In this area he found his greatest expression. In all his writing, Schiller was never unfaithful to the mission he felt as a youth. Even while the last of his health was giving way, he still wrote with wholesome and cheerful dramatic fire. He could do so because his heart and intellect were based on sound principles.

In the winter of 1805 Schiller, now only forty-five years old, became totally bedridden. One early May day he asked that the curtains be drawn to allow in the sunshine. When his sister-in-law asked him how he was, he whispered, "Cheerful, ever more cheerful."

The next day he momentarily gained consciousness and his last conscious act was to kiss his beloved Lotte. Then he experienced a convulsion like an electrical shock. As his head fell back and he rested, a most perfect peace came over his face; his mission was complete.10

Word of Schiller's death was sent to Goethe's house, but none had the courage to give so dreadful a message to the master. However, something in the behavior of the members of the household made Goethe uneasy, but he refused to ask a direct question of anyone. "I observe," he said to his wife, Christiane, "that Schiller must be very ill." During that night he was heard sobbing. The next morning he again asked Christiane, "Is it true, is it not, that Schiller was very ill yesterday?" Christiane burst into tears." He is dead?" asked Goethe. Christiane, still crying, at last told him the bitter truth. "He is dead!" Goethe repeated, and covered his eyes with his hand. He had lost a friend and the world a great writer.[11]

NOTES

[1] Carlye, Thomas. *The Life of Frederick Schiller.* Boston: Dana Estes, 1825, p. 249.

[2] Ibid., p. 251-52.

[3] Ibid., p. 216

[4] Boyesen, Hjalmar H. *Goethe and Schiller: Their Lives and Works.* New York: Charles Schribner's Sons, 1911, p. 303.

[5] Spofford, A.R. Lamberton, J. P., and Frank Weitenkampf. *The Library of Historic Characters and Famous Events of All Nations.* Boston: J. B. Millet, 1902, p. 347.

[6] See Carlyle, p. 221.

[7] Boyesen, p. 352.

[8] Boyesen, p. 374.

[9] Ibid., p. 383.

[10] See ibid., p. 423.

[11] Sime, James. *Life of Johann Wolfgang Goethe.* London and New York: The Walter Scott Publishing Co. Ltd., 1910, p. 154.

Sir Walter Scott

POET, NOVELIST   *1771-1836*

"I will not doubt—to doubt is to lose."

THE FIRST GREAT BRITISH WRITER OF THE ROMANTIC SCHOOL, SIR Walter Scott was the first writer to turn the thoughts and hearts of his Scottish countrymen towards their heritage and the middle ages. After reading his historical novels, people felt proud of their ancestry and their homeland. Goethe called Scott "The first novelist of the century."[1]

Only one other man of the day shared Scott's enormous popularity—Lord Byron. Their bust or pictures were in almost every cultivated home. Their most famous lines were repeated at evening gatherings as a sign of culture. When compared to Burns and Byron, Scott called them "the most poetical geniuses of my time, and half a century before me. We have, however, many men of high poetical talent, but none, I think of that ever-gushing and perennial fountain of natural water."[2]

In 1820 King George IV made Scott a baron, the first person to receive a title because of literature. And his fame was not limited to the British Isles. He was beloved in America as well. America's first author, Washington Irving, sought the presence of the great man of literature and was treated with utmost courtesy and kindness.

Scott was a prolific writer, so prolific as to be almost incomprehensible. He could write forty or more hand written pages a day. He wrote two, and sometimes three, novels a year, as well as many reviews and other sundry writings. Some of his novels were printed with as many as fifty thousand copies. He produced twenty-seven novels in seventeen years.

Scott's writing was aided by his keen observation of men and manners. He also had an exceptional gift of memory, which he often said worked only on things that interested him. He was able to reproduce what he heard, read, or saw with vividness and oftentimes freshness. He also had a vivid imagination, which played with the things he learned to produce the themes of his historical romances. So great were the wanderings and twisting of his imagination that he said he had no more idea than the man in the moon of what would come next out of his brain. While he often called mortals the "children of imagination," he also felt great reverence for humankind, calling them "the emblem[s] of deity."[3]

In spite of the abundance of his works, writing was not his profession. Following his father's wishes, he became a lawyer. During his years of writing he was also sheriff of the county and at the same time a judge of the court. He served in a volunteer regiment, and he was devoted to his wife and four children.

Scott was known and respected for his honesty, absolute integrity, and his benevolence. He was not, however, without his weaknesses, his greatest one being his desire to obtain more land than he needed. At times he referred to this desire as his "mistress," a mistress who, as all mistresses do, got him in trouble. His love of nature and all that she possessed sometimes overcame his better judgment, and he foolishly spent a great deal of money buying land he could not afford.

Politically, Scott was a staunch Tory supporting the royalty and all of her nobility. He was deeply attached to the past and felt it an integral part of the British heritage. Consequently, as a youth, he was adamantly against the Americans and their revolution. As he matured however, he felt Britain should exert every effort to promote goodwill between America and the mother country. When the war between them had ended, he advocated getting along and building a strong relationship with their former enemy.

Scott's life reflected the saying: "Act well your part, there all the honor lies." He knew well that the greatest happiness is not in being praised, but in doing right and acting in goodness of character. This he endeavored to do all his life.

Sir Walter Scott and his literature are a product of his early life with his family. Not only his immediate family, but also his grandparents, cousins and particularly an old maiden aunt were very important and influential.

Walter Scott was born on 15 August 1771, in old Edinburgh and was of Scottish lowlander heritage. He was one of twelve children, but only five survived early childhood. He was the second child to be named after his father, the first one having died. His name was also the name of his great-grandfather and his great-great grandfather. Every Scot has a pedigree and Scott was proud of his. His father was a lawyer of the greatest integrity. He was religious to the extreme, except for a liberality towards the theater. His mother was a descendent of the famous Swintons, the great warriors in the medieval days. One of his ancestors had been a border chief.

Although Walter was a robust healthy child, he nearly died from exposure to tuberculosis. His first nurse had consumption but concealed it until she feared for her life. She went to see the noted physician, Dr. Black, who immediately informed the family. The nurse was promptly dismissed. Shortly thereafter, one night when Scott was about eighteen months old, he was chased about the room in an effort to put him to bed. Finally, the little renegade was caught and put into bed. By morning he was running a fever. The family, however, was not overly concerned because they felt this was due to teething. It lasted for three days, and on the fourth day, when he was given a bath, it was discovered that he had lost the power in his right leg. At the time they could not establish the cause , but scholars now feel that he had polio.

Scott's maternal grandfather, Dr. Rutherford, was summoned. After an examination, he recommended he be sent to his paternal grandfather's farm at Sandy Knowe for fresh air and sunshine.

At Sandy Knowe his relatives went to great lengths to restore his health. Scott recalled some of the remedies and cures that were tried on him, especially that of being wrapped in the skin of a freshly slain lamb: "In this tartar-like habiliment I well remember lying upon the floor while my grandfather, a venerable old man with white hair, used every excitement to make me try to crawl. I also distinctly remember ... a relation of ours, and I still recollect him in his old-fashioned military habit ... kneeling on the ground before me, and dragging his watch along the carpet for me to follow it.

The benevolent old soldier and the infant wrapped in his sheep skin would have afforded an odd sight to interested spectators."[4]

The cure that had the greatest effect was to be carried among the flocks and over the fields by the young ewe-milkers. They carried him through the beautiful scenery and among the crags, and he grew to love the sheep. His quick memory served him well, and he soon came know to every sheep and lamb by their head-mark. Old Sandy Ormistoun, the chief superintendent, would give the young invalid a ride upon his shoulders to the tower above the little loch, where Scott spent the day. He was content to lie hour after hour on the heather-scented hill, under the floating clouds. One day Sandy had left him among the knolls to lie and learn, when a thunderstorm came up. His Aunt Jenny, suddenly remembering his situation, ran to collect her little charge. She found him lying on his back , clapping his hands at the lightening, and crying out, "Bonny, bonny!" at every flash.[5]

Even though his relatives worked diligently to restore his health, he did little but crawl the first years of his life. In the old farmhouse where he stayed there was never a still moment. Milk buckets clanged and swarms of cousins came and went. In the evening his grandfather sat on one side of the fire and his grandmother with her spinning wheel on the other. Little Scott lay on a rug at their feet, listening to the Bible stories and good books that his aunt read them. He particularly remembered the reading of Josephus. His grandmother told him thrilling tales of his ancestors and of earlier days. Scott loved to hear of his great-grandfather, "Beardie." Like Sampson, "Beardie," determined not to shave until the Stewarts returned to the throne. "Beardie" died with a full beard. These and other stories enthralled young Scott.

When he was four years old, his aunt took him to Bath, hoping to find a more effective remedy. A year later he was no better, he had, however, learned to compensate for his stiffness and could walk and run. During this time his mind was not idle. His uncle took him to the theater and his aunt taught him rudiments.

Finally, when he was seven years old, he was returned to his family. Fitting in the middle of four other siblings required some getting used to after the attention he received at the farm. But being at home offered him new opportunities to learn. Many of Scott's most tender memories were of moments with his mother, sleeping in her room and listening to her stories. She, too, had an excellent memory. She knew all the Scottish oral genealogy and could recite from memory the ancestry of everyone she knew or had ever heard of. She also had a proverb for every occasion. She lived to be eighty and to see her crippled son become world famous.

When Scott was about twelve he attended a social gathering where a number of literary figures were present. Robert burns, the famous Scottish poet, stood admiring a painting under which was written a couplet of poetry. He asked who was the author and no one seemed to know. Then young Scott very shyly gave not only the author's name, but also quoted the rest of the poem. Burns placed his hand on the young boy's and looking him in the eye said: "Son you will be a great man in Scotland some day."[6]

Years later, Scott recalled Burn's encouraging words as the turning point in his life. These kind words of encouragement touched the young lad in such a way as to help him on the road to greatness.

Scott attended school until his fifteenth year. He was an ordinary student, but one teacher said of him that while others could read the Latin authors, Scott could better understand their heart. In his fifteenth year he became critically ill with a broken blood vessel and had to stay in bed most of the year. This year became, in Scott's opinion, one of the best years of his educational experience. Because of his illness he could do nothing but read, and read he did, storing up in his mind large amounts of material from which he was later able to draw from for his own writings.

Once, Scott reached manhood, he became a lawyer and married Charlotte Carpenter, a French refugee. They had a happy marriage, and she promoted his works even before the editors saw them. They had four children.

Scott seemed to have two missions—his first, to paint Scotland with such vividness and beauty as to almost create a new country, and to paint all that was good of the Scottish character, its strife, and its courage; his second, to give life to its heritage and people.

In Scott's day both Scotland and England were entering the nineteenth century with its quick and often turbulent changes. Scott's historical novels allowed the people to enter into the nineteenth century with a compassionate sense of their past. In giving the people this heritage Scott did his greatest work.

In 1826, terrible financial reverses hit the printing houses in London and Edinburgh. Scott was greatly involved in these houses and stood at the edge of bankruptcy. Rather than give in, he chose to work off his indebtedness through his writing. "I will be their vassal for life," he said, "and dig in the mine of my imagination to find diamonds to make good my engagements, not to enrich myself."[7] The debt was large—$700,000. He worked unceasingly at reducing it, thus hastening his death in 1836. At his death, when his life insurance and royalties were applied to the debt, it was paid in full.

The following poem, written by Scott, reveals his belief in an afterlife and speaks of man's longing for his native home. The poem warns that the ability to return to that home lies within each person's own unselfish actions.

> Breathes there the man, with soul so dead,
> Who never to himself hath said,
> this is my own, my native land!
> Whose heart hath ne'er within him burned,
> As home his footsteps he hath turned
> From wandering on a foreign strand?
> If such there breathe, go, mark him well!
> For him no minstrel raptures swell;
> High though his titles, proud his name
> Boundless his wealth as wish can claim,—
> Despite those titles, power, and pelf,
> The wretch, concentrated all in self,
> Living shall forfeit fair renown,
> And, doubly dying, shall go down
> To the veil dust from whence he sprung,
> unwept, unhonored, and unsung.
> ("The Lay of the Last Minstrel")

Scott shed mortality happily, after giving Scotland a heritage and dignity from which she has never departed.

NOTES

1 Scott, Sir Walter. *The Journal of Sir Walter Scott.* New York: Harper, 1890, 2:485

2 Ibid., 1:112

3 Ibid., 1:316.

4 Oman, Carola. *The Wizard of the North: The Life of Sir Walter Scott.* London: Hooder & Stoughton, p. 19.

5 Mackenzie, Shelton R. *Sir Walter Scott: The Story of His Life.* London: Focroft Library Editions, 1977, 1:20.

6 Brown-Steve. *How To Talk So People Will Listen.* Grand Rapids, Mich.: Baker House, 1993, p. 15.

7 Mackenzie ,1:94

William Henry Seward

AMERICAN STATESMAN *1801-1872*

> *"There is a higher law than that of the Constitution which regulates our authority."*

AS THE GREAT POLITICAL DEFENDERS HENRY CLAY, JOHN CALHOUN, and Daniel Webster neared the end of their lives, many wondered if there would ever again arise such men of destiny. The younger men seemed unlikely candidates, and the public took little note of them. They were nevertheless men of integrity and devotion. Abraham Lincoln was then almost unknown, and William Seward, who was to play a key role as Lincoln's Secretary of State, was just entering the U.S. Senate.

As Secretary of State, Seward's superb diplomacy kept the European nations from taking advantage of this troubled land during the Civil War. His loyal support to Benito Juarez finally helped drive the French out of Mexico. After the death of Lincoln he helped implement Lincoln's ideas for peaceful repatriation of the South. Seward's gifted diplomacy saved his country in many instances, and his iron will helped restore a badly shattered nation. Seward is perhaps best known for his purchase of Alaska from Russia. This purchase is often referred to as "Seward's Folly," for many at the time thought the purchase was worthless. However, Alaska has returned to this country many times the value of the purchase price.

William Seward was born in Florida, New York, on 16 May 1801. His father was Samuel Seward, and his mother, Mary Jennings. His father's family were of Welsh descent, and his mother's family were English-Irish.

Seward was not a strong child and his health was poor. However, his mind was extremely active, so his father determined to get him an education. His thirst for knowledge sometimes got him into trouble. Once it almost cost him his life. When he was about twelve years old, and driving the cows home from the field, he read a book as he walked, glancing now and then at his charges. A group of boys spied the young scholar abstractly driving his herd and tried to attract his attention by tossing rocks at him. Seward was resolved not to be disturbed in studies, and he merely turned his back towards them and walked backwards with his eyes still on the book. Not knowing that he had come to a bridge over a small stream, Seward missed the bridge and fell into the creek, hitting his head and knocking himself unconscious. An elder brother had been watching the incident, and he rescued Seward from downing.[1]

Like other boys of the day, Seward had many chores. "It was my business to drive the cows, morning and evening to and from distant pastures, to chop and carry in the fuel for the parlor fire, to take the grain to mill and fetch the flour, to bring the lime from the kiln, and to do the errands of the family generally."[2] He was a hard worker, but he wanted to attend school. He ran away to school before he was old enough to attend.

Still, although he loved to learn, school did not always go smoothly. One day when he felt overloaded with Latin assignments, he rebelled and threw away his books. His father appealed to his sense of the future, telling him that some day he might become a great lawyer like some of the famous men of his day. Interestingly, this argument seemed to reach young Seward, and he began to double his attention to his studies.

When Seward was fifteen he passed the entrance exam at Union College. He did so well on the examination that he would have been placed as a junior, but because of his age he had to enter as a sophomore. His favorite studies were rhetoric, moral philosophy, and the ancient classics. He accustomed himself to rise at four in the morning, a habit that he maintained throughout most of his life.

Seward was well liked. One of his father's friends observed in a letter that "the confidence which he [Seward] has in himself and the ease of his manners renders him quite pleasing."[3] But his pleasantries did not quell his strong will, which at times bordered on stubbornness. One day Seward thought an instructor of his had not treated him fairly, and he refused to give his recitation. He was so adamant that only with the personal intervention of the president of the college was the matter settled.

He was also sensitive to the opinion of his fellow students. When they ridiculed him because he spent extra time being tutored by the Latin teacher, he promptly quit and used his extra time in tutoring some of the students in other subjects. When they commented on his country clothes, he visited a tailor shop and acquired a new set of clothes. He had the bill sent to his father. His father was a rather stern and strict man, and the purchase was not in accordance with his wishes. He refused to pay the bill. When the creditors came knocking at his door, Seward resolved to abandoned his college career and seek employment. Without notifying his family, he left Union College with a friend and sailed south to Savannah where teaching jobs were being offered. Seward obtained a teaching job and stayed in Savannah, observing firsthand the oppressive nature of slavery.

Soon his father found out where he was and sent a letter demanding his return to college. Seward, however, was in no hurry to leave. He remained in Savannah six months before he returned to college, where he graduated with the senior class with honors at the age of nineteen.[4] The title of his commencement address was *The Integrity of the American Union.*

Seward pursued his law degree and accepted an offer in the law office of Elijah Miller. Not long after, Seward married Elijah's daughter, Frances. They had a happy marriage. Seward was a successful lawyer, and his fame grew fast. In 1830, he was elected to the state senate and later became the governor of the state of New York. He became known for his support of internal improvements and his advocacy of the abolishment of imprisonment for debt. He also advocated new and better organization of the public schools, supporting certain claims of the parochial schools for help. In 1844, he supported Henry Clay for the presidency and made speeches for him at public meetings.

One of his recurring themes was the immorality of slavery. In a memorable speech in 1848, he stated, "The party of slavery upholds an aristocracy founded on the humiliation of labor as necessary to the existence of a chivalrous republic."[5] In 1849, he was elected to the U.S. Senate receiving three-fourths of all the votes. Then in 1850, while promoting the admission of California as a free state, he uttered these immortal words: "The Constitution regulates our stewardship; the Constitution devotes the domain to union, to justice, to defense, to welfare, and to liberty. But there is a Higher Law than the Constitution, which regulates our authority over the domain, and devotes it to the same noble purposes."[6] He contended that the country was involved in an "irrepressible conflict" that would end only in the nation becoming all free or all slave.

Because Seward was the organizer of the Republican Party, Lincoln chose him to be his Secretary of State. This proved a providential choice, for during the Civil War Seward's "brain was pitted against all Europe and always won."[7] It was through his diplomacy that the efforts of the Confederates to gain recognition by foreign powers were frustrated.

In the spring of 1865, Seward was thrown from his carriage, breaking his jaw and arm. Later, on 14 April 1865, just five days after the close of the Civil War, Lincoln was assassinated. One of the co-conspirators burst into Seward's bedroom with a bowie-knife and slashed and stabbed him in the face and throat. Seward's son was injured in the attack and his daughter helped to drive the man off. Seward survived, but his wife, who was an invalid, received such a shock that she died within two months. His only daughter, who helped to fend off the assassin, never recovered from the effects of the scene and died within the year.

When Seward recovered he returned to serve under President Andrew Johnson. Seward and Johnson stood virtually alone in pursuing Lincoln's ideals of peaceful reparation and immediate and full recognition for the Southern states. Seward's stand offended a majority of his own party, and he was banished from national public life. Johnson's and Seward's policy, however, was triumphant, and a new spirit of nationalism took root and began to grow.

Throughout the Civil War, Mexico was also involved in a civil war, fighting for her very survival against the French and their appointed Emperor, Maximilian. Seward steadfastly refused to recognize Maximilian's government. His diplomacy did much to keep supplies from reaching the French in Mexico. In a symbolic gesture, he held a presidential ball to honor Margarita, Benito Juarez's wife, who had fled with her children to the United States for safety. This act declared to the world that the U.S. stood firmly behind Juarez as the rightful leader of Mexico.

Early in his career Seward had been a key supporter of "Manifest Destiny," a policy which sought the extension of our boundaries. But when Mexico was freed from her civil war, a war which was caused by the intervention of the French, Secretary Seward became Mexico's greatest ally and defender of her territory. Always he was a devoted friend of Juarez.

Seward's private life was impeccable. His public career spanned stormy times, but he always maintained a steady course in the pursuit of liberty for all men. He stood for the abolishment of slavery, and was always ready to help the poor and defend the needy. He was not afraid to take a dangerous position, even if it meant standing alone. His headstone reflected how he wished to be remembered. It said simply: "He was faithful."

NOTES

[1] See Baker, George E., ed. *The Works of William H. Seward.* New York: Redfield, 1853, p. xvi.

[2] Bancroft, Frederic. *The Life of William H. Seward.* New York: Harper & Brothers, 1900, p. 3.

[3] Ibid p. 5.

[4] Lothrop, Thornton Kirkland. *William Henry Seward.* New York: Houghton Mifflin, 1899, p. 9.

[5] Spofford, A.R., Weitenkampf Frank, and J. P. Lamberton. *The Library of Historic Character and Famous Events of All Nations.* Boston: J. B. Millet, 1902, p. 48.

[6] Duyckinick, Evert A. *Portrait Gallery of Eminent Men and Women.* New York: Henry Johnson, 1873, p. 463.

[7] Morris Charles, *Heroes of Progress in America.* Philadelphia: Lippincott Co., 1919, p. 275.

George Stephenson

1781-1848

"Do as I have done—persevere!"

ON 4 JUNE 1881, IN A SUPPLEMENT TO THE LONDON NEWS, A former acquaintance of George Stephenson wrote:

> All that is great and good in the English character found expression in the career of George Stephenson. He will go down to posterity a type of the physical and moral virtues of his race.

> An athlete, he was a lover of birds [and a] giant in strength.... The greatest practical engineer the world has seen, he maintained his supremacy with unaffected modesty. With opportunities to amass a colossal fortune, he put gold aside as dross compared with honour.

The article then quoted Stephenson's response to a request for his name and address. The request had compared him to royalty. Stephenson said: "I have dined with princes, and peers, and commoners—with persons of all classes, from the highest to the humblest.... I have seen mankind in all its phases, and the conclusion I have arrived at is—that if we were all stripped there's not much difference between us."[1]

George Stephenson was the second son of Mary Carr and Robert Stephenson. His father was a fireman of a coal pit engine, near Newcastle. Stephenson was born on 9 June 1781. As with other great Englishmen, Stephenson had a mother of remarkable character who had a great concern for the welfare of her son. Those who knew Mrs. Stephenson referred to her as a "canny body" which was a way of saying that she was clever, good, and very reliable. The family existed in rather poor circumstances and there was no money to send George to school. One historian remarked that had Stephenson had an education, he would have made his mark on the world, but would probably not have been the father of the railway. It was his very surroundings, the environment of the mining community that helped his mind to concentrate on what his hands and mind could do.

At the age of eight he had to help the family by going to work herding cows for a nearby neighbor. This job was a great stimulus to his love of the outdoors and particularly to his lifelong attachment to birds. His responsibilities included not only herding but also opening and closing the gate on the main road for wagons. He acutely observed everything that passed by. Another young boy, named Thirwall, helped young Stephenson herd the animals. The two boys loved to play on the banks of nearby streams, building tiny windmills at each opportunity. These interests and activities led them to design model engines out of clay, using hemlock stems as steam-pipes. They made small wagons out of cork and ran them by means of a miniature winding-machine. From his job of tending cows, he moved to hoeing. Finally, he got a job he greatly desired driving the "gin" horse, adjacent to the coal pit.

At fourteen he obtained the position of assistant fireman under his father at the coal pit. It was here that his engineering mind began to blossom, yet he still preserved his great love for birds and knew every local nest in the area. His great ambition during this time was to become the engineer man on the old steam engine that pumped water out of the mine. To become familiar with the machine, he spent hours studying it and taking it apart to help repair it. His mind thrived on such exercises, and they prepared him to realize his potential. Then at the age of seventeen, he was promoted over his father to the office of engineman.

Although, Stephenson excelled in many areas, by the time he was 18 years od, he still could not read. He often sat listening as others read him the latest news. He finally concluded that if he was to advance, particularly in his skill as a mechanic, he would have to read. He signed up for a class by a local minister to learn the basic skills of reading and writing. He learned with great rapidity and even learned his "sums" while working. Mathematics seemed a natural part of his genius.

Stephenson had great plans for the future. He did not waste time at the local pub with the other miners. He wanted his future family to have a better lot in life than he himself had experienced. He had three basic goals: to become a skilled workman, to win the confidence of his employers, and to have the respect of his neighbors. In order to add to the meager wage he earned from the mine, Stephenson mended shoes in the evening. He repaired clocks and watches as well. He fixed anything he could "put a hand to." He was known in the village for holding the record for throwing the hammer the greatest distance.

Among the shoes he mended were those of a beautiful young woman named Fanny Henderson. Fanny was a servant of one of the more well to do families. It didn't take much for these two exceptional people to fall in love. But Stephenson's wage was so small that they could not marry. They waited a year. By then Stephenson had purchased a small cottage and they were married at Newburn Church. After the ceremony the young couple traveled together on a single horse to pay their respects to Stephenson's parents. They then rode over fifteen miles to their new cottage.

On 16 October 1803, a son Robert was born. Soon after this the family moved to Killingsworth, where Stephenson worked in the West Moor Coal mine. They had been married just twelve months when Fanny died. Stephenson was devastated. She had been the bright star in his life. She believed in his hopes and dreams, even his "impossible" dreams. He lost himself in his work superintending a Boulton and Watt spinning gin.

He was called to Scotland to apply his practical knowledge to a coal pit engine that kept drawing sand. After studying the situation for a time, Stephenson ordered a twelve-foot box built and placed in the well. He set the pump inside, and it worked without drawing sand. When he returned home with a goodly sum of money, he found that his father had been blinded in a mine accident. Stephenson paid off his father's debts and took his parents under his care. About this time he was drafted into the Continental Army. Working at extra jobs he was able to pay a "substitute" to serve for him, allowing him to stay home and take care of his little son and parents.

In 1808, with two other men, Stephenson took a small contract for managing all the engines at West Moor Pit. Saving all he could,

Stephenson was able to send young Robert to school. He worked hard and made little. His luck soon changed. A new engine had been put in at Killingsworth, and for some reason no one could keep it running. Like all the neighboring engineers, Stephenson examined the machine. He turned the subject over and over in his mind. At last he felt quite sure that he knew the solution to the problem.

One day the "sinkman" of the pump asked Stephenson if he thought he could repair the machine. Stephenson replied that he could and that within one week he could have the shaft emptied of water so men could go to the bottom. Stephenson's claim was reported to the owner, who was so desperate that he was willing to try anything. Stephenson gently took apart each piece of the engine, taking four days to put it back together—it worked! This success brought his ability wide acclaim, and his engineering ability and reputation began to precede him. Stephenson was now paid in pounds instead of schillings, and his abilities began to out distance regular engineers. However, because of his lack of education other engineers often called him a "quack."

In 1812 the engine-wright at Killingsworth was accidently killed and Stephenson was appointed to the position. His salary was now one hundred pounds a year, a considerable sum for the time.

About this time many began to experiment with the application of Watt's steam engine to propulsion. Several designs and contraptions had been tried but none successfully. A Mr. Trevethick was the first to attempt to use steam to move a carriage. In 1804, he constructed an engine that was suppose to run on rails dragging some ten tons of iron at the rate of five miles an hour, but the design did not work. Mr. Trevethick's conclusion was that a smooth-wheeled engine would not "grip" or "bite" on smooth rails. This conclusion became an established law of engineering for many years. In 1812, a Mr. Blackett experimented with an engine that crept at a snail's pace along the road taking as long as six hours to travel five miles.

During this time Stephenson was not idle. He was trying to find the best way to deliver coal from the mine to the river. The high price of corn was making it terribly expensive to keep the horses that had been pulling the cars. He visited Mr. Blackett and viewed his engine. After examining the engine, he decided that he could make a better one. The owners of the mine authorized him to proceed on the construction of a locomotive. With little regard for the established theory of resistance, he made all his engines' wheels smooth. It was the first engine ever to have smooth wheels. On 25 July 1814, the engine was tested. It succeeded in pulling eight loaded coal cars, of some thirty tons, at four miles an hour, and the coal was efficiently delivered to the river.

Stephenson spent many nights studying and learning with his son. Their first of many engineering projects together was the building of a sun dial. Robert inherited many of his father's great traits and he became an engineer in his own right. The two spent time together improving the joints of the rails, designing lighter and more durable wheels. They studied resistance and gradients, concluding that the power of the locomotive adapted best to level roads. Stephenson also invented a safety lamp for his fellow mine workers. He tested it for safety by first wearing it himself in a tunnel. Ironically, Sir Humphrey Davey had at the same time presented a similar lantern, and Stephenson was accused of stealing the idea. History has been able to put the controversy to rest; neither had knowledge of the other's invention until it became public. Stephenson conducted himself with great dignity throughout the entire ordeal though he was denounced as an impostor because he did not have an engineering degree. It took considerable chemical knowledge to produce the lamp, many reasoned, and so they doubted his ability.

Stephenson's projects did not interfere with his job at the mine, Several mines began to ask for delivery lines, usually to the closest canal. By 1825, with the help of a Mr. Pease, he established a "railroad" line. On 27 September, the first locomotive, driven by Stephenson himself, pulled thirty-eight cars with four hundred and fifty passengers and some ninety tons of merchandise. The highest speed attained was twelve miles an hour.

Soon after a bill was introduced into Parliament to help lay a line from the north for the more rapid and expedient transportation of coal to London. The bill was vehemently opposed, particularly by the canal companies and land-owners. Of this occasion Stephenson wrote:

I had to place myself in the most unpleasant of all positions—the witness box of a parliamentary committee. I was not long in it before I began to wish for a hole to creep out at! I could not find words to satisfy either the committee or myself. I was subjected to the cross-examination of eight or ten barristers, purposely, as far as possible to bewilder me.... But I put up with every rebuff, and went on with my plans, determined not to be put down.[3]

The construction of the railways was opposed not only by the leading men and scientists but also by the local people as well. The project was denounced in public speeches, newspapers asserted that locomotion by steam was most damaging and would poison the birds as they flew over. They said it would destroy the preservation of pheasants, and burn up the farms near the lines; oats and hay would become unsalable because horses would become extinct; boilers would burst and kill hundreds of passengers. In spite of such opposition, the bill passed through Parliament.

The proposed railway lay across an immense bog, and all of the noted engineers of the day said it could not be done. But after weeks of work and design, and after almost having the project canceled, Stephenson was able to sustain tracks on the bog. He wrote, "An immense outlay had been incurred,... so the directors were compelled to allow me to go on with my plans, in the ultimate success of which I myself never for one moment doubted."[4]

The following newspaper article illustrates how Providence worked upon his mind:

> On one of the Sundays which he spent under the hospitable roof of Tamworth Hall, the residence of Sir Robert Peel, he and Dr. Buckland were loitering in conversation after church on the terrace near the house, when a railway train was seen in the distance, a long white wreath of steam marking its rapid course. Now, said Stephenson, What is the power that is driving yonder train? One of your big engines, I suppose, answered Buckland. But what drives the engine? Oh, one of your canny Newcastle fellows, no doubt. What do you say to—the light of the sun? How can that be? the Doctor asked. That's what it is, said the engineer. It is light bottled up in the

earth for tens of thousands of years—light, absorbed by plants and vegetables, being necessary for the condensation of carbon, during the process of their growth, if it be not carbon in another form—and now, after being buried in the earth for long ages in fields of coal, that latent light is again brought forth and liberated, made to work, as in that locomotive, for great human purposes.

Stephenson's biographer, Samuel Smiles, said the idea was striking and original and like a flash of light, it illuminated in an instant a whole field of science.[5]

Stephenson did what all the "learned" engineers of the day could not do. The advancing world will ever hold a debt of gratitude to this brilliant, humble, and gentle soul.

NOTES

[1] Hatton, Joseph "The Centenary of George Stephenson The Father Of Railways" *Supplement to the Illustrated London News.* Printed & Published by George C. Leighton.Vol. 78, 4 June 1881, p. 553

[2] Ibid.

[3] Duycknick, Evert A. *Portrait Gallery of Eminent Men and Women.* New York: Henry J. Johnson, , 1873, p.439.

[4] Ibid., p. 442.

[5] Hatton, p. 554.

William Makepeace Thackeray   *1811-1863*

ENGLISH HUMORIST, SATIRIST, NOVELIST

> *"Indeed, it is something noble I think to think that God has a responding face for every one and sympathy for all"*

WILLIAM MAKESPEACE THACKERAY, AUTHOR OF THE SOCIAL SATIRE *Vanity Fair*, was one of first writers to use literature as a means of social commentary. In his day, reactions to his writing were strong—both for good and ill. People could not read him without responding to him. Charlotte Bronte, who dedicated the second edition of her novel *Jane Eyre* to him, spoke eloquently in his favor:

There is a man in our own days whose words are not framed to tickle delicate ears ... who speaks truth as deep, with a power as prophet-like and as vital ... and as daring ... I think if some of those amongst who he hurls the Greek fire of his sarcasm, and over whom he flashes ... his denunciation, were to take his warnings in time, they or their seed might yet escape a fatal Ramoth-Gilead.

Why have I alluded to this man? I have alluded to him, Reader, because I think I see in him an intellect profounder and more unique than his contemporaries have yet recognized; because I regard him as the first social regenerator of the day—as the very master of that working corps who would restore to rectitude the warped system of things.[1]

Anthony Trollope, who was a friend of Thackeray, wrote of him; "Thackeray tells us that he was born to hunt out snobs."[2] Thackeray chose to dissect the middle and the upper classes—to turn the morality and mores inside and out. "You, dear reader," wrote Thackeray, "have faults and petty vanities and I know them well for have I not those same frailties myself?"[3] He is recognized as the first writer to have held a mirror up to society. His most valuable gift was his ability to observe. This gift was so keen that he was able to portray the hypocrisy of society and to strip off the layers of pretense.

The experiences of Thackeray's life gave him abundant material from which to draw for his writings. He traveled to France many times and to Ireland. He associated with people in all walks of life. He was born with status, but fell into poverty, and then rose to be one of the most famous men of the era. Although Thackeray was a product of the Victorian age, he felt and expressed the hypocrisy of the times. He held with the Victorian view of women, whom he saw as having great hearts, but little minds. He wrote that women were set apart as a higher order of moral beings. His early writings are full of parodies—the affectionate attack on accepted norms. A close friend wrote that the two secret keys of Thackeray's great life were disappointment and religion. The first was his poison, and the second was his antidote.[4]

In his youth, upon a request by a newspaper, he wrote an article criticizing an eminent man who was becoming a baronet. Later, he wrote that he regretted having written the article, for the man was a great man. He readily admitted his mistakes as a youth and strove to never make the mistake again.

Thackeray's family history is as interesting as any novel. The family's ancient name was Thakwra, which was eventually changed to Thackeray. Thackeray's grandfather transferred to India, where his son, Richmond, became one of the high officials of the East Indies. As a wise manager, Richmond was able to accumulate a modest fortune. Richmond was Thackeray's father. His mother was Anne Becher.

Anne Becher had been sent to India by her stern grandmother. Anne had fallen in love with a young lieutenant she had met at a ball in Bath, England. He was of a good family, but as the second son, had no inheritance. Anne's grandmother disapproved of the match and sought someone of higher status for her granddaughter. In spite of the grandmother's protest the youths continued to see each other. When their meetings were discovered and stopped, they smuggled letters to each other. Then one day Grandmother came into Anne's room and told her to prepare herself for a shock. She then told Anne that her young lieutenant had died.

Heartbroken Anne was sent to India to stay with relatives. English beauties were rare in India and dashing seventeen year-old Anne Becher was much sought after. She soon accepted Richmond Thackeray as her suitor and married him. The birth of Anne's first child was extremely difficult and almost took Anne's life. She was unable to have any more children after this birth. Her only child was a boy, William Makepeace.

Because of her husband's position, he and Anne gave many balls. One evening as Anne, the hostess, entered the dinning room to greet her guests, she was startled to see the man who had been the object of her love but a few years before and who was supposed to be dead. One can only imagine the feelings of these two people at this first greeting for as it has been said, love does not die in death, but only in separation and hatred. As fate would have it only in fiction, Richmond Thackeray died three years later and Anne married her lieutenant, now Major Carmichael-Smith.

When Thackeray was just five years old he was sent with another little cousin back to England. Many believed that the climate in India was bad for young children, so they were all sent back to England to live with relatives or in boarding schools. The parting with his mother at this time was almost more than his little soul could bear. He had been the focus of her total affections since his birth, and he idolized his mother.

In England he was greeted by kind relatives with whom he stayed a short time. One day his aunt, placed her husband's hat on young Thackeray's head, and found that it fit. Concerned that he might have water on the brain, she took him to the local physician, who told her not to worry. He had a large head the doctor said, and plenty in it. After his short stay with relatives, he then was sent to a private boys' school which was highly recommended to the parents in India. Thackeray wrote of this experience:

> We Indian children were consigned to a school of which our deluded parents had heard a favourable report, but which was governed by a horrible little tyrant, who made our young

lives so miserable that I remember kneeling by my little bed of a night, and saying, "Pray God, I may dream of my mother!"[5]

Although Thackeray was generally well liked by his peers, one day two older boys forced him into a fight. During the fight Thackeray's nose was broken and permanently flattened.

Thackeray was not motivated in school and showed no promise except in drawing. He continually drew his teachers and fellow students in caricature. In the evenings he drew scenes from his lessons.

When Thackeray was nine, his mother and husband returned to England. The exchange between mother and son at this greeting must have touched Thackeray deeply, for later he wrote: "A veil should be thrown over those sacred emotions of love and grief. The maternal passion is a sacred mystery to me."[6]

When Thackeray was near the age of eleven, he was sent to public school. English public schools at that time were in urgent need of reform and later received some sharp attacks from Thackeray's pen. The poor quality of education was a frequent theme in Thackeray's journalism. The school Thackeray attended was called Charterhouse. The experience there was so bad that later when he wrote a satirical article on education, he renamed the school, calling it "Slaughterhouse." In the article he wrote of the evils unsupervised boys were exposed to, for the boys at Charterhouse were boarded near the prostitute-haunted streets round about. "Boys used to go ... out of their way to see the wretches hanging at Newgate [prison];... books of the vilest character were circulated in the long-room... Both morality and religion were ignored."[7]

Thackeray was concerned about the deep and lasting effect on young boys of the exposure to brutality and prostitution. He was later to write of the university:

> I should like to know how many scoundrels our universities have turned out; and how much ruin has been caused by that accursed system which is called in England "the education of a

gentleman." Go, my son for ten years to a public school, that "world in miniature"; learn "to fight for yourself" against the time when your real struggles shall begin... You have learned to forget (as how should you remember, being separated from them for three-fourths of you time?) the ties and natural affections of home... My friend ... had gone through this process of education and had been irretrievably ruined by it.[8]

Thackeray never sent his two daughters to public school.

Throughout his entire educational experience, Thackeray was never a motivated student. However, at Cambridge he did read and enjoy the classics, and he loved Greek plays. After a couple of years at Cambridge, he came of age and received his inheritance. He spent it most unwisely. So-called friends introduced him to gambling, and he spent much of his time and resources in its pursuit. Gambling became a parasite to his nature which took him years of struggle to overcome.

Thackeray left the university and moved to Paris in order to become an artist. He traveled to Wiemar where he met with the aging Goethe and reveled in the influence left by the great Schiller. When he returned to Paris, he discovered that the investment house in which his father's money was invested had failed. Because of the failure, Thackeray was forced to live for the next several years on what he could make He had to rely on his own talents, something he probably would not have done without this seeming tragedy. He began to write short illustrated essays for magazines, but he received only a pittance for his work.

In Paris he met and fell in love with seventeen-year-old Isabelle Shaw, the daughter of an Irish man and woman. Her father had served in the army in India and died there, and Isabelle lived with her overbearing mother, who opposed the young couple from the start. At last, however, she relented and signed the consent form that was required because her daughter was under age.

Theirs was a happy marriage. They had three daughters in three years. The responsibility of a family made Thackeray become very serious about his work. His marriage gave him stability and greater meaning in life.

Soon, however, tragedy struck when their second baby died at eight months. Isabella was especially affected. After the third baby was born, Isabelle had several fevers and did not recover from the depression that accompanied the birth. Deeply concerned, Thackeray took her on a series of trips. Each trip seemed to bring a little temporary relief, but nothing cured it. Little was understood about mental illness in Thackeray's day so when she became so ill that she could not take care of herself, Thackeray arranged for her to live in a home with a couple.

Losing his wife in this way was Thackeray's greatest sorrow of life. He never fully adjusted to his loss. An elderly Irishman once accused him of writing a book which made fun of the Irish. "God help me!" said Thackeray, turning his head away as his eyes filled with tears, "all that I have loved best in the world is Irish.... I was a happy as the day is long with her."[9] As trying as this experience was for Thackeray, he did not allow it to sour his life nor did he sink in despair. Rather, the experience mellowed him, filling him with courage and great tenderness for all human sorrow and suffering.

Thackeray's greatest work was *Vanity Fair*, which rose to great popularity. After its publication he was invited into the highest social circles.

Although he now made good money, he felt he needed to provide for his daughters after his death. These feelings made him sensitive to others who might also be in need and he spent much of the money he did have helping those in need. He began giving a series of lectures in an effort to increase his income. Twice he came to the United States and was well received as a lecturer. He was sympathetic to the history of this country. When asked what he thought of Washington he said: "I think the cause for which Washington fought entirely just and right, and the champion the very noblest, purest, bravest, best of God's men."[10]

Near the end of his life Thackeray's health was not good and some of his later work began to show signs of his illness. On Christmas Eve, 1863, having worked until evening, he returned to his home to rest. Later that evening he died.

Thackeray's good friend Mr. Synge described how Thackeray,

sensing his death, gave him a book to comfort him when he died. Synge said,

> I took from its shelf the book he pointed out; out of it fell a piece of paper on which Thackeray had written a prayer, all of which I do not pretend to remember.... He prayed that he might never write a word inconsistent with the love of God or the love of man: that he might always speak the truth with his pen, and that he might never be actuated by a love of greed.... The prayer wound up with the words "for the sake of Jesus Christ our Lord."[11]

NOTES

[1] Merivale, Herman and Frank T. Marizials. *Life of W. M. Thackeray.* New York: The Walter Scott Publishing Co., n.d., p. 141-42.

[2] Ibid., p. 132.

[3] Monsarrat, Ann. *An Easy Victorian: Thackeray the Man, 1811-1863.* London: Cassell, n.d., p.2.

[4] See Merivale, p. 18.

[5] Peters, Catherine. *Thackeray's Universe Shifting Worlds of Imagination and Reality* London: Faber and Faber, n.d., p.7.

[6] Ibid., p. 9.

[7] Ibid., p. 11.

[8] Ibid., p. 90.

[9] Merivale, p. 111.

[10] Duyckinck, Evert. *A Portrait Gallery of Eminent Men and Women.* New York: Henry Johnson Co., 1873, p. 137.

[11] Merivale, p. 248.

Amerigo Vespucci 1454-1512

ITALIAN NAVIGATOR

> *"Those new regions which we found we may rightly call a New World."*

AMERIGO VESPUCCI IS ONE OF THE TWO MEN INCLUDED IN THIS research who are not of the eighteenth or early nineteenth century. Amerigo played a significant role in the establishment of America. He was the first to establish that America was a new continent and not a part of Asia.

Amerigo was born in Florence in 1454. He was the son of Nastagio Vespucci, whose family was among the most cultured and respected of the region. Amerigo's father was the secretary of the Signori, the Senate of the Republic of Florence; his uncle Juliano was the ambassador to Genoa; and a cousin, Piero Vespucci, was the ambassador to the King of Naples. Interestingly, Leonardo da Vinci was so impressed by the noble manly features of Amerigo the elder that he followed him about the streets until he had memorized his features. Da Vinci later drew a crayon portrait of him.[1]

Shortly after his birth, Amerigo was taken to the Cathedral of the Saints for his baptism. Custom dictated that all babies blessed in that parish be named after a saint, but Amerigo's father departed from the tradition and named the new baby after his grandfather, a name which now the world knows as two of its continents.

Amerigo Vespucci's family, position, and education were vital for the purpose which he was to fulfill. Most of Amerigo's education was under the tutelage of his uncle Georgio Antonio Vespucci, a monk and distinguished scholar. This uncle collected manuscripts and was the owner of a splendid library. His intellectual circle included the leading thinkers of Florence, and he felt it wrong to limit learning and knowledge to that which was approved by the Church. Therefore, Georgio Vespucci spent much time studying the Greeks and the ancients. These elements combined put Friar Georgio in the midst of the Renaissance.

Under his instruction Amerigo became acquainted with Vergil, Dante, Plutarch, and most importantly, Ptolmey, whose astronomical calculations helped establish the meridians, or the beginning of the longitude and latitude system. Amerigo also studied classical lore, mathematics, and grammar. When Amerigo left his uncle's tutelage, he was an accomplished scholar—a rarity in his era. Along with scholarly instruction, Friar Georgio also gave his nephew a "profound sense of dependence upon the protection of God."[2]

Amerigo became friends with Piero Soderini, with whom he remained good friends throughout his life. Piero eventually became the head of the powerful Medici family. In his letters to Piero, Amerigo detailed his four voyages to the new world and his observations of what he found there. These letters are among the few documents left of these important events.

In 1478, the unsanitary conditions of Florence caused a terrible plague to spread throughout the region, forcing Friar Vespucci to shut down his school. Amerigo's parents took him to the countryside until the plague passed. While there, he wrote letters expressing his love of adventure. Amerigo also wrote of the kindness and generosity with which he was raised: "Georgio Antonio, commends to your consideration a poor and wretched neighbour of his whose only reliance and means are in our house.... He asks you, therefore, that you would attend to his affairs, so that they may suffer as little as possible in his absence."[3]

During this time Lorenzo the Magnificent made Florence a major attraction to all of Europe. Many of the notables of the time passed through this city of the Renaissance. Festivals of Enlightenment were celebrated there.

One of the most noted scholars in Florence at this time was Paolo dal Pozzo Toscanelli. For Amerigo and others in this advancing community, Toscanelli was the "fountainhead of inspiration," whose most noted student was Leonardo da Vinci. Toscanelli was a medical doctor who would not accept pay for his services for the poor. Like Friar Giorgio, he collected old manuscripts. He was also a great cosmographer and astronomer. He established a meridian line for use in determining dates of "movable feasts" such as Easter. His method was extraordinarily accurate for his day.

In 1474, Toscanelli proposed to a Portuguese friend, Fernando Martinez, the idea of reaching India by sailing westward. It was not long after this that he received letters of inquiry from a young Italian living in Portugal—Christopher Columbus. Toscanelli sent Columbus a copy of the letter in which he proposed the idea to Martinez. The letter to Martinez declared that "there is a very short route from here to the Indies ... by way of the ocean."[4] Toscanelli wrote back saying: "I note your noble and ardent desire to go to the western ocean, which is indicated upon the map I sent you."[5]

The impact of this man's far-ranged studies upon da Vinci, Columbus, and Amerigo revolutionized the world. Like Toscanelli Amerigo became engrossed in collecting the best maps and charts available. Maps were very scarce, and his collection became an expensive hobby. He paid the equivalent of 500 dollars for a map made in 1439.

When Amerigo finished his schooling he became a clerk in the commercial house of the Medici, the ruling family of Florence at the time. During his services as clerk, one of the leading men of Florence was assassinated. Retribution was swift. Anyone who had any connection with a suspect—including his relatives—was punished. Friar Piero Vespucci helped one of these men escape and was arrested and sentenced to life in prison. However, two years later, the King of Spain interceded on behalf of the Vespucci family, and Piero was released. Piero was not the only Vespucci to benefit from these strong connections with the King of Spain. They benefited Amerigo as well. The ruling Medici family sent him to their bank in Spain to become their branch manager. This was a position of great trust and responsibility, for the Medici fortune was thought to be the greatest in all Europe.

Amerigo was thus in Spain in 1492 when Columbus discovered America. During this time Amerigo changed employment to work for the house of commerce of Berardi, another Italian family. Their main business was to equip and supply ships. After Columbus's first trip, Ferdinand and Isabella contracted with the house of Berardi to outfit four different groups of ships to be sent to the New World. From business transactions, it appears that after the death of Berardi, Amerigo managed all the affairs of outfitting the ships ordered by the king and queen.

Amerigo was greatly excited by the report of Columbus's discoveries. However, he disagreed with Columbus' theories about the new world, who felt that the new land was the eastern-most coast of Asia. For some time Amerigo held that the measurements of longitude established by Toscanelli were incorrect and that this new land was actually the fourth part of the world. Through correspondence he tried to communicate his ideas to Columbus.

Columbus wrote to Amerigo, expressing concern about his belief that he did not discover Asia: "With your well-known skill in cosmography, I fear me, you combine more of doubt than becoming to a Christian navigator." In reply Amerigo wrote:

> Far from undervaluing the effect of the discoveries ... I am rather disposed to place a greater estimate upon them, than does the Admiral [Columbus] himself... My own thoughts lead me to the conviction, that there exists near unto the lands you have visited, an immense country, ... being according to my calculations as large, if not larger, than the whole of Europe.[6]

Columbus's next letter reminded Amerigo that even Toscanelli's views were in accordance with his own. Amerigo responded that Toscanelli based his calculations upon some of the exaggerated observations of Marco Polo.

He closed his correspondence to Columbus with these words: "I am strongly moved to tempt the ocean myself, in the hope of adding something to the knowledge of mariners."[7] Despite the disagreement between the two men, who remained friends throughout their lives, each was able to perform their providentially assigned tasks. Although Columbus may not have understood that the new land was a new continent, he was able to break through the cloud of ignorance, boldly opening the way that others might follow. It was Amerigo's calling to know that the land Columbus saw was a new world even before he sailed. His abilities in using the quadrant and astrolobe established that the new land was, in fact, a hitherto unknown continent.

In May 1497, King Ferdinand was anxious to be reassured that the reports of Columbus were true, as certain if, in fact, this new land was Asia. To this end and to "assist in the discovery," after Columbus' second voyage the King outfitted four ships for the new lands. Vespucci's assignment to sail with the fleet appears to have been his first major sailing adventure. This voyage was supremely important, for it firmly established that the new land was really, as Amerigo called it, the "New World."

This little fleet of Spanish ships was the first to reach the mainland. (Columbus did not reach the mainland until his third journey.) Amerigo described the journey to his friend Piero of Florence:

> What we suffered on that vast expanse of sea, what perils of shipwreck, what discomforts of the body we endured, with what anxiety of mind we toiled.... And that in a word I may briefly narrate all, you must know that of the sixty-seven days of our sailing we had forty-four of constant rain, thunder and lightning—so dark that never did we see sun by day or fair sky by night. By reason of this such fear invaded us that we soon abandoned almost all hope of life. But during these tempests of sea and sky, so numerous and so violent, the Most High was pleased to display before us a continent, new lands, and an unknown world.... We knew that land to be a continent and not an island.... God's mercy shone.... To Him be honor, glory, and thanksgiving.[8]

When the fleet reached the mainland, it went down the coast, Amerigo making notations of all that was in sight. He dramatically improved the known maps of the time. This voyage not only established the existence of the New World and a new continent but also a whole new hemisphere. Some have said that his two words, "New World," were actually the first Declaration of Independence for America.

Amerigo's training from his uncle and the knowledge he gained from Toscanelli saved the ship at a precarious moment. In a letter he wrote of the experience:

> Partly owing to tempest and winds which kept us from the proper course and compelled us to put about frequently.... For we were wandering and uncertain in our course, and only the instruments for taking the altitudes of the heavenly bodies showed us our true course precisely; and these were the quadrant and the astrolabe... For this reason they subsequently made me the object of great honor; for I showed them that though a man without practical experience, yet through the teaching of the marine chart for navigators I was more skilled than all the shipmasters of the whole world.[9]

In his correspondence he described a small book into which he was placing all his information. But the little book was lost. In a letter, he said he had given it to the King, and he hoped it would be returned. Apparently, it never was.

Amerigo's knowledge and skills were well respected. After only four voyages to the New World the King of Spain made him Pilot Major and decreed that no man could become a captain without attending Amerigo's school. In this way, Amerigo promoted exploration.

During this time and unbeknownst to Amerigo, the New World was being given his name. At the time his letters became known in the courts of Florence, a group of advanced thinkers at the university of St. Die in Lorraine set up a printing shop to print scientific information. These scholars obtained copies of Amerigo's letters to Piero and published them. In the ninth chapter of the book *Cosmographie Introductio,* one of the scholars suggested naming the New World America:

> But now that these parts of the world have been widely examined and another fourth part has been discovered by Americu Vesputiu, ... I see no reason why we should not call it America, that is to say, land of Americus, for Americus its discoverer, man of sagacious wit, just as Europe and Asia received in days gone by their names from women. It is fitting that ... in as much as Americus discovered it (and mapped it) it

be called Amerige, or let us say land of Americi that is: america.[10]

The idea spread. People liked the name and began to be refer to the new land by it.

Amerigo's legacy is not only his name, but in his dignity and devotion to the divine. Amerigo had believed for years before any actual discovery that there was a New World.

NOTES

[1] Arciniegas, German. *Amerigo and the New World.* New York: Alfred Knopf, 1955, p. 26.

[2] Lester, Edward. *The Life and Voyages of Americus Vesupcius.* New York: New Amsterdam Book Co., 1903, p. 62.

[3] Pohl, Frederick J. *Amerigo Vespucci, Pilot Major.* New York: Columbia University Press, 1944, p. 17.

[4] Pohl, p. 23.

[5] Ibid.

[6] Lester, p. 78.

[7] Ibid., p. 83.

[8] Vespucci, Amerigo. Trans. by George Tyler Northrup. *Mundus Novus.* New Jersey: Princeton University Press, 1916, p. 2.

[9] Ibid., p. 2-4.

[10] Arciniegas, p. 296.

Daniel Webster 1782-1852

> *"The most important thought that ever occupied my mind was that of my individual responsibility to God."*

DANIEL WEBSTER, DEFENDER AND EXPOUNDER OF THE CONSTITUTION, was born in 1782, at the end of the Revolutionary War. His father was Colonel Ebenezer Webster who at eighteen enlisted in the Rodgers' Rangers during the French and Indian War. After the war, he moved his family to the remote frontier of New Hampshire. Although providing for his growing family was difficult on the poor farm land, Ebenezer's colonial spirit thrived on the frontier.

When war broke out, Ebenezer went out among his neighbors with patriotic fervor, enlisting men in his New Hampshire company. He was soon made captain over this company, and when his little band of soldiers joined Washington's army, Ebenezer was selected to head the proud columns of the Sons of Liberty.[1]

Ebenezer was twice George Washington's personal bodyguard. Daniel Webster told his son Fletcher of this experience, saying: "I should rather have it said upon my father's tombstone that he guarded the person of George Washington, and was worthy of such a trust, than to have emblazoned upon it the proudest insignia of heraldry that the world could give!" Later Daniel spoke of those who joined his father's company: "I was gratified to find who [joined].... Among [them] was he from whom I am immediately descended, with all his brothers, and his whole kith and kin. This is sufficient emblazonry for my arms; enough of heraldry for me."[2]

Ebenezer was elected a representative from his area to New Hampshire's convention that met to vote on the Constitution. He was bonded to vote no, as were most of the delegates. When Ebenezer arrived at the convention and read the Constitution, he saw George Washington's name affixed to the bottom of the document.

During a recess Ebenezer returned home and asked to be released from his bond. The people responded, releasing him to be a free representative. When the convention reconvened Ebenezer stood to make his yes vote, stating: "I have followed the lead of Washington through seven years of war, and I have never been misled. His name is subscribed to this Constitution. He will not mislead us now. I shall vote for its adoption.'"[3] His vote, along with other like-minded soldiers did much to bring about the adoption of the Constitution.

All these events did not escape the keen observation of young Daniel Webster. His impressionable mind was being carefully shaped by Providence to prepare him for a later work—that of defending the Constitution.

Daniel Webster's mother was Ebenezer's second wife, Abigail Eastman, his first wife having died. There were five children at the time of this second marriage, and Abigail bore five more. Daniel was the ninth child. Like many other great men, Daniel entered this world with an extremely fragile body. So frail was this new little baby that the neighborhood women attending Mrs. Webster could only shake their heads and prophesy a short life for him. But Abigail Webster thought otherwise; she caught him to her bosom, wept over the child, and resolved in her heart to do all that she could so that he might live.[4]

As a toddler, Daniel still could not sustain himself on his feeble legs. One day his father brought him in, carrying him in his arms, and said to his wife: "We must give him up; we never can raise this child." Undeterred, Abigail once again took young Daniel in her arms and let her tears fall upon his cheeks.[5] Then she did all she could to help him, even carrying him in her arms as she rode a saddled horse the long distance to the beach. There she worked his frail limbs in the salt water, seeking to strengthen them. Her commitment to her son was great for she had great expectations of him. When Daniel was only ten years of age, she prophesied that he would become an eminent leader among men.[6] Years later, Daniel remembered the work of his mother in his behalf and declared: "There was a mother for you!"[7] With such perseverance on his parents' part Daniel survived childhood.

Referring to his childhood he wrote that, "here, in the meadow land by the river, with rough high hills hanging over, was the scene of my earliest recollections; or, as was said in another case, 'Here I found myself.'"[8] He played in the woods and fields, where he learned to love nature and to wonder at nature's offspring.

One day Daniel was mowing in the fields, but he didn't do very well. His scythe would sometimes get stuck in the ground or over the top of the grain. He complained to his father that his scythe was not hung right. His father tried to help him arrange it so that it would hang better, but had no success. He finally told Daniel to hang it to suit himself. Daniel promptly walked over to a tree and hung it on a branch, saying, "There, that's just right."[9] His father laughed and told him to let it be. Daniel returned to his own outdoor pursuits.

His companion in these pursuits was an old British sailor named Robert Wise. This elderly gentleman and his wife lived in a small cottage on the edge of the Webster property. Wise would often carry young Webster on his back as they hiked through the forest, and he spent hours teaching the young boy the art of fishing. Wise also used these hours to tell his young companion endless stories of the adventurous life he had had in the wars in Europe as a sailor of Admiral Byng and Lord George Germaine, of Minden and Gibraltar, of the yellow-haired Prince Ferdinand and of General Gage and Bunker Hill. He often told him of his own decision to leave the British lines and join the armies of Washington. In return for his friend's companionship, Daniel read the newspaper to him.

Daniel wrote in his autobiography that he could not remember a time when he did not read, so early was he taught by his mother. Using the Bible as her text, she taught him to read. It was his mother who gave him his first copy of that sacred book.

When a school was opened in their area, Daniel and his brother Ezekiel entered as advanced scholars. Master Tappan, the teacher of the school was amazed at Daniel's mind, and he told the following story about him:

> One Saturday I held up a handsome new knife to the scholars, and said that the boy who would commit to memory

the greatest number of verses in the Bible by Monday morning, should have it. Many of the boys did well; but when it came to Daniel's turn to recite, I found that he had committed so much that, after hearing him repeat some sixty or seventy verses, I was obliged to give up, he telling me that there were several chapters yet he had learned. Daniel got that jackknife.[10]

Master Tappan further stated that Daniel could learn more in five minutes than another boy in five hours.

When Daniel was about eight years old he found for sale in the country store a handkerchief with the Constitution printed on both sides. With careful patience he was able to save enough to purchase the handkerchief. That evening while seated before the fire near his mother and father he read and reread with care this wonderful document. Before he went to bed Daniel had memorized the entire Constitution. Like Napoleon, who as a boy played with a cannon and Martin Luther who found amusement in a Latin translation of the Bible, Daniel was attracted even as a boy to the words and materials that would allow him to perform his mission.

Daniel's parents, knowing of the boy's talent and having an inkling of his destiny, decided to do all they could to send him to college, even if it meant selling every acre of their farm.

I remember [said Daniel Webster later] the very hill which we were ascending, through deep snows, in a New England sleigh, when my father made known this promise to me. I could not speak. How could he, I thought, with so large a family, and in such narrow circumstances, think of incurring so great an expense for me? A warm glow ran all over me, and I laid my head on my father's shoulder and wept.[11]

His education allowed him to follow in the steps of such men as Henry Clay, John C. Calhoun, William Seward, and others who implemented the divinely inspired Constitution. His purpose was to stand as a bridge between the Revolutionary and the Civil War, laying up strong support for the Constitution so that it could withstand the test of the Civil War. In fact, one of Webster's speeches in the Senate is said to have delayed the Civil War by thirty years.

Many of his speeches made reference to future generations, for whom he felt a deep affection. He said:

> And when, from the long distance of a hundred years, they shall look back upon us, they shall know we possessed ... gratitude for what our ancestors have done for our happiness.... Future generations we would hail you as you rise ... to fill the places which we now fill.... We welcome you to the immeasurable blessings of rational existence, the immortal hope of Christianity, and the light of everlasting truth.[12]

Man's greatest work, said Webster, lay in teaching others of love and goodness. He said,

> If we work upon marble, it will perish; if we work upon brass, time will efface it; but if we work upon immortal minds, if we imbue them with principles, with love of others, we engrave on those tablets something which will brighten all eternity.

As a senator, legislator, and secretary of state, Webster's greatest triumph was the convincing of the Supreme Court and the people of the United States that the federal government was a union and not a league. "Liberty and union," he said, "now and forever, one and inseparable." Daniel Webster gave all that he had in support of his country, including his son Edward, who died from sickness while serving in the Mexican War, and his only other son, Fletcher, who was killed at the second Battle of Bull Run.

Not since the time of Washington's death had the country mourned as deeply as they did over Webster's death. At his request his grave bears his name and a scripture from the Bible, his first textbook, which reads:

"Lord, I believe, help thou my unbelief."

NOTES

[1] See Harvey, Peter. *Reminiscences of Anecdotes of Daniel Webster.* Boston: Little, Brown, & Co., n.d., p. 4.

[2] Harvey, p. 6.

3 Curtis, George Ticknor. *Life of Daniel Webster.* New York: D. Appleton & Co., 1870, 1:9-10.

4 See Lodge, Henry Cabot. *Daniel Webster.* New York: Houghton Mifflin, n.d., p. 9.

5 Harvey, p 397.

6 See Lanman, Charles. *The Private Life of Daniel Webster.* New York: Harper & Brothers, 1852. p. 13.

7 Harvey, p. 317.

8 Lewis, Walker. *Speak for Yourself, Daniel Webster: A Life of Webster in his Own Words.* Boston: Houghton Mifflin, 1969, p. 4

9 Lanman, p. 20.

10 Ibid., p. 15.

11 Bartlett, Mabel and Sopia Baker. *Mothers of the Makers of Men.* New York: Exposition Press, p. 23.

12 Spofford A. P., Weilienkemph Frank, and J. P. Lamberton. *Library of Historical Characters and Famous Events of All Nations.* Boston: J. B. Millet, 1902, 7:100.

John Wesley 1703-1791

> *"What are termed afflictions in the language of men are in the language of God-styled blessings."*

MONTESQUIEU WROTE OF PRE-WESLEYAN ENGLAND: "IN ENGLAND there is no religion and the subject, if mentioned in society, evokes nothing but laughter."[1] John Wesley wrote of the results of this loss of religion in his journal: "Life was cheap. I've watched them hang ten and twelve a day from the gallows. They hung a ten year-old boy one day for stealing a loaf of bread."[2] Into this spiritual desert was born one of the great spiritual revivalists and reformers of all times, John Wesley.

His history covers almost the whole of the eighteenth century, and his importance goes beyond a narrow definition of organized religion and more broadly to education and literature, prisons and poverty.

Wesley's desire to do good gave him great energy. He traveled approximately five thousand miles on foot or horseback each year. He generally preached fifteen sermons a week. He wrote over four hundred publications and aided his brother in the compilation of some six thousand hymns. With the help of his sister he made good books available at low prices. The two wrote books of their own and rewrote others in easier diction so that people of limited education could read them. Wesley's concern for the poor put him far in advance of his time in social reform. He supplied the poor with clothes and food and helped make arrangements for the satisfying of their debts. He established a lending fund to help struggling businesses. He opened dispensaries in London and Bristol and was often the only medic the poor ever saw. In all these actions, Wesley felt that he was "called of God."

Because of his public activities, however, he was viewed as a threat to ministers of the gospel who collected their fees and spent their time hunting or fishing. Wesley's promotion of the value of human souls was seen as politically incorrect. As early as 1732 he was decried in the press, and not more than five years later his character was publicly slandered and attacked in court.

Of these experiences Wesley, said: "All crimes have been laid to my charge of which a human being is capable, except drunkenness." Wesley had no sooner uttered these words when a ragged wretch jumped up, exclaiming that Wesley had made a trade with a lady friend of hers for a considerable amount of whisky. Having made her case she sat down amid a thunderstruck assembly. Mr. Wesley, unmoved, merely "thanked God that his cup was now full."[3]

Because Wesley marched in advance of his time, he advanced the people of his time. Fortunately he was not alone in his quest. His work was complemented and supplemented by eminent men and women such as Samuel Johnson, Hannah More, David Garrick, Maria Edgeworth, Edmund Burke, Sir Edward Gibbons, and Oliver Goldsmith.

John Wesley was the fifteenth of nineteen children, only ten of whom survived infancy. He was born in 1703 to Samuel and Susanna Wesley. Distinguished by character and moral fortitude, they were not fettered by a love of the things of this world. Susanna was known for her beauty, brilliance, and strong headedness. Like her husband she was well educated for her day.

Samuel Wesley was assigned as a preacher to the rectory at Epworth in England after the birth of their first child. The farmers there were a bitter lot, angry that the crown had taken nearly two-thirds of their land. Their anger was often vented upon tax collectors. It was said that not even Oliver Cromwell was able to subdue the people of Epworth. They were a brawling and a riotous group, their actions reflecting the hopelessness they felt.

The people of the town were not happy to welcome a new preacher to their town, and they were often cruel to Samuel Wesley and his property. His crops were burned, his grain stolen, and the rectory set on fire and partially burned. Wesley was but two years old when he watched his father dragged off to debtors' prison for a debt that could have been paid had his crops not been burned. There he remained for four months until friends could raise the necessary money to pay his debt. Through Susanna's careful management, the little family had enough to eat. The forbearance of both parents was a significant factor in the development of their children's character.

Because Samuel and Susanna were both gifted and knowledgeable, they each had strong opinions that sometimes conflicted. Samuel once shared with his son the following sentimental story. Susanna would not say "Amen" when Samuel prayed for King William II, because she did not support the king. This disturbed her husband, who called upon his wife to change. She refused. Susanna wrote that Samuel

> immediately kneeled down and imprecated the divine vengeance upon himself and all his posterity if ever he touched me more or came into a bed with me before I had begged God's pardon and his, for not saying Amen to the prayer for the king. [4]

So adamant was Samuel about this issue that he departed for London under terms of separation, promising to send money for the care of the children. Near the end of summer Samuel returned to visit, intending to stay but a few days. A partial rectory fire, among other things, encouraged him to stay on. John Wesley's birth was the result of their reconciliation. The evil one seemed to know that the next Wesley child would shake his domain, and did all he could to stop John's coming.

One winter when John was six years old, the parsonage was set on fire at midnight. Samuel was awakened by the cry of "fire, fire" from someone in the street. As he opened his bedroom door, he was astonished to find the entire house full of smoke and the roof so burned that it was ready to fall in. Susanna burst into the nursery, gathered up her youngest child, and called to the others to follow. All the children heard her call but John, and in the confusion he was forgotten. After gathering the children, Susanna "waded through the fire" to safety.

When little John was heard crying up in the nursery, his father ran to the stairs. He found them so badly burned that they would not sustain his weight. In despair, he fell upon his knees in the hall and in the agony of a loving parent commended the soul of his small child to his God. John, finding it impossible to escape by the stairs, climbed upon a chest that sat under the window where he could be seen from the yard. There was no time to obtain a ladder, so one man hoisted another upon his shoulders in an attempt to reach the child. John was plucked from the flames just as the roof fell in with a tremendous crash.

When Samuel saw that his child was safe he exclaimed: "Come, neighbors, let us kneel down; let us give thanks to God!"[5] After Wesley's narrow escape, Susanna resolved to be "more particularly careful of the soul of this child, which God had so mercifully provided for."[6]

Some twenty years later Wesley reflected upon the influence and the teaching his of dear parents. He wrote his mother and asked her to write and relate her method of teaching her children. She reminded him that she kept them close to her and to the truth by carefully teaching them in their early years. She cautioned him that "no one can, without renouncing the world in the most literal sense, observe my method."[7] She further stated:

> There are few, if any, that would entirely devote above twenty years of the prime of life in hopes to save the souls of their children, which they think may be saved without so much ado; for that was my principal intention, however unskillfully and unsuccessfully managed.[8]

Although Susanna was often criticized by many in the village for teaching her children, she remained undisturbed, saying "that she had long taken leave of the world, and that everything which conduces to the salvation of the souls appears odd to others."[9] Susanna's devotion to the souls of her children blessed the world; all of her children were gifted and good. But her sons John and Charles were such great missionaries that they forever altered the Christian world.

Susanna was so determined to teach her children that she sometimes employed unconventional, even unorthodox, methods.

An example of this type of departure occurred when Samuel was called to London for a time. In his place came a temporary curate whose sternness did more to empty the church than to fill it. Susanna, sensing a need for her little family to have adequate instruction, began holding Sabbath evening service in her kitchen. She reviewed and delivered interesting sermons that she found in the rectory storage. She also read the Bible. Soon close friends began to gather with her family, and they in turn began bringing their friends. It was not long until Susanna Wesley had more attending her "kitchen fireside services" than the curate had at church.

The curate promptly wrote Samuel informing him of his wife's indiscretions, and Susanna soon received a letter of rebuke from her husband. She replied to Mr. Wesley that she had sought the will of God in the matter and that she would gladly let a man do the reading but could not find one that read well enough. She concluded with this powerful statement:

> If after all this you think fit to dissolve this assembly do not tell me you desire me to do it, for that will not satisfy my conscience; but send your positive command in such full and express terms as may absolve me from all guilt and punishment when you and I shall appear before the great and awful tribunal of our Lord Jesus Christ.[10]

Samuel gave no reply to such boldness and upon his return the rectory was returned to its normal procedures.

Wesley's father, Samuel, also played a role in his children's growth. He was a good father and helped his children pursue higher education. When Wesley was about to take his orders for the ministry, he wrote his father and asked which commentary on the Bible was the best. His father's reply was simply "the Bible."[11]

As a young man Wesley attended school at Charter house and then Oxford University, where, with his brother, he formed a small study group to further the religious principles upon which the university was founded. This group formed the nucleus of the Methodist movement.

Upon graduation Wesley felt that he should travel as a missionary to America in order to bring the gospel of Christ to the Indians. On the way to America he sailed with a group of religious men called Moravian Brethren. He was so touched by their calm faith during a storm which nearly destroyed the ship that he began to desire such a faith. He remained in Georgia two years and later wrote that his mission to America was not, he realized, for the conversion of the Indians but for the conversion of himself.

On his return to England he met another member of the Moravian Brethren, Peter Bohler. Wesley shared with Bohler that he felt he should cease preaching until he truly had faith. Bohler replied: "Preach faith till you have it and then, because you have it, you will preach faith."[12] In further discussions on the long trip back to England, Bohler led Wesley to see that although he was fasting twice a week, reading the scriptures, and visiting the prisons, these were outward expressions of faith and that he must also find an inward expression.

Wesley felt that he understood what he lacked: "I fixed not this faith on its right object: I meant only the faith in God, not faith in or through Christ."[13] Not long while listening to someone reading from "Luther's Preface to his Epistle to the Romans," he experienced a transforming revelation that changed and strengthened his faith.

> About a quarter before nine, while one was describing the change which God works in the heart through faith in Christ, I felt my heart strangely warmed. I felt I did trust in Christ— Christ alone—for salvation. An assurance was given me that he had taken away my sins, even mine, and saved me from the law of sin and death.[14]

Wesley's strength and his power of touching large masses of people grew from that moment on. When Wesley first began to preach, he felt that it was sinful to preach outside of a church, but a Reverend Whitehead convinced him otherwise. Wesley eventually taught in the fields, drawing crowds of as many as ten to thirty thousand listeners.

His meetings were often met with severe opposition and

interruptions. Once while preaching in a church, a mob was so furious that they pulled out the window, tore down the doors, and even pulled up the planking of the floor. Another time, when a mob came to take Wesley to a judge, his clothes were torn and the skin ripped from his hand. He received several blows to the head, but he was saved by many believers around him who defended him. While he was preaching in a field, a mob even ran a mad bull through the crowd. When it would not do what they wanted, they beat and whipped the bull until it was bleeding and weary. The mob was finally able to get the bull near the table on which Wesley was standing. The bull knocked the table over, and the ruffians beat the table, tearing it apart piece by piece. Wesley moved to a new location and continued his preaching.

At a conference in 1770, he drew a rebuke from rigid Calvinists by presenting resolutions which stated that the heathen who had never heard of Christ could be saved if they feared God and lived up to such light as they had.[15] However, although Wesley was continually subjected to such persecution, he never wavered from what he considered as his call from God to "feed His sheep."

At nearly 50, Wesley was briefly married to a widow, but it was not a happy union and she left without notice. He continued to work, up to the last moments of his life. He died when he was eighty-eight.

Wesley felt the sum of religion was expressed in the words: "We love him, because he first loved us," (John 4:19). He lived that religion, extending love, his own and Christ's, to all.

NOTES

[1] Tuttle, Robert G. *John Wesley: His Life and Theology*. Grand Rapids, Mich.: Sondervan Publishing House, 1978 p. 61.

[2] Ibid., p. 32.

[3] Wakeley, Rev J. B. *Anecdotes of the Wesleys: Illustrative of Their Character and Personal History*. New York: Carlton & Llanahan, 1871, p. 146.

[4] See Tuttle, p. 42-43.

[5] Wakeley, p. 79.

[6] Ayling, Stanley. *John Wesley*. London: Collins, 1979, p. 20.

[7] Heitzenrater, Richard P. *The Ellusive Mr. Wesley: John Wesley as Seen by Contempories and*

Biographers. Nashville: Abingdon Press, 1984, p. 16.

8 Tuttle, p. 37.

9 Ibid., p. 45.

10 Wakeley, p. 66.

11 Heitzenrater, p. 23.

12 Wakeley, p. 100.

13 Introduction by Alderman, Edwin A. *Autobiograph in the Days of Frederick the Great,* n.p., 1918, p. 8.

14 Wakeley. p. 102.

15 See Fitzhugh, Harriet And Percy K. *Concise Biographical Dictionary.* New York: Grosset & Dunlap Publishers, 1935, p. 726.

William Wordsworth

ENGLISH POET *1770-1850*

> *"Every great poet is a teacher; I wish either to be considered as a teacher or as nothing"*

WILLIAM WORDSWORTH IS CONSIDERED THE GREATEST POET OF HIS age. Upon his death he held the position of Poet Laureate of England. Though his work was at first rejected and criticized, Wordsworth persevered in his unique poetic style of magnifying the ordinary and cloaking the common in royal robes of description.

Wordsworth's appearance was not extraordinary except for a high forehead and penetrating eyes that revealed an unusually perceptive personality. His eyes, according to one description, shone with a "light that never was on sea or shore, a light radiating from some far spiritual world."[1] With this light he was able to discover through careful observation the beauty around him, which he then expressed in the humblest of terms. While beauty had for decades been sacrificed for purely moral content, Wordsworth delighted not only in knowing truth and morality, but in portraying them in beautiful language.

At only fourteen years of age, Wordsworth developed his style when he suddenly awoke to the beauty of the simple things around him:

> This is feebly and imperfectly expressed; but I recollect distinctly the very spot where this [recognition] first struck me. It was on the way between Hawkshead and Ambleside, and gave me extreme pleasure. The moment was important in my poetical history; for I date from it my consciousness of the infinite variety of natural appearances which had been unnoticed by poets of any age or country, so far as I was acquainted with them; and I made a resolution to supply in some degree the deficiency.[2]

Feeling that poetry was his "office upon the earth," Wordsworth acted on this resolution through his poetry as he said in one poem:

> Earth's materials wait upon my step,
> Pitches her tents before me as I move.

Some time after Wordsworth's death, a stranger asked one of his servants to show him the poet's study. The servant replied as she showed the room, "This is my master's library, where he keeps his books, but his study is out of doors."[3] Although many believed that nature was Wordsworth's god, it is more accurate to say that Wordsworth worshiped nature for there he found God.

Wordsworth is known not only for his descriptions of simple beauty, but also for his belief in immortality and his allusions to the influence of a higher power. These beliefs brought great criticism upon him, even from his old friend and fellow poet, Samuel Taylor Coleridge. But Wordsworth had an inflexible loyalty to truth and he refused to depart from impressions of an afterlife, which he held as a "revealed truth." His influence eventually changed the character of the poetical literature of his country.

Another prominent theme in Wordsworth's poetry was patriotism. Many of his poems dealt with issues of tyranny and liberty. This was no doubt the result of having been born in 1770, during the reign of George III, and having lived through the fateful years of the American Revolution, the French Revolution, the Irish issue, and the Napoleonic Wars. Young Wordsworth was particularly influenced by the French Revolution. He ardently sympathized with the revolutionaries but drew back sharply when their fight for liberty spilled into cruel excesses. These subjects were so important to him that in writing about them he felt he tread upon "holy ground."

Wordsworth felt a great responsibility to fulfill the call of his youth. He wrote that the purpose of his poetry was "to console the afflicted; add sunshine to daylight by making [the] happy happier; to teach the young and the gracious of every age to see, to think, and feel, and therefore to become more actively and securely virtuous."[4] Fulfilling this purpose meant that he never gave utterance to feelings of discouragement or despair. His desire was to purify and exalt

English poetry, and the results of this desire can be seen in some of his finer works; such as "Ode to Intimations of Immortality," "Ode to Duty," "My Heart Leaps Up," and in a declarative statement announces the sacred calling of a poet: "If thou Indeed Derive thy light from Heaven." Although Wordsworth was not widely read in his lifetime, the future makers and shapers of England read his works and he became a reforming spirit of the age.

Born to John Wordsworth and Anne Cookson, William Wordsworth was one of five children in a warm and loving home. To Wordsworth, his mother was the personification of intuitive wisdom. She who was his first teacher had not

> ... falsely taught,
> Fetching her goodness rather from times past
> Nor did by habit of her thoughts mistrust
> Our nature, but had virtual faith that He
> Who fills the mother's breast with innocent milk,
> Doth also for our nobler part provide.[5]

Wordsworth's mother died when he was eight years old. Although his memory of her was dimmed by the years, his most tender feelings were always associated with her. Her philosophies of childhood did much to further his poetic interests. She gave him, even in his earliest years, access to nature. As soon as young Wordsworth was capable of walking outside the kitchen door, she left it open to him. He was left on his own to explore and discover the outside world, and his realm grew with each passing year.

In spite of his mother's delight in his growth, she had some concern for this particular child. She once expressed to a friend of hers that of her five children, she was most anxious about William's future. She understood in an intuitive way that he would be remarkable either for good or for evil, and sometimes she saw evidence for the latter. Wordsworth himself acknowledged that in his formative years he was often stiff, moody, and violent. He described how once, while at his grandfather's house, he and his eldest brother Richard were whipping tops: "The walls were hung round with family pictures, and I said to my brother, 'Dare you strike your whip through the old lady's petticoat?' He replied, 'No,

I won't.' 'Then,' said I, 'here goes,' and I struck my lash through her hooped petticoat for which, no doubt I was properly punished."[6]

Wordsworth's education was not based entirely in nature. His father was careful to acquaint his son to the great literary masters. William memorized portions of the works of the best English poets and at an early age could repeat lengthy portions of Shakespeare, Milton, and Spenser.

His first formal education was under the care of one of the village dames who also promoted memorization and gave a great deal of freedom in educational tasks. When Wordsworth was nine, he was sent to Hawkshead school in his village. There, although in school, he was still surrounded by those favorable influences of nature that had such a beneficial affect upon his moral and intellectual development. His experience at Hawkshead was made even better by the fact the he was able to live there with a most affectionate and motherly person named Anne Tyson. Her kind attention he gratefully remembered and celebrated in his autobiographical poem, "Prelude."

The headmaster of Hawkshead loved nature and appreciated Wordsworth's attempts to depict nature in writing. He was the first to detect and stimulate Wordsworth's earliest efforts in poetry. These early experiences in nature and writing convinced Wordsworth that all children are born as natural poets, but they gradually lose that power through the habits formed in this life.

When Wordsworth was fourteen, his father died having never fully recovered from the shock of his wife's earlier death. Some biographers have passed lightly over the death of both parents commenting that Wordsworth was little affected. However, one cannot but help wonder if these losses led to his understanding and belief in the principle of immortality.

After his father's death Wordsworth remained at Hawkshead until he was eighteen years old. Concentrating little on Latin and Greek, he loved to read Goldsmith, Cervantes, Shakespeare, and others.

In 1787, Wordsworth entered St. John's College at

Cambridge, where, much to his relatives' dismay, he was little motivated. Although Cambridge was noted for its scholarship in mathematics, Wordsworth instead devoted most of his time to the poets. After graduation he visited France with a fellow student and quickly aligned himself with the early workings of the French Revolution. Had he not been forced to return to England because of a collapse of his financial affairs, he might have met with the guillotine.

While in France, Wordsworth fell in love with a young French girl, Annette Vallon. As was the accepted custom of the day in France, they shared a common-law marriage. He returned to England, anticipating only a short stay; his common-law- wife, who was expecting their first child, stayed with her family. But after Wordsworth left, the French Revolution broke out and soon reached its height. It was impossible for any Englishmen to enter France.

Once again bereft of a family, Wordsworth spent the next few years aimlessly. His relatives tried to buoy him up by encouraging him to go into law or the ministry, but neither interested him.

A friend of Wordsworth's, whom he had once helped, died, and willed him £1000. This was characteristic of his life, as money always seemed to become available just when he needed it. His sister, Dorothy, who by this time had become his traveling companion and an inestimable influence on his poetry, managed the money so well that they were able to live a number of years before the money ran out. When it was finally gone, a large sum of money that was owed his father's estate came through. This money left Wordsworth free to pursue his writing. It was during this time that Wordsworth met and collaborated with Samuel Coleridge.

When the French Revolution quieted and Wordsworth was able to return to France, so much had changed between him and Annette they agreed to permanently separate, even though he felt a deep concern for his child. He returned to England and noticed that a friend of his sister's, Mary Hutchinson, had grown into a lovely lady. With encouragement from Dorothy, Wordsworth married Mary. It was a perfect match. She was a good woman in the purest sense, and she bore Wordsworth five children. Wordsworth expressed his feelings in "She was a Phantom of Delight."

Wordsworth spent his life recounting the human experience in poetry. It was therefore fitting that his death on the 23 April 1850 occurred on the anniversary of Shakespeare's birth and death.

Summarizing Wordsworth's influence Matthew Arnold wrote "Memorial Verse":

> Time may restore us in his course
> Goethe's sage mind and Byron's force;
> But when will Europe's late hour
> Again find Wordsworth's healing power?

NOTES

[1] Cochrane, Robert. *The Treasury of Modern Biography*. London and Endinburgh: William P. Nimmo, 1916, 1:23.

[2] Encyclopedia Britannica, 11th ed. 1911, 28:826.

[3] Duyckinck, Evert A. *Portrait Gallery of Eminent Men and Women*. Henry J. Johnson, New York, 1873, p. 563.

[4] Ward, Thomas H. *The English Poets*. New York: Mcmillan & Co., 1894, 4:2.

[5] Harper, George Mclean. *William Wordsworth: His Life, Works, and Influence*. Charles Scribner's Sons, New York, 1916, 1:23.

[6] Cochrane, p. 99.

Index